An
Unchanged
Mind

2008
Lantern Books
One Union Square West, Suite 201
New York, NY 10003

Printed in the United States of America

Library of Congress Cataloging-in-Publication Data

McKinnon, John A., MD.
An unchanged mind : the problem of immaturity in adolescence / John A.
McKinnon.
    p. ; cm.
ISBN-13: 978-1-59056-124-9 (alk. paper)
ISBN-10: 1-59056-124-4 (alk. paper)
1. Adolescent psychiatry. 2. Maturation (Psychology) I. Title.
[DNLM: 1. Adolescent Psychology—methods. 2. Adolescent Behavior.
3. Adolescent Development. 4. Professional-Patient Relations. WS 462
M4775u 2008]
RJ503.M362 2008
616.8900835—dc22
                          2008014165

An Unchanged Mind

The Problem of Immaturity
in Adolescence

John A. McKinnon, MD

Lantern Books • New York
A Division of Booklight, Inc.

green press

INITIATIVE

For
Rosemary

Contents

Acknowledgments

In retrospect, it is often hard to know just where an idea came from, what friend listened at a critical time, gave the idea a hearing, what colleague contributed in a chance remark the germ of a novel concept. In this case, however, I know and acknowledge my debt to John Santa, PhD, my partner and friend, who always was at the blackboard with me to debate and refine every idea of any import in this book. These were *our* ideas, not only my own. No doubt when he writes his account of Montana Academy he will remember to add what I have forgotten to say.

I have dedicated this book to my wife, who has been my best friend for forty years. She, too, has helped give birth to any understanding that may be new here. I sincerely thank my daughters, with all my love, who over the years have put up with my helpless need to write. I am grateful to my eldest daughter in a particular way—for her skilled surgery with a sharp blue pencil, her untiring effort to tighten my prose. All remaining flaws in diction, taste and imagination are my own. Fiona did her best.

Over the years of the writing of this book, I have put upon friends, who have patiently read various drafts and reacted to them—and so taught me what I needed to know: Peter Banys, MD; Christie Woodfin, MEd, CEP; Nadia Bacon, DVM; Tim Corson, PsyD; Vince Gaudiani, MD, and his wife and my friend, Candace Plummer Gaudiani, MBA; John and Carol Santa, PhD; Paul Case, PsyD; Arlene Bush, MSW; Victoria Creighton, PsyD; Susan Zegans, MSW; and not least, Rick Klausner, MD. I appreciate their many efforts, blunt suggestions, and tactful silences. A friend who reads is a friend indeed.

I am particularly indebted to Jane Isay, who became a friend over the writing of this book. She believed these ideas were important enough to engage me in editorial therapy. I particularly recall her interpretation: "Stop writing like a damned professor!" She pushed me to express my thoughts in plain English, which is of course the most difficult kind of prose to write. She said that there were "parents out there who need these ideas and who didn't go to Yale"—and for years she offered patient, witty, skillful, and considerate help. I am grateful for all of it. I hope she will not be disappointed.

I thank my friend Ben Mason for taking the trouble to introduce me to Gene Gollogly, publisher of Lantern Books, who knows about places like Montana Academy and generously tried to "get the word out" even before we agreed that he himself would publish this book. I have found him to be a man of good humor and integrity. I am grateful to his staff—in particular, Kara Davis, my editor, and Evander Lomke, who winnowed my words and, with notable editorial diplomacy, turned them into a book.

Finally, not least, I acknowledge all those who have taught me most of what I know about teenagers—the students at Montana Academy. I hardly need add that their parents were my teachers, too, for this book will make that obvious. Some parents of Montana Academy students took the trouble to read this manuscript and have encouraged me. All of them bestowed upon me (and on my colleagues) the highest honor parents can give to a clinician: the care of their children. I hope in this book I manage to give a little back to them. I doubt they have any idea know how grateful I am.

Author's Note

Whenever a clinician describes a professional experience, he risks indiscretion. To avoid this risk I have chosen to present composite cases, rather than to detail the lives of actual teenagers and parents. These composites are true to life, insofar as I could make them so. They are typical and plausible. Yet none is a portrait, or even a good likeness or deft sketch, of any particular person. None contains details that will permit the reader to identify any particular person—other than myself. Any resemblance to any person known to the reader will be unintentional and coincidental.

In the final chapter, however, I present letters in which a few parents describe their own experiences—and use their own words. I do so, with permission, to provide vantage points, other than my own, of the personal experience and clinical consequences of growing up. Throughout this book, however, I camouflage the details and change the particulars—names or nicknames of people, names of schools, descriptions of places or persons—so as to guard the privacy of young people and parents.

I ought also to note that, as a matter of taste, I have chosen to alternate the use of personal pronouns that imply gender. Rather than invariably to use the masculine form or repetitively to employ an awkward locution, such as, "him or her," I prefer to alternate "him" in one context with "her" in another, to use "he" on one occasion and "she" on another, so as not to distract the reader with a clumsy diction.

—jamck

Preface

I was trained sufficiently long ago to find it congenial, as a psychiatrist, to think of teenagers' problems in a developmental way. Thirty years ago when I was a resident at Yale, I was taught to think of adolescence as a spectacularly noisy, sexy, amusing, and sometimes precarious transition between the childhood and adult stages in the human life cycle. In this education Erik Erikson was a gruff avuncular presence—a blue-eyed, silver-haired professor who was, at that time, an intellectual mentor whose account of the "eight ages of man" topped the reading lists in our seminars.[1]

From a developmental point of view adolescence is but one stage—but a key step—in a sequential progress from birth to death. This portentous stage is an integral part of the larger lifespan, and so what happens in adolescence is firmly connected to what came before and to what will follow. This being so, a disrupted childhood makes adolescence less smooth, less secure, and less likely to accomplish what needs to be accomplished to prepare for adult life. A botched adolescence can permanently wreck the infrastructure of adult character. Between childhood and adulthood the adolescent "identity crisis" is a prolonged moment of truth.

The developmental point of view, of course, was not and is not the only legitimate psychiatric point of view upon human behavior. There are other useful ways to describe what happens in the brains and minds of young players who strut and fret their hours on that stage in the life cycle. The Yale department of psychiatry, in days gone by, was divided among these various clinical and research viewpoints—and was, for this variety, a better place to train. There were in New Haven, at that time, a psychoanalytic institute, the world-renowned scholars of which would debate psychological meta-theory and excitedly contemplate the laws surrounding child custody and innovations in linguistics; a public mental health center framed on social systems theory; nationally-funded laboratories for biochemical bench research; a famous child study center; hospital clinical research units doing controlled studies of drug efficacy; a veterans' hospital, where Vietnam vets struggled with the psychological aftershocks of combat; and an adolescent hospital whose young inmates were floridly psychotic or locked into an intractable proclivity for antisocial delinquency.

From this smorgasbord I chose to train to do psychotherapy. I had been an English major in college, had written about Wallace Stevens's notion that human beings shaped the mental world they inhabited by means of acts of the imagination, and so I was drawn to all the ways— sensible, sane, and otherwise—that human beings tried to imagine a world in which they could find solace and live vigorous lives. A psychiatric resident with my clinical ambitions, in those days, got assigned to the Yale Psychiatric Institute, the remarkable university hospital for profoundly disturbed teenagers. This peculiar institute, whose young patients were referred from across the nation, was one of Yale's two primary training sites for therapists. There, I spent my training years learning to foster relationships and to understand and help a motley collection of profoundly disturbed teenagers, who were—as we said among ourselves—sad or mad or bad, or all of the above.

The variety among the teaching units seemed only an advantage in those days. After all, a resident who took an interest in one aspect of mind was still expected to learn all the others. A bench researcher still worked the ER when on call, caring for hallucinating, suicidal, confused or inebriated men and women who came in out of the night. A psychotherapist still had to be competent with medications. The director of the Yale Child Study Center did research on the pharmacology of Tourette's syndrome, but also had trained as a psychoanalyst. This was the ideal, in those days, the Renaissance Man, the well-rounded clinician capable of thinking about human beings in all of those disparate theoretical ways. It was understood in those days that some human problems were best assayed in psychological terms; others in biochemical terms; and others as organizational, economic, or political problems. In that exhilarating Tower of Babel, with its profusion of different kinds of diction, what I did not foresee was a radical splintering of my profession and a coming mortal struggle—fought in economic terms, in the end—as to which clinical view would prevail at the expense of the others.

I should have seen this coming. There were plenty of signs. In the same month I started as a new resident at the Yale Psychiatric Institute, for example, the entire forty-bed hospital—professional staff, grumpy, confused patients, med students and residents, nurses, consulting psychoanalysts, battered furniture, athletic equipage, pots and pans, pantry supplies, pharmacy, even the ash trays (for in those days teenagers and staff both were permitted to smoke)—moved out of Yale Medical School's headquarters on Cedar Street. For years that venerable psychiatric hospital had been located down the hall from the dean's office; but now its famous clinical service, where developmental and object-relations understandings of schizophrenia and adolescent delinquency had been pioneered, was relocated to a rented dormitory four miles away on the campus of Albertus Magnus College. If I then considered the meaning of this exodus, I probably saw it only as a paltry squabble over university real estate—which no doubt in part it was.

But this exile was more than a shuffling of departmental office space and furniture. It was a portent of what would soon happen in the professions of psychiatry and psychology. For that expulsion was a symbolic displacement, also, which anticipated the banishment of psychoanalysis, the demotion of developmental psychiatry, and the loss of prestige of the "talking" therapies. A few short years after I trained at Yale, the diagnostic nomenclature would be revised. A psychodynamic nosology, revised in 1973, was to be further displaced in 1982 by descriptive syndrome diagnosis. Innovations in neurotransmitter psychopharmacology called for a more objective nosology, and so the psychoanalytic model of mind, with its preoccupation with semantics, its mental model of conflict, got pushed aside. Out went the "neurosis"—and in came the "disorder." Out would go psychotherapy, in coming years, and in would come the clinical psychiatry of the synapse: prescription pad, brief office visit, and pills.

In this professional turmoil after I departed New Haven's leafy streets, I have struggled to find a dignified, effective context for clinical practice. In the end, with a little help from my friends, I have had to imagine and create my own—a story I tell at the opening of this book.

In the meantime I felt a little like Daniel Boone lighting out for the frontier when I saw the encroaching cooking fires of new neighbors and sensed the loss of elbow room. At the University of California in San Francisco, where I took my first job, I was a well-supported and encouraged young professor and teacher in a fine medical school, helping direct the training of young psychiatrists and psychologists, happily managing an ambulatory clinic in an urban VA medical center. Then abruptly, as it seemed to me, my boss, the department's chairman, a famous psychoanalyst, got replaced by a bench researcher whose expertise was all about the biochemistry of slime mold. I then moved to Texas, where I helped to start a new adolescent and adult hospital—until I was so offended by intrusive "managed care" that my practice no longer seemed to be my own. In Montana I was, for a decade, a small town shrink in private hospital and outpatient practice—until… well, I will tell you about it in chapter 1.

What has *not* changed in me, in thirty years, is an abiding curiosity about teenagers and their troubles. What also has not changed in three decades is a young person's need for adult help to grow up straight and strong. Adolescents regularly need their parents—and other adults who inhabit the village it takes to rear a teenager. When they get into serious trouble, teenagers still need a psychiatrist who understands their troubles and can talk straight with them. Moreover, despite the wonders of a modern understanding of the synapse, neuroscientific discoveries have not replaced the skills of deft parenting. No pill substitutes for a mother or father. Nor will pills ever replace the psychiatric conversation that troubled teenagers need when they get stuck and cannot grow up. The skills of parents and psychotherapists are congruent, closely related. And treating developmental troubles in children and adolescents, I will argue, is a parental task. Helping kids to grow up is, after all, what parents *do*.

After these introductory remarks it will not surprise you to learn that, in this book, I will urge that a developmental point of view is necessary for parents—and for psychiatrists, psychologists, and teachers—if they are to make sense of the many troubles of many troubled teenagers. Immaturity often is the explanation. Not that delayed maturation is always the problem. Nor is it that immaturity is the only problem that can disrupt the life and frustrate the potential of a modern teenager.

Yet, much more often than contemporary clinicians seem to realize, a global breakdown in adolescence—with repetitive failures at school, at home, and among social peers—is best explained not as an acute mental disorder that calls for a pill, but as a disrupted maturation that calls for sustained parental intervention of a very different kind.

Kalispell, Montana
February 29, 2008

Part 1
Breakdown

1　Point of Departure

A DECADE AGO, during a time when I still tried to care for troubled teenagers in a conventional psychiatric practice, I awoke one midnight to an insistent beeping from my pager, a summons from the emergency room. I pulled on my trousers and shirt and drove to the hospital, where a weary ER doctor had just finished suturing the forearm of a slim teenager I will call Pauline—a frightened, angry sixteen-year-old girl who had lacerated her own wrist with a razor-edged shard of broken glass.[1]

The ER doc, a friend, took me aside. "There were some old, scarred, superficial scratches," he said, "but those fresh cuts were deep. I couldn't get her to talk. But boy, she looks unhappy. The officers had to break down the door because she wouldn't open it. There was blood everywhere, because she nicked a small artery. On an unlucky day she might have succeeded."

When the others cleared out, I told her my name. "You did quite a job."

Pauline did not meet my gaze. She just rubbed at her bandage, not smiling, and impassively looked down at her arm, letting her hair fall across her eyes like a veil.

"You weren't kidding," I tried.

She rubbed absent mindedly at the gauze, shaking her head.

"Very much pain?"

She kept slowly shaking her head, not looking up.

"Want to say what happened?"

She shook her head.

I waited.

3

"I want to go home," she murmured.

"You do?"

She nodded now, still not looking up.

"Go on," I said. "What's at home?"

I took a chair beside her bed. This would take time. We needed a relationship—not so easy with a girl who would turn out to have little use for adults. It would take hours to learn the details of her history.

Perils of Pauline—Before

Yet, looking back, it does not require hours to explain her predicament. Nor is every detail necessary to an understanding of her story.

> Pauline's stern, affectionate dad had been killed in a car crash almost exactly two years prior to that night in the ER. Her grieving, demoralized mom, unable to pull herself together, felt overwhelmed by her new financial worries. Heretofore the family had two paychecks, and she had relied upon her husband to discipline the children.

> Out of her loneliness, the second year of widowhood, Pauline's mother accepted the friendship of her dead husband's workmates, who invited her out with them to drink at their bar. They cheered her up with affectionate reminiscences about her husband, but she had begun to drink to excess—returning home only with a little help from a new male friend. When her mother passed out that inebriated friend began to make a habit of slipping into Pauline's bedroom (age fifteen) to climb into bed with her.

> Pauline began to skip school to smoke with some of the naughty girls, who were always in trouble. Her grades collapsed. She began to scratch her wrists with a piece of glass from one of her mother's broken wine bottles—a sharp curved sliver that she kept hidden, wrapped in a Kleenex, in the pocket of her jeans—worried that she might forget to conceal it, and her mother might discover it.

> When she whispered her dirty secret to a girl at school, who told another friend, who told another friend, who told her boyfriend, who told his mother, who told a teacher, who

mentioned this rumor to the vice-principal, who called the sheriff, a social worker came to talk with Pauline, and then the child protective authorities removed her from home, pending an investigation.

They settled her into a foster home an hour's drive away. Pauline began to attend a new, local junior high school, where she had trouble breaking into the established cliques. She missed her little brother. She began spending time with kids dressed in black and drinking alcohol on weekends.

As a part of the youth authority's procedure, Pauline was sent for an evaluation by a psychiatrist, whose diagnoses were:

I   *Oppositional Defiant Disorder*
     Dysthymic Disorder
     Cannabis Abuse
     R/O Other or Unknown Substance Abuse
     Sexual Abuse of a Child
     R/O Neglect of Child
     R/O ADHD
II   *No Diagnosis*

The psychiatrist noted, for the official report, that Pauline had been difficult to evaluate because she did not wish to talk about her mother's boyfriend or her mother's drinking, that she probably was not to be trusted in her accounts of her own use of drugs and that, in the absence of all of her school records, it was difficult to evaluate Pauline's recent difficulties with concentration and academic performance at school. He also recommended an antidepressant medication, which he suggested that another clinician, not involved in her court evaluation, prescribe. Finally, he urged that the youth authority further evaluate whether there was sufficient supervision in the home—and not rush to return her to an unsafe environment.

Time passed. The youth authority was busy, and the evaluation took many weeks. A detective came to the fos-

ter home to ask about those encounters in her bedroom. He pushed her to say how much her mother had been drinking, but otherwise she was not told what to expect.

She did not like her foster parents, who insisted she come to church with them. They got very angry after she came home drunk on a Saturday night.

Pauline had not had much to say to them—or to anyone else. And she did not like it that her foster father criticized her friends. After she came home intoxicated a second time he came to her bedroom when she arrived and warned her sternly that if she did not make better choices she could "end up a slut like your mother." Pauline promptly locked herself in the bathroom and refused to come out. Her foster parents called the sheriff, but before they could get the door open, she had sliced open her arm with a jagged piece of glass.

A Threshold

About a year after that ER encounter with Pauline, I ceased to admit patients to the hospital, and I closed my office. I had been treating teenagers in hospitals and in my outpatient office for twenty years. For some of that time I had been an academic professor, teaching residents and running a university hospital outpatient clinic in San Francisco. For some years I helped to start a private hospital in Texas. And for most of a decade I had been practicing office and hospital psychiatry in a Montana town just outside the western entrance to Glacier Park. I was fifty, too young to retire and in no mood to quit. But I no longer wanted to struggle to help troubled teenagers in the conventional ways my colleagues (and me) around the nation had been trying to help them.

Why not? Because too often that treatment was ineffective. There were many teenagers we could not help very much. After insurance companies accomplished a hostile takeover of psychiatry, they drove those kids out of the hospital—so that, in effect, clinicians lost the use of that safe haven. For the security of a hospital psychiatric unit, insurance companies had substituted "managed care"—a way to reduce the cost of a teenager's care and so to pocket the savings. Aside from ultra brief emergency stays after a suicide attempt, managed care had left us with only an outpatient approach—usually a limited number of weekly psychotherapy visits—and pills. These outpatient gambits proved helpful for some troubled teenagers, but not for all.

About a year after I met Pauline, I made my decision to resign from the staff of the regional hospital, where I had been medical director for psychiatry inpatient services. I also shut down my comfortable outpatient office on a leafy street in downtown Kalispell, Montana. I mention these events, Pauline's admission and the closing of my conventional practice, because they were not entirely unrelated. I do not mean that I gave up my practice because of one sad girl. But my failure to help her very much was exemplary—a symbol for so many other failures. In my mind she remains the exemplar of a common American clinical problem, which I just could not figure out how to solve in conventional ways.

An Inpatient

I transferred Pauline from the ER to the adolescent unit at Kalispell Regional Hospital. This locked psychiatric unit is the sort of safe place a psychiatrist needs to be able to put a troubled girl when he cannot send her home or back to a foster home where she had worn out her welcome and obviously was not safe; when he cannot be sure anyone else will protect her, night and day, as she needs to be protected; when he cannot be sure she will survive another day.

Our unit was typical of adolescent psychiatric facilities across the country. Such units, in my experience, have a standard layout: a corridor with doors on either side that open into double-occupancy bedrooms; a cafeteria for kids, staff and visitors; and a nursing station, the glass walls of which overlook a day room with easy chairs and a giant television. In the nurses' station the staff sit along a counter writing notes and orders. From there, the ward secretary pushes a button to unlatch a magnetic lock to admit to the unit an approved visitor.

On such units there is a classroom, where a part-time teacher presides over study hall and young patients work (or do not) at problem sets or essay assignments that have been obtained from counselors at their own high schools. For physical exercise, young patients play basketball or volleyball in a half-court gym, or on sunny days play in a narrow exercise yard enclosed by a cyclone fence. On secure units like this one, all the doors lock when they close. No window can be opened without a key.

An inpatient unit is a fishbowl. Even when a young patient has little to say, it is possible for a psychiatrist to learn much about her from observation—his own, and the noted experiences of nursing and therapy staff. On such a ward psychiatrists make daily rounds, sitting down in private to talk with young patients—as I did with Pauline. On rounds I heard the social worker report about group therapy, read the nurses' notes, and checked lab results. In the chart, as attending psychiatrist, I documented my own observations, cited objective data, made clinical inferences, defined the treatment plan, and wrote orders.

Over that week, in these various ways, I got to know Pauline—a reticent girl who missed her mommy and could not sleep; a pretty teenager who thought she was ugly; a high school student of average intellect who believed she was stupid. She had little idea about the future: no plans. She was sensitive to criticism, quick to tears, then anger, sputtering with denials and fibs, trying to shrug off the blame. She reminded me of a kitten tossed into a rain barrel, who came out hissing, back arched, claws ready, frightened but determined to defend herself. I liked her spunk. Also, she was loyal to the other young people on the corridor. She would not tattle about their lies, evasions, or rule-breaking. Like them, she considered this collusion to be ethically honorable, and proudly proclaimed she would not rat—and so became one of the gang, and less lonely.

When I arrived to make rounds, she rushed to ingratiate herself— and then wanted special privileges, reduced constraints, a suspension of ward rules in her favor—extra phone calls to her mother, the freedom of town outings, a chance to call a friend. When told no, she pouted. When I was distracted by another patient she hid in her bedroom to see whether I would look for her. When I came late, she pretended not to notice I had arrived. But I would catch her checking to see whether I had noticed her snub. It did not occur to her to wonder about my other duties, my family, my fatigue, or any other adult wish or need. It did not occur to her to say thank you.

Yet I liked her. I saw a girl who had been bereft, after her father's vanishing, then startled by her mother's despair and drinking. Her memories of her dad were idealized, childish in their obliviousness to what sort of adult he might have been. She was still grieving, spending hours at a dayroom window while others watched television/and staring at the snow-capped mountains where she recalled camping with him. She imagined that she would meet him again in heaven, which she imagined would resemble Glacier Park. She entertained fantasies about getting hit by a car or overdosing on her mother's pills, so she and her dad could be together again.

She had little idea what to do with her life—no ambition about higher education or a career. She wanted what she wanted *now*. She could not wait long without a humiliating meltdown. It was hard to miss her unworldliness. She realized that her age-peers at home were attending school, getting on with their lives, rapidly leaving her behind—and about this she was baffled and frightened, sensing a relative failure, but she did not know how to organize her own progress. She could not anticipate the course, let alone pace herself for a marathon. Plans for tonight, tomorrow, next week? None. How did the past make sense? It did not make much sense, and it did not much matter. How had she arrived at this place—and did she contribute to her own troubles? Not interested.

Her mother arrived for a visit after I called to ask her to come. She reported that her daughter had drifted apart from her. Even at home she had been ducking rules and had become evasive, insubordinate. At school, her mother thought, she was a capable but indifferent student. She lied about homework. She seemed always to create "dirty secrets she tried to keep from me." Pauline's education meant little to her, her mother said. She recalled how Pauline averted her gaze from all talk about her failings, from teachers' stares, waiting out the adults. She would stay home from school with a stomachache if her mother would let her. Her mother seemed depressed, distracted by her son's ADHD and her own health problems. Pauline seemed to have trouble holding her mother's full attention.

In fact, Pauline had no meaningful relationship with any other responsible adult, and she seemed to recoil from counting on any adult, yet she also seemed hungry to do so. Her solitary sadness touched the nurses, who dug up a frayed teddy bear another young patient had left behind and gave it to Pauline. Pauline made a beginning with me, too. She saw that I liked her. She knew I was amused by her peek-a-boo, her pretense not to be interested in whether I came or went. She knew I liked it that she wanted to just sit in my office while I wrote in charts—just to be together in silence. She could connect. She did connect. And then she began to tell me about her dad.

I began to look forward to our talks.

Managed Care

What to do with her? I worried about the suicide risk. Her reunion fantasies, the depth of her self-lacerations, the multiple traumas—all recommended great care about her safety. I believed there was no home in which she could be secure, as yet. It seemed reasonable to call a time-out in her life—to make her safe while she settled down, to bring her mother back into her life, to goad Child Protective Services social workers to complete their assessment and get this girl home, if possible. I started her psychotherapy, laconic as it began. She had much to talk about. Moreover, it would make sense to increase the dose of her antidepressant, for I planned to follow her when she left the hospital, and I could assess whether, in the weeks it required to have its full effect, it did her more good than harm.

I knew that it would take time to get to know Pauline's mother, to watch them together on the ward, to talk with the psychiatrist who worked with her mom, to figure out how to restore her to full participation in her daughter's parenting, if that made sense. I wanted to use the hospital as a haven while we assembled the parts of what could become a sound outpatient plan. The hospital protected her from drugs, the internet, broken bottle glass, knives, ropes, poisonous antidepressants, and predatory men. It seemed the right container. Given the level of risk, there was no local alternative.

Yet within the first two days of Pauline's stay, a stranger's voice on the phone began to lobby to eject her from the hospital. This person, unknown to me, unknown to Pauline or her mother, worked for a managed care company with a profitable franchise—to "manage" benefits available under Pauline's insurance plan. When Pauline was registered in the ER as a hospital patient, a nurse called this company for authorization to treat—i.e., a promise that the insurance company would pay the bill for a specified increment of care. The unknown person's voice agreed only to "certify" two days in the hospital. When by the end of the second day I had not already obediently discharged Pauline, this now-annoyed voice left an 800 number and a message: if the doctor failed to respond by 4 P.M., Pauline's insurance reimbursement would end on that day.

I did call back. But a different voice announced that the first voice was unavailable. Clicking keys in the background, this person asked me how "our patient" was doing and then wanted to know exactly when I proposed to discharge "Paul." This bonhomie persisted through my correction ("we're talking about a girl, Pauline"), but not beyond my intention to discharge Pauline (or, for that matter, any other patient) only when we had sufficiently improved matters, when we had put together the elements for a plausible treatment. This plan turned out not to be acceptable. The annoyed stranger lectured me—if Pauline had not "vocalized imminent suicide intent" in the last twelve hours, she no longer "met criteria" for a hospital's level of care. He could authorize only one more (a third) day "strictly for discharge planning." I asked where he was calling from—New Jersey? Did he have a map locating other facilities near Kalispell, Montana? Within a hundred miles? Could he find Montana on a map? The now-hostile voice stayed on message: he had "determined" there no longer was a "medical necessity" for Pauline to remain in a hospital.

By this late stage in my career I had already lost patience with managed care. This was not my first conversation with a reviewer. So I said, not very politely, that I really did not care what he authorized or did not authorize, Pauline would leave the hospital when I said so, and that this would happen when I was satisfied that she had a reasonable chance of staying alive—which I would have to judge, inasmuch as I had met her, and he had not; and inasmuch as I was responsible for her, and he was not; and inasmuch as I had her mother's informed consent to make treatment decisions for her, and he did not. Already I knew that, as a result of this conversation—as a result of my refusal to permit this reviewer to determine the course of Pauline's treatment—I would never get paid for Pauline's care.

My friend Kenny Pannell, Pauline's hospital therapist, looked at me gravely when I put the phone down. "They're getting to you, doc," he said. "You are not going to make it to retirement."

This was not a new idea.

Minutes later the hospital administrator called the nurses' station. He complained that an insurance company reviewer had just reported to him (a) that I had been uncooperative, and (b) that I had failed to justify any "medical necessity" for further days in hospital—and did I understand that the hospital now would not get reimbursed beyond today? He doubted the hospital itself would continue to exist if I did not find a better way to cooperate. He wondered, while we were discussing this patient, what was the earliest date on which I might consent to discharge Pauline?

"She needs a locked unit and 24/7 nursing supervision," I said. "Were you volunteering your house?"

Scribbling in a chart, Kenny muttered, "Never going to make it, doc."

Days later, without enthusiasm but without an alternative that met the conditions of all the involved parties, I signed a discharge order. The hospital's social worker, a Child Protective Service social worker, a managed-care reviewer, and Pauline's mother, who could not afford to pay an unreimbursed hospital bill, agreed to Pauline's transfer to a residential treatment center (RTC) in Butte. There, as I insisted, Pauline could be protected on a locked unit while whatever would happen next could be arranged. The reviewer, I was told, had been "reasonable," meaning that he had agreed to certify an RTC step-down (at lower cost to the insurance company, of course) for "up to seven days" with the proviso that, were Pauline still there at the end of that week, there would be yet another review of "medical necessity."

When the nurse called her to get ready, Pauline made a wise crack. But I saw that she was frightened. She knew where she was going—to another program, a four-hour drive from Kalispell and a five-hour drive from her mother's home. She was going to a "less restrictive" venue, a point the reviewer seemed to think on his side of the debate, as if less supervision were what this girl needed. The new venue would be 240 miles from my office. I would no longer be able to preside over her care.

I bid her farewell. The ward secretary pushed the button to open the magnetic door. Tears welled in her eyes when she hugged a nurse awkwardly and turned away from me, murmuring, "Thanks." I watched her follow the driver out the door, clutching her teddy bear, not looking back.

A Matter of Ethics

I did not hear about Pauline again for months. In that time there were other Paulines, other Pauls. My disquiet about managed care became serious. I began to resist talking with insurance company employees on the phone at all, for any reason. I had signed no contract involving them in my practice. I had accepted no obligation to them. It was true my patients and the hospital wanted me to tell insurance companies what they wanted to hear so that the reviewer would authorize payment of (at least part of) the bill. But what did this have to do with me? I had never agreed to let anyone manage my care for my patients.

Moreover, I had begun to think it unethical to cooperate. Just talking on the telephone—in an undocumented conversation with a stranger whom I could not identify, who had not been vetted for privileges in my hospital, who might not be licensed in my state, and who certainly did not have informed consent to take part in decisions affecting my patients' care—began to feel unethical. Even if I did not do exactly what these strangers prodded me to do, I knew these conversations affected my judgment. I could feel my dread of the next call, a distaste and annoyance that poisoned hours of my day, and I did not doubt that, even unconsciously, those people were successfully rushing me. Worried only about their own profit, pretending to a phony concern for my patients, these insurance company employees felt no fiduciary responsibility for my patients' clinical best interests.

How could I let them intrude?

Flying Blind

In that frame of mind I received a phone call from a young therapist who asked me, somewhat out of the blue, whether I knew where Pauline was? I did not. The woman told me she had been seeing Pauline weekly, that Pauline on occasion had spoken about me with affection, so when she vanished from a group home in Missoula, and failed to call her therapist or her mother, she had wondered whether I might have heard from her. I had not. I told her that if I did, I would let her know.

She sounded so upset and worried that I asked if she was all right, and she said, "No." She only had known Pauline a few weeks. Their sessions had been so friendly she believed they were getting started all right. But after Pauline's disappearance she talked to staff and some of the young group home residents who knew Pauline—and was told that "while we were chatting about her favorite reality TV show" and how sexy Matt Damon was (or wasn't), Pauline had been truant repeatedly at her high school, had been failing all her courses, had been having sex with near strangers, and was shoplifting to pay for hard drugs.

"I have learned the hard way," I said, "that office therapy requires a cooperative patient. For most kids it's just a game of Blind Man's Bluff."

"She never told me *any* of it," the woman said ruefully.

I knew how she felt. Watching an adolescent catastrophe happen from an outpatient office, she had failed to help, yet she felt responsible.

Again

A second encounter began much as had the first. My pager awakened me after midnight to a summons from the ER.

"One of yours, doc," the ER nurse announced. "You had better come in."

They were trying to wake up "a young single white female who won't say her name." The girl had no wallet or ID, mumbled that she lived in Missoula, but "all we got was that somehow she got dumped off in front of the ER up here." The girl was sleepy, had taken pills—maybe an overdose.

"You're doing the usual drill?"

"Yep. She's groggy now, but awake. They're giving her the charcoal."

"Be down soon."

"Bring your gloves," she said.

I was still groggy, too. "Gloves?"

The nurse giggled. "She bit the paramedic."

I spotted Pauline when I came in—on a bed in a side room hunched over an emesis tray, the curtain pulled back so the nurses could keep their eyes on her. On the station desk I found her old chart with my summary. An EMT wheeling his gurney out through the automatic doors grinned at me, shaking his head. "Good luck with *that* one, doc."

Pauline remembered me. "*You* again!"

"You," I said. "Again."

Noisily she threw up, muttering, "This is disgusting."

The room stank of vomit. "It is," I agreed.

Absentmindedly, staring into middle distance, she wiped her mouth with a towel.

"The nurse says you aren't friendly."

Pauline spat into her bowl. "Bitch."

Watching her, I saw that she was still pretty, but her features seemed harder, fixed in an expression of wary defiance that did not relax even after she vomited. She glanced up at me through a stringy curtain of unwashed auburn hair. One of her eyes was bruised, all but swollen shut. She still looked small and feline, but more solid—no longer a kitten. Over faded blue bra and dirty jeans the nurse had tied on an exam gown like a bib, which now was wet and stained down the front with the gray slurry. Halfheartedly, knowing the futility of the gesture, she kept brushing her hair out of the brackish liquid.

"Downers?" I said.

"Yeah. And Everclear."

"You were drunk?"

"Not drunk enough." She made an exaggerated grimace, as if eating garbage.

I took her meaning to be sexual. "A boyfriend?"

"Nah," she said. "Some jerk just wanted head for coke—liar said he *had* coke." She put up a hand, "Excuse me," and heaved again—more ashen liquid and pale pill shapes. Again she wiped her mouth. "The guy tried to pass me off with ex.[2] I got so mad I grabbed his stash and ran. He caught me"—she hooked her thumb at her black eye—"but I ate a handful first."

"Trying to kill yourself?"

"Maybe. If I'd of thought of it."

"Did you take enough to kill you, do you think?"

She shrugged.

"Did that cross your mind?"

She shrugged.

"How did you get here?"

"He was scared I might die, so he drove here and pushed me out."

"A real friend in need."

"Yup." She threw up again.

Perils of Pauline—After

A few days later on the unit, I saw that she had changed considerably—and not for the better. She was contemptuous, loud, shameless, and rude with the nurses, whom she noisily called "dicks" (the men) and "bitches" (the women). She ignored the rules, refused to do her chores, got sent to her bedroom for defiance and refused to go—and so provoked confrontations with nursing staff. At night she sneaked into other bedrooms as leering young men egged her on. She was a sexual debacle waiting to happen.

Placed into the program she made no effort to do school assignments. She disrupted study hall with sexual jokes and insulting attacks on the teacher. She had little self-restraint, playing only to adolescent applause. When criticized or told "no" or asked to leave a room, she shouted imprecations at the teacher or nurse, or she threw a book or cup of juice at the nurses' station window. In the day room she had to be told again and again to get her hand out of a boy's trousers, to get a boy's hand out from under her T-shirt. She was defiant and irascible, sometimes impossible to contain on an open unit. When physically removed from the community, so as to sit alone in a cleared bedroom to calm down, she became morose. She tried to cut her arm on a vent. She banged her face against the Plexiglas window.

In a time-out room, sitting on the floor together, we traced the past year of treatment. She had spent 9 weeks in the RTC in Butte, where she settled in gradually, began working in the classroom, getting good grades, and making friends. As soon as she began to look better and to feel OK about the RTC, however, her managed care reviewer refused to authorize more weeks of residency. He insisted she be transferred to a "less restrictive" (i.e., cheaper) foster home— with partial-hospital schooling, and prescribed medication. In the new school she had trouble making friends. Her loneliness led to another suicide gesture. She had to be admitted to a hospital unit in Missoula. There, once again, she settled down within firm structure. But as soon as she did, a new reviewer insisted she be transferred back to the RTC. Weeks later, when she again had made herself at home, a manager insisted she be sent to a "less restrictive" (i.e., cheaper) group home—and attend another partial-hospital school program plus secure prescriptions for Prozac.

She grudgingly adapted to the group home, but there was not enough supervision. She made the acquaintance of neighborhood "skaters," who admired her tank tops and offered marijuana for blow jobs. She found their friendly come-on irresistible, and went truant with them. Then she ran away from the group home and, for twelve weeks, she had traded sexual favors for food, shelter, and drugs—on the lam on the streets of Missoula. When a department store called the cops about her shoplifting, the arresting officer discovered that she belonged in the local group home—and sent her back.

She lasted there only a week. Hitching a ride, she reached Kalispell and accomplished the evening's sexual chore in the back of an old Blazer. Then she had run, gobbling a fistful of sedatives before she was caught and beaten. And so I had admitted her to a locked hospital ward for the third time in a year.

~

Reflecting upon Pauline's return, I was not sure who felt more queasy. I had not had to drink charcoal slurry. Yet I quickly saw that at the end of her picaresque, in which I had participated, she was much worse off psychologically than when I had first encountered her a year before. Her personal deterioration was the cost she had paid for a profoundly mediocre approach to her treatment. I was upset to have taken part in it. The wretchedness of her life, the socioeconomic debacle I could anticipate in coming years, turned my stomach. She now was crowding eighteen, and the opportunity to help her had been squandered.

This happened to be a turning point in my life, too. By the time she showed up again I already had been planning to try something different. I wanted to see whether we couldn't do better with troubled teenagers.

After meeting Pauline again, I told Kenny, "Surely we could have done better on a ranch if we had a structured life for her—school, chores to do, horses to care for and to care for her, some camping and nights under the stars and, oh by the way, some competent psychiatry. What if we could sustain a girl's treatment and let her hold onto her close relationships for many months, and not jerk her around?"

"Medicaid would never pay for it," Kenny said. "Their case managers would see it as a luxury and never agree to it."

"That's because they would think of it in the short run," I said. "If it changed the prognosis it would be a bargain in the long run."

"Maybe even in the short run."

This idea gave us pause. For we did not know the cost, but could find out. In the year she spent in Butte and Missoula, her mother had lost her job and her employer's medical insurance, so now Pauline had only Medicaid. The details of Medicaid's low reimbursement scale is in the public domain. We could call the group home, the RTC, and find out our own hospital's inpatient charges, so as to calculate what Medicaid had paid for Pauline's grotesque merry-go-round year. After some phone calls, Kenny had the answer.

The *dollar cost*? Medicaid would have spent seventy-two thousand—in discounted dollars[3]—for forty weeks of Pauline's "treatment." For another twelve weeks (of one year) she had managed her own care on the streets of Missoula. So when Kenny adjusted for the missing weeks, Pauline's treatment ran the Medicaid meter at $94,000 per year[4]—and presumably an insurance company would have paid even more. In all that time, her reviewers never set eyes on her. They controlled her life, but never bothered to visit a Montana RTC or inpatient unit or group home, never had to look at the result.

And the outcome was terrible. A troubled, traumatized, neglected fourteen-year-old girl had been jerked out of her daily life six times—and in that time had learned not to count on adults. Thrice she had been uprooted when her symptoms got worse, three times when her symptoms supposedly got better. No transfer was ever motivated by an informed clinical concern for Pauline, but rather her reviewers, spouting Orwellian excuses,[5] yanked her from higher- to lower-cost settings as soon as they could get away with it, so as to pocket whatever portion of her prepaid premium they could not spend on her. If a program worked, and she began to feel "better," she got pushed to a cheaper venue. By this psychotic logic a doctor would stop an antibiotic as soon as a child felt a little better, so as to substitute a cheaper medicine known to be less effective.

Surely, the savings were imaginary. Managed musical chairs rendered every step in the sequence ineffective. All year, Pauline could not settle down and stay. She could never attach, never commit to a school from which she had no prospect of graduating. She could never invest emotionally in adults, for they were here today, gone tomorrow. All her caregivers learned about her got squandered every time she moved on to start over. Unstable relationships made her despair, and then a suicide gesture bounced her back to a costly inpatient unit.

These monetary calculations left out the personal costs. They also failed to account for the social costs that, in the end, would have to be paid by the rest of us: her ignorance, her unemployability, her low productivity; her failed marriages, the costs for the police, prison and ER services she would need; and the opportunity cost of yet another wasted generation (her inevitable children), reared incompetently.

Only a managed care company or a fool—surely no sane parent—would purposely inflict upon a child this instability in key relationships. Pauline's treatment could make sense only to someone who ignored Pauline herself. It could make sense only to someone mindlessly tracking symptoms—as if symptoms ("Is she suicidal *today*?") offered a sensible metric. The result? An unhappy, molested young girl had been transformed into an angry, ignorant, alienated, addicted, self-loathing whore.

Goodbye to All That

By the time we did this calculation, I already knew I wanted no further part in this. Soon after I encountered Pauline for that second time, and she went back to the group home in Missoula, I shut down my practice—to join a few good friends to start a new kind of therapeutic school on a ranch west of town.

I found it wrenching to close my office. I had been a psychiatrist for twenty years, practicing in conventional ways, and collaborating with other physicians, who had become friends. I liked that leafy street in Kalispell, which was close to restaurants and stores and colleagues' offices. I was sad to leave it behind.

For all those years, I had carried a pager to sound the alarm when a neighbor was in trouble or a colleague wanted my help. All those years I had been radio- or phone-connected to a hospital and answering service. Certainly there were times when I wished to be free of it, when sleeping beside my pager felt like sleeping next to a ticking package. But on my last day in town I came home feeling cut loose, unmoored.

Not that I would go it alone. My wife, Rosemary, threw in her lot with me—she would direct admissions. Two friends already had shared with us the risk of the purchase of our ranch. Carol Santa, an educational psychologist who was expert in the ways kids learn, would lead our school. Her husband, John Santa, a clinical psychologist, would give up his practice in town, too, so that together we could create a novel clinical structure. Kenny Pannell would lead the ranch program.

I had already transferred my outpatients to my colleagues. I had resigned as the psychiatric medical director at the regional hospital. The phone company had disconnected my office telephone. I had canceled my answering service, for there were no cell towers forty miles from town. When I arrived home that last day, I had disengaged from my old professional life—unplugged.

My wife, Rosemary, saw it on my face. She followed me upstairs. I hung up my coat, and then we just looked at each another. I unclipped my pager from my belt, switched it off, and put it down.

2   Global Disarray

TEN YEARS AGO, WE LEFT TOWN. Within a year we had encountered a riddle, the answer to which would change everything.

Anticipation

At the time we knew only that we wanted to create an affordable, open-air residential treatment program for troubled teenagers. To this end we purchased a 400-acre cattle ranch in a remote Montana valley called Lost Prairie. There we hoped to protect parents from the crushing overhead of a medical center. We wanted to emancipate our adolescent patients from the antiseptic confinement of a hospital lockbox. On an open ranch we wanted to situate a sustainable clinical collaboration among teenagers and their parents.

We were in flight, too—refugees from managed care. We proposed to elude those phony intruders by shifting venue: from hospital to ranch. Clinically, we wanted to change set: from weekly outpatient visits to the intensive 24/7 culture of an enlightened boarding school. We planned to banish insurance companies from the doctor-patient relationship. We were determined to repel managed care at the cattle guard. At the ranch, only parents would authorize our work with their children.

All this we anticipated, more or less. We could picture a healthy community of adults and adolescents. We were itching to set free our clinical work from insurance company interference. We could imagine the ranch as a developed campus—lodge, cabins, bunkhouses, classrooms, barn, pastured horses, soccer field, shop—long before we re-mortgaged our homes and hung up our beepers. With an irrational faith we imagined that, if we built it, they would come.

Yet it was what we did *not* anticipate that changed everything. What we could not foresee would alter the way we understood every teenager entrusted to our care. What we did not see coming would transform our approach to treatment.

Unplugged

Oddly enough, we did not know ahead of time precisely *who* would come. And so we could not anticipate the makings of a clinical riddle that—along with fishing rods and backpacks—our new students would carry with them to Lost Prairie. We did not anticipate that when parents came to visit they would present us with a rebus that, for a time, we would be unable to decipher.

We encountered this enigma in the context of a unique ranch society. Over the years all our students and professional staff arrived from American cities or suburbs. But for various reasons, the ranch community evolved into a distinctive social order—distant in space, a throwback in time, and as different from American mass culture as Prospero's island.

And so, to introduce this clinical conundrum I must first pause to describe this remote society, the outcome of a peculiar anthropological experiment: a throwing together of well-meaning adults and troubled teenagers, who were strangers to one another, but would have to live and work together on a remote Montana ranch. It would be here that students would attend classes, study, do homework, play in vigorous sports, accomplish chores, hike and ski, make their own music, create art, act in theatrical productions, and pursue outdoor adventures. It would be in the ranch dorm and at the dining-hall table that they would struggle to make and keep friends, to help each other and learn to get along. It would be on the ranch campus that they would engage affectionate adults and, in time, reengage their parents.

It would be here, also, that we would encounter the clinical riddle, the solution to which is the subject of this book.

∾

At the ranch we unplugged from the matrix. On the new campus there would be no satellite dishes, no televisions—no sitcoms, no casual, repetitive violence; none of television's mind-numbing idiocy; no shifting images and sound bytes, which shorten the human attention span. These choices were deliberate, of course. We knew that, instead of their watching *Friends*, we wanted our students to make friends. Instead of experiencing a community vicariously on *Seinfeld*, they ought to create a community and belong to it.

To protect this fledgling culture from the barrage of media stimuli—whether ads for vodka or military shock and awe—we disconnected from network feed, so that the tidings of battle filtered into the ranch after a lag of days, much as the ancient Greeks received news from Thermopylae. We admitted political debate, but only after the bombast had been flattened onto the page, the ranting muted by distance. We banished sexy consumer ads, except in the classroom, where they could be analyzed. We turned off MTV's erotic peepshow. We took control of our own hi-fi speakers, and turned down the mind-boggling volume, so as to make it possible to listen to one another, to hear one another's words, to speak in completed paragraphs.

In short, we banished those noisy intrusive sound bytes that distract young people from personal relationships with other human beings. We banned Walkmen and Discmen. We permitted no iPods or cell phones, got rid of instant messaging and video games, forbade Net surfing and i-porn, and provided no car keys to automobiles in which teenagers could go elsewhere, vanishing into the night and leaving adults behind. Absent these intrusions and distractions, there soon came to be *conversations*. Young people and adults talked to one another over meals, in the lodge, in class, in team groups, and in private encounters with therapists.

To join this community wholeheartedly, we discovered, each student would also have to unplug, or to be unplugged, from the old school, from old friends, from drug dealers, and, at least briefly, from home. Deliberately we barred distractions so that students would attend to their relationships here, and encounter their thoughts and feelings now.

Some reading this account may wonder, as we did ourselves, whether we would best help our students by controlling these elements in their lives. For they would have to return to that American mass culture and would have to learn to handle those distractions. Yet our students were not teenagers who had done well despite temptations. Every student who ever came to the ranch already had failed to thrive in that larger social order, already had been victim to intrusive come-ons and too-available distractions from all the tasks of adolescence. Moreover, we learned the hard way that if we permitted students to bring Discmen and headphones to Lost Prairie, if we turned the television back on, allowed cell phones or permitted free use of e-mail, we would never capture our students' full attention—and they would never listen to one another. We had to turn off mass culture so as to hear one another's words, to take note of each other's presence. For social reasons, in part, the ranch community began to feel different from American mass culture—less harried, less intruded upon, less hurried.

This altered atmosphere also had to do with a sustained close encounter with the natural world. On a remote ranch weather intruded. Time slowed. The diurnal cycle and change in seasons, encountered every day as students worked and played outdoors, became prominent rhythms in their lives, just as the motions of the planets once preoccupied the proto-Indians who left their petroglyphs on outcroppings below Meadow Peak. Each new student, having to go cold turkey from the incessant noise, chatter, flashing lights, and commercial come-ons of city life, experienced a squirmy withdrawal. The tranquility of Lost Prairie, set off by the sibilance of wind in the pines, made it hard, at first, for new students to sleep. Students had time and scope for thinking and feeling, for loneliness and regret, for anger and shame—and had no ready access to drugs or other distractions from those immediate feelings. There were no video games, no city lights to dim the night's starry vastness.

This slower pace was amenable to talk, however. Students had a lot to do, but few scheduled events that required rushing off somewhere else. A typical ranch day provided structured occasions for discussion—hours set aside for group and individual talks that often included adults. Dining-hall noise was but talk and laughter undisrupted by text messages, lyrics in a headset, video games, rant radio, or the woozy siren song of intoxication. No one was selling anything. And no one with a cell phone sat across the table like a hallucinating lunatic talking to someone who was not there.

Adults were in charge. At the ranch, teenagers were supervised. We only enrolled students who had not been assaultive, and rules limiting aggression were enforced. Therefore, the ranch became a peaceable kingdom, where students and staff were safe, and adults insisted that it remain so. We did not tolerate assault, and there was little thuggish behavior or reason for a student to fear to say what was on her mind. We also enforced rules about sexual behavior. There were no unsupervised beds, no parties without adults. Although romance and erotic fantasy were rampant, the grown-ups in a friendly way refused to provide opportunities for adult sexual encounters for which adolescents are neither emotionally ready nor economically competent to take responsibility. Nor did adults permit the sexual bullying that vulnerable girls regularly described in their home communities. Boys and girls at the ranch have always been as beautiful and sexy as young people anywhere, but they lived at the ranch in an erotic calm, about which, oddly enough, they seemed to be relieved.

In this protected context, conversation among students shifted into a frank and honest key. Therapeutic conversations between teenagers and adults became less stilted, more affectionate, informal, and parental. Students, teachers, team leaders and therapists dined together, and heard the news and encountered rumors simultaneously. All witnessed the same squabbles and social operettas. Staff knew each student's roommates, teammates, friends, lovers, and rivals. Parents visited, so that other students and staff knew a student's family, too. Moreover, a therapist talking with a student in her office was not left in the dark about the quotidian events in the student's life, since teachers and team leaders talked with therapists regularly. Therapists knew how much a girl was eating, because they shared meals together. Team leaders knew whether a boy was turning in his homework and whether at night he was crying himself to sleep.

Once that intimate culture emerged, adults and adolescents felt close, talked frankly, knew each other's opinions, and understood how the other thought and felt. Without mass media, instant communications, and up-to-the-minute gadgets, without automotive mobility, without drugs or laptops or unsupervised space for hooking up, the ranch felt as different from American mass culture as an extended visit to Lilliput.

Although Lost Prairie was but forty miles from town, located only an hour's drive from a modern airport where big jets land, the ranch seemed to be situated in a time warp, hidden behind a piney ridge, stuck in a time zone located fifty years behind contemporary Los Angeles and

New York. For students and staff at the ranch it might as well have been 1956—and Eisenhower just reelected.

Three Ironies

At the time Montana Academy opened, there were three ironies that we had little time to notice. All we knew was that, from the start, the ranch filled and we were working harder than we had ever worked in our lives. All we could focus on were the risks and the problems, which were greater than we had anticipated. We had no time to consider what it meant that, even as our capacity doubled and tripled and quadrupled, even as tens of other adolescent programs opened over the ensuing years, our beds stayed full. Starting at twenty, our student body grew to eighty-five. In ten years we enrolled some 500 troubled students from thirty states—and these were but a fraction of the young people that educational consultants wanted to refer to us.[1] As we got busy, in those first years, we were naïve enough to congratulate ourselves on the excellence of our model, the quality of our staff and the virtues of our clinical work. It did not occur to us that another force was shifting the ground under adolescent psychiatry.

We did not make the connection—that insurance company tactics, which we had so resented, were successfully emptying the nation's adolescent hospitals and RTCs. In effect, managed care companies were successfully pushing troubled teenagers out of psychiatric facilities, which were supposedly covered in their policies, and into alternative residential programs like Montana Academy—not covered in the fine print of those same medical insurance policies. Troubled teenagers still needed this level of care. Parents who could afford to pay out-of-pocket were searching out alternative programs, such as Montana Academy. But medical insurance companies simply shrugged off the duty, as part of medical insurance, to provide sustained residential care for disturbed teenagers.[2]

In a second irony, we imagined that Montana Academy was an innovation. We thought we were inventing something, that the ranch school was a fresh idea, albeit an innovation that started from extant programs in the remote mundo of alternative schools and programs. Yet in retrospect, this convivial, intense therapeutic community of trained adults and struggling pilgrims—eating, sleeping, studying, working, conversing, recreating, and resolving intrapsychic problems together—was not new. The ranch community was simply another expression of a venerable idea—of utopian retreat to an asylum, removed or walled off from a troubled society. Such communities, in the ideal, were guided by wise and experienced elders, structured with firm discipline, and constituted a haven from a stressful or a corrupted world—and so became places where balance, inner strength, and peace of mind might be recovered. This idea, implicit in the cloistered mediaeval abbey, was also the avatar of a benevolent, more recent era in hospital psychiatry.[3]

Finally, in a third irony, our flight into the outback actually put us, for the first time in our professional lives, at the informational hub of contemporary urban-suburban American psychiatry and psychology. The ranch school, located forty miles from the nearest town, immediately provided a ringside seat on modern clinical practice—a vantage, all but unique in the nation, from which we could see one of psychiatry's most striking errors.

Why? Because each student arriving at Montana Academy brought to the ranch, along with spare shorts and skis, a detailed account of an unsuccessful contemporary psychiatric treatment. Parents themselves, at our request, reconstructed detailed developmental histories, which we read carefully. But also, along with their applications, parents forwarded records—outpatient work-ups, psychological testing reports, educational assessments and hospital discharge summaries—that constituted a national sample of American clinical thinking about unhappy teenagers. These records—hundreds of them—invariably described failed treatments. For if our students had not already been treatment failures, their parents never would have paid the emotional price or would have born the out-of-pocket tuition expense to send them to the ranch.

Of course, parents had not started their search for help in Montana. On the contrary, they arrived in Lost Prairie months and years after that first attempt—usually after a second or third try. When they journeyed to Lost Prairie they were making what they usually considered to be a desperate last attempt in the short time remaining before their sons and daughters turned eighteen, and it would be too late to find a remedy.

These failures begged the question *why?* Why did all that conventional expert outpatient (and occasionally also brief inpatient) treatment fail to remedy the psychiatric problems of all those troubled teenagers? From our vantage, forty miles from town, this was the first articulation of the riddle.

27

Who & What

To find a solution to that puzzle, one must first ask not why, but *who* and *what?* Who were those students? What parents sent their troubled children so far away? Was this act careless or irresponsible? And what troubles? What problems had contemporary psychiatrists and psychologists failed to solve?

Who? The answer begins with our admission criteria. In brief, we welcomed troubled girls and boys between the ages of fourteen and eighteen. Invariably they had many problems, not only one or two. By serendipity, one criterion came to be intelligence.[4] But quickly I must add that, despite good intelligence, our students usually arrived at the ranch school after protracted and intractable academic failures, whether at large public high schools or in intimate private day or boarding schools. They came from more than thirty states, from most of the urban-suburban hubs of the nation. Prior to their arrivals almost all had ceased to try at school, were not doing or turning in homework or classroom assignments, had stopped showing up for school at all, or were intoxicated in class. Many of them had been suspended or expelled.

We also selected parents. We welcomed mothers and fathers who agreed to participate in treatment from start to finish. Most of our parents were intelligent and well-educated, energetic and well-meaning—criteria that, of course, only deepened the clinical enigma. For surely it has always been less of a mystery when a failing teenager emerged from a family devastated by drink, drugs, illiteracy, unemployment, poverty, or mental illness. Among our parents these handicaps were rare. These parents could and would pay a steep tuition and they insisted on participating. They were competent in their own challenging careers—as attorneys, teachers, professors, researchers, inventors, district court judges, surgeons, internists, editors, entrepreneurs, psychiatrists, psychologists, psychoanalysts, investment bankers, venture capitalists, CEOs, engineers, and artists. The prevalence of university degrees—BAs, MAs, MBAs, JDs, PhDs and MDs—and advanced training were off the chart.

These criteria also gave new emphasis to the riddle—why did *these* teenagers have so many troubles? After all, their parents had worked hard and traveled far at great expense to look for solutions. Their parents already had consulted experts, had tried conventional therapies, including bushels of pills. They had looked elsewhere and could afford to take their children anywhere on the planet where they found effective help. Surely no plausible explanation for these teenagers' troubles could be based upon a lack of parental good intentions, intelligence, or education. These parents had all that—and their sons and daughters nevertheless had serious, multiple problems.

What? Oddly enough, we did not foresee, before they arrived, the panoply of problems our students would bring. We probably had a choice in this matter, but we did not take it. For some consultants, who were trying to figure out what kids to refer to us, asked us whether we wanted to specialize in particular symptoms? Did we aspire to treat mood disturbances? Low self-esteem? Eating disorders? Learning differences? Other consultants, who had less use for the *Diagnostic and Statistical Manual of Mental Disorders (DSM-IV)*, employed their own informal lexicon. Did we want soft kids, or hard? Internalizing or acting-out teenagers? Cutters? Did we wish to treat trauma? What about young people already taking medications—could we handle that?

At the start, we were reluctant to say. We refused to limit enrollment to specific symptoms. It simply went against the professional grain. In all those years when we practiced on the medical or psychology faculties of universities and hospitals, our colleagues would have thought it presumptuous—either for me, or for them—to mention a preference for particular symptoms. Within the general category of psychiatry, who cared what symptoms I liked? If her patient became suicidal, a surgeon wanted my help ASAP, and the last thing she cared about was whether suicidal thoughts happened to be among my favorite presenting symptoms. So, out of habit, we kept mum. Apart from exclusionary criteria, we would take any referred problem.

Our exclusionary criteria were merely scruples about safety—the defining qualities of young people we thought we ought not to risk treating on an open ranch, given that there would be knives in the kitchen, axes and rope in the barn, gasoline in mower tanks, and winter weather that would quickly freeze an impulsive or careless runaway. We would not accept parents who would not cooperate, who would not commit to go the distance. We did not want to start if we would not be permitted to finish. Otherwise, in those first months, we did not preselect our students.

This being so, we had no excuse to be surprised when our first students brought to the ranch an array of problematic symptoms and wretched behavior. A casual survey produced this cumulative list:[5]

> *Deflated mood; self-loathing; anxiety; insomnia; nightmares; mood swings; tantrums (with or without property destruction); threats; fights; brandished weapons; assaults; vandalism; theft; shoplifting; self-injury (covert or overt) including scratched, cut, abraded or burned skin on wrists, thighs, ankles or breasts; pulled hair; suicide gestures, threats, hints or serious attempts; school anomie; truancy; collapsed academic effort; poor concentration; classroom squirminess; disruptive talking in class; failure to do or turn in assignments; falling or failing grades; suspension or expulsion; rudeness with adults and peers; oppositionality or defiance with teachers or parents; eating disturbances (binging, purging, self-starvation, compulsive use of laxatives); drug or alcohol intoxications or addictions; arrests for intoxication or possession; drunk or intoxicated use of motor vehicles; drug dealing; sexual harassment; compulsive looking at pornography; sexual promiscuity; rape (perp or victim); family discord, including alienation from parents; mean mistreatment of siblings; family squabbles and fights; destruction of belongings or property; failure to keep curfews; compulsive playing of computer games; compulsive instant messaging or web surfing; hacking; chore refusal; running away; pilfering to pawn; lying; and other sneakiness.*

Traditionally, psychotherapists considered symptoms, signs, and misbehaviors to be grist for the mill. Outpatient therapists had to trust that a patient who agreed to say whatever came to mind soon would bring to the therapeutic hour the thoughts, feelings, memories, and associations that were relevant, whatever the underlying theme. That is to say, surface symptoms and signs would recede in importance and abate eventually as therapy revealed an underlying conflict, buried trauma, or repetitive leitmotif. This, no doubt, was our traditional expectation, when we began. On this basis we anticipated that we would treat any student, whatever the signs and symptoms, to a common regimen of individual and group psychotherapies supplemented by a pragmatic psychopharmacology to target key symptoms.

Nevertheless, we found daunting this long list of symptoms, signs, and misbehaviors. How could we adapt our scheduled program to touch upon all these troubles? How could our program achieve coherence if each student's symptoms or misbehavior needed a unique remedy? How many staff would it take? And how could we train our team leaders to deal with a chaotic collection of symptoms and not have them simply flailing in all directions? How could we schedule psychoeducational groups if separately and simultaneously we had to address a girl's low self-esteem, a boy's shoplifting, a girl's bald spots from hair-pulling, and a boy's defiant rudeness in the classroom? Did these symptoms hang together? Was there any rhyme or reason?

But formal diagnosis, we presumed, would reduce this complexity. After all, the *DSM-IV* is but a large collection of laundry lists of signs and symptoms and misbehaviors. The psychiatric nomenclature bundles signs and symptoms into commonly occurring clusters and calls each cluster "a disorder." Therefore, inasmuch as our students already had been evaluated at home by competent psychiatrists and psychologists, and all had been given syndrome diagnoses, we might have expected this welter of signs and symptoms to reduce to a few key disorders that could provide a logical basis for programming.

This did not happen. On the contrary, along with water bottles and fly rods, each of our new students brought along (usually multiple) diagnoses.[6] By the third year after we opened, we had collected a cumulative list of those formal diagnoses, which included:

> Cyclothymic Disorder (301.13); Panic Disorder (300.01); Post-traumatic Stress Disorder (309.81); Adjustment Disorder with Mixed Disturbance of Emotions and Conduct (309.4); Generalized Anxiety Disorder (300.02); Social Phobia (300.23); Obsessive-Compulsive Disorder (300.3); Factitious Disorder Not Otherwise Specified (NOS) (300.19); Anorexia Nervosa (307.1); Sleepwalking Disorder (307.46); Hypochondriasis (300.7); Dissociative Disorder NOS (300.15); Somatization Disorder (300.81); Conversion Disorder (300.11); Body Dysmorphic Disorder (300.7); Gender Identity Disorder in Children (302.6); Frot-

teurism (302.89); Bulimia Nervosa (307.51); Primary Insomnia (307.42); Narcolepsy (347); Pathological Gambling (312.34); Intermittent Explosive Disorder (312.4); Trichotillomania (312.30); Identity Problem (313.82); Adverse Effects of Medication NOS (995.2); Parent-Child Relational Problem (V61.20); Neglect of Child (V61.21); Sexual Abuse of a Child (995.53); Physical Abuse of a Child (995.54); Bereavement (V62.82); Reading Disorder (315.00); Mathematics Disorder (315.1); Disorder of Written Expression (315.2); Asperger's Disorder (299.80); Attention-Deficit/Hyperactivity Disorder (314.01); Conduct Disorder (312.8); Oppositional Defiant Disorder (313.81); Enuresis (307.6); Encopresis (307.7); Separation Anxiety Disorder (309.21); Reactive Attachment Disorder (313.89); Alcohol Abuse (305.00); Sedative, Hypnotic or Anxiolytic Dependence (304.1); Amphetamine Abuse (305.70); Cannabis Abuse (305.20); Cocaine-Related Disorder (NOS) (292.9); Hallucinogen Abuse (305.30); Inhalant Abuse (305.90); Polysubstance Dependence (304.80); Hallucinogen Persisting Perception Disorder (292.89); Dementia Due to Head Trauma (294.1); Schizoaffective Disorder (295.7); Schizophrenia, Undifferentiated Type (295.9); Brief Psychotic Disorder (298.8); Major Depressive Disorder (296.33); Bipolar Disorder (296.65).

To complicate matters, the majority of our new students, on the basis of these diagnoses, already had been prescribed (usually multiple) psychotropic medications. Most students arrived taking some combination of antidepressants, stimulants, mood stabilizers, atypical and typical antipsychotics, or hypnotics—usually two or three different medications per student, and as many as nine.

Three Sketches

In sum, our new students arrived with multiple symptoms, signs, misbehaviors, and functional failures. They were bright. Their parents were intelligent, well-educated, and concerned. Many of our students had been hospitalized, but only briefly, of course. In all cases their parents already had consulted experts who had prescribed medications, outpatient psychotherapy, and family interventions. Yet they were still floundering and—from their parents' vantage and in the judgment of experienced educational consultants—they no longer safely could be permitted to live at home. Neither parents nor educational consultants, nor therapists themselves, thought it made sense to perseverate in an out-patient treatment that had failed.

In her application a mother wrote about her son, **David**:

By his second year of high school, David's risk-taking worried us. We were shocked to realize that, at sixteen, he still had so many problems. We thought he would begin to fend for himself, but instead he seemed at risk to cause an awful debacle. He should have been getting ready to steer down the road of life, but instead he kept driving into the ditch.

He was so bright. In childhood he was precocious. But in the three years since middle school his grades dropped from A's and B's to D's, even a few F's. He quit the band, refused to practice his sax at all, and stopped his lessons. He became less communicative with us, angrier. His tantrums were pretty hard to take. We knew he had joined a wrong crowd. We discouraged his new friendships with skaters, who had a rep for using marijuana and maybe other drugs. To us, they looked like trouble. …

David stopped showing up at all at dinner time. As his tenth grade began, his relationship with his father became very tense. He just seemed so mad all the time, especially with his father, while he was calm and affectionate when he was just with me. With his dad he was so hostile.

His girlfriend broke up with him. He had been affectionate about her, but he picked a fistfight with a senior boy she had met and just got talking to—as if David just could not stand any competition for her attention. The boy hit David's mouth, knocked out a front tooth, and we were upset that David had been hurt—and complained to the principal. But although David was very polite and reasonable, she concluded that David provoked the fight—and so she had to suspend him from school. She said she thought we should get him some help. He agreed to see a psychiatrist and take medication, if need be.

I took him to see my own psychiatrist, who diagnosed bipolar disorder and oppositional defiant disorder and substance abuse sisorder NOS—and prescribed various mood stabilizers and anti-depressant medicines. But no medication seemed to make much difference. He agreed to take the medication and for a few months he did so, carefully, but he remained as defiant and unhappy as before.

One evening when he did come home for dinner, his father told him we would not sign a permission slip for him to go skydiving with his new acquaintances, because we thought it too dangerous. David got so angry he threw his plate of food on the floor and punched a hole in the dining room wall— right through.

I was frightened, so his father called 911. David was very polite when the officers arrived, but he kept shouting that his father was "driving him nuts." When one of the officers suggested he come along, and get out of the house, he tried to shove the officer away, and so the policemen wrestled him down and handcuffed him and put him in their cruiser and took him away. We had to call a lawyer friend and go before the court. Oddly enough, when he had to face a lady judge, he became subdued and courteous, even though she insisted that, if he did not cooperate with residential treatment, she would send him to juvenile hall.

Even from this brief sketch it becomes clear that this bright boy, who had concerned, intelligent parents, was symptomatic, misbehaving and failing in various areas of his life. Outpatient consultation and intervention had not improved matters. David was removed from his parents' home in handcuffs.

In another application, a father described his daughter, **Helen**:

When she entered high school, she was not really a problem. But in her sophomore year Helen began cutting classes. In December she got in trouble for truancy, lack of work, late arrivals, and fast friends whom the vice-principal suspected of drug use and wild parties. Helen came home indignant after the vice-principal described her friends as "losers." She seemed angry at any and all adult authority.

That spring she was arrested for shoplifting. A month later the police showed up at school with warrants to search Helen's locker and the lockers of her friends. He removed a small bag of marijuana and charged Helen with possession. We got a good lawyer, who got her off because of an error in the warrant. But Helen was rude to the judge.

We thought she had learned her lesson. She went back at school, and we thought the problem had blown over. But only a few weeks later she overdosed on pills and cough syrup.

The psychiatrist at the hospital diagnosed major depression; marijuana abuse disorder; sedative, hypnotic and anxiolytic abuse; rule out polysubstance abuse—and parent-child problem. (We agreed with this last part, for sure.) He started an antidepressant, but we have not seen any change.

Here, again, an intelligent girl with concerned parents had become polysymptomatic. Her sneaky misbehavior and risk-taking prompted her parents to banish her from home and from her community, where she had repeatedly gotten into trouble. Conventional diagnosis and psychopharmacology had not rectified these problems.

In these words a worried dad described his sixteen-year-old son, **Phil**:

Sending Phil off to a wilderness program will be the hardest thing we ever have to do.… But it seems to us that things with Phil are entirely out of control. We have no control over him, and he has no control over himself, certainly none over his acid tongue.

Phil did all right in grade school, but he was asked to leave two high schools within six months—because of his threatening behavior. At home he has become more and more angry, defiant and verbally abusive. His relationships with his schoolmates and family has been deteriorating. Phil is argumentative and dismissive of all authority. And he has an enormous sense of entitlement. He is unable to take responsibility for his actions.

A neurologist we consulted thought Phil had a post-traumatic neurological lesion maybe from a head injury he sustained in an accident when he was ten, and he got knocked out. The doctor wondered if he had some ADHD, too, and diagnosed oppositional defiant disorder. He prescribed anti-seizure medicine and put him on Ritalin, but none of the pills fixed his many problems or changed his attitude.

The house has been in turmoil. My wife and I have tried everything we could think of. But things have only become more dysfunctional. Everybody in the family has suffered.

In Phil's case, too, a family was in turmoil. At school, at home, and among his social acquaintances, bad had gone to worse. Other interventions had been tried. All had failed.

Global Failure

Taken together, the surface features of these three accounts differ. Superficial troubles, in each case, are not the same. Symptoms and misbehaviors were not equivalent. No dominant emotional tone was shared in common. David seems angry, and he was throwing tantrums; Helen seems wary and sneaky, and defied authority beneath the parental radar; and Phil is a resentful, smoldering, acerbic, impulsively threatening young man. Specific misbehaviors differ. Helen smokes dope and overdosed on sedatives. Dave did not use drugs, insofar as we know, but had traded reputable friends for disreputable pals. And Phil was taking medications meant to address a remote neuropsychological head injury and to damp down his labile moods; he also took stimulants for a presumptive neuropsychological deficit in attention and focus. None shared the same diagnostic profile, and no two took the same prescribed medications.

Yet these vignettes share a common deep structure. For a start, each teenager's troubles were so diverse that no Axis I diagnosis tidily could tie it all together. None of them struggles in only one adolescent venue, either. They seem to be failing in every typical adolescent setting.

That is, they all struggled *in school*—not showing up, not working effectively, not turning in work, not getting along with educators. They all also struggled *at home*—alienating parents and siblings, defying rules, resisting parental authority, lying, sneaking, hiding in their bedrooms, not coming home. They all struggled *socially* among age peers—unable to make or keep friends, unable to sustain romantic relationships, switching to affinities with disreputable teenagers who also were not doing very well—and so slipping down the adolescent social register. And they all were unhappy even when *alone*—angry, sad, ashamed, guilty, mercurial in mood, tuned out, uncommunicative, filled with self-contempt. In the disparate details of their interpersonal pathology, too, they were a lot alike—uncooperative, intoxicated, injuring themselves, suicidal, out of control, abusive, defiant, threatening, and refusing to let anyone help— in the protean variety of their unpleasant attitudes and interpersonal failures. They all suffered a broadly based disarray.

The students discovered this commonality themselves. Groping for shared grounds for conversation in group therapy, for example, they discovered common themes in their lives, similar experiences, equivalent attitudes, cognate mistakes, and a lot of the same self-defeating errors. Over and over they said aloud to one another: "I can relate to *that*, because I did [or thought, or felt] the same thing." They noticed that all of them had failed in much the same ways at all the tasks of adolescent life—at school, at home, and among their classmates. They recognized that all had suffered, during the crises that preceded their exiles to Montana, a global breakdown.

Shared Deep Structure?

We, as staff, also sensed this latent resemblance. In clinical conferences, as we talked about these stroppy teenagers whose lives we now shared, we shook our heads at the inventiveness of a particular student's misbehavior, the eloquence of another's defiance, how cleverly a third student made points in noisy debate. Yet there also emerged among us a consensus that, for all their diversity, our students shared something that was fundamental. We did not yet have a diction to name this common denominator. But for all the surface differences, we sensed that, having met one, we had encountered them all. These sketches illustrate this similarity. For all the disparate details, the story lines are the same: a progressive, repetitive debacle, ultimately an act of violence or risk-taking or lost self-control that finally prompts reluctant parents to take drastic action.

This emerging consensus got reinforced by our early, somewhat inadvertent clinical successes. On occasion a student would get "better" and abruptly begin to do very well. Such students began to make sustained academic efforts, became leaders in their classes and in the dorm. They handled parents with diplomacy. The generational friction subsided. They began to like their parents, to understand adult feelings, to respect mothers and fathers, to repair relationships. Their parents willingly reciprocated, startled by a son's or daughter's new graciousness. Successful students began to make friends with other successful students, implicitly recognizing something they shared. They felt better, complained less, liked what they were doing, cared about friends in new ways, fell in love, and felt new energy and ambition. They began to plan for college, met application deadlines, and began to look forward to lives they would live beyond the ranch, which they began to imagine.

What struck us was that this improvement was also global. Students did not improve piecemeal, only in one narrow dimension. They did better in school *and* with adults *and* among age-mates *and* they felt better about themselves—all at about the same time. Just as collapse happened in many dimensions, so did these recoveries. Their improvement was global. These radical improvements in adolescent functioning looked very much alike from one student to another, no matter what the formal diagnostic profile had been.

We puzzled about these observations, asking ourselves what sort of problem would cause a global breakdown in adolescence? –and what kind of a psychological problem, when remedied, produces a global recovery, too?

Doubts

We did not find the answer in the conventional wisdom. In fact, we came to be skeptical of *DSM-IV* diagnoses in struggling teenagers. For example, if David's supposed bipolar disorder, a genetic psychophysiological diathesis, was supposed to explain his aggressive misbehavior, why were his outbursts tied so closely to his father's attempts to say no? Or again, if Helen's depression was supposed to make sense of her academic ennui, what explained her shoplifting and defiance of authority, which are not routinely or necessarily associated with a fallen mood? And how could Phil's childhood concussion, for years of no consequence in his history, now explain an abrupt adolescent collapse in academic effort? Or his bitter threats? We could not make formal diagnoses explain the history or predict our own relationships with David, Helen, or Phil. Parents who would visit also seemed to have become skeptical.

This skepticism has also been reflected in the lay press—for example, in a series of contemporary articles on the front pages of the *New York Times*, called "Troubled Children." In "What's Wrong with a Child—Psychiatrists Often Disagree," reporter Benedict Cary painted an unflattering portrait of contemporary diagnostic practice and polypharmacy.

> *Paul Williams, thirteen, has had almost as many psychiatric diagnoses as birthdays.*
>
> *The first psychiatrist he saw, at age seven, decided after a twenty-minute visit that the boy was suffering from depression…*
>
> *What followed was a string of office visits with psychologists, social workers, and psychiatrists. Each had an idea about what was wrong and a specific diagnosis: "Compulsive tendencies," one said. "Oppositional defiant disorder," another concluded. Others said "pervasive developmental disorder," or some combination. Each diagnosis was accompanied by a different regimen of drug treatments.[7]*

Unimpressed, Carey summarized:

> *A child's problems are now routinely given two or more diagnoses at a time, like attention deficit and bipolar disorders. And parents of disruptive children in particular—those who might once have been called delinquents, or simply "problem children"—say they hear an alphabet soup of labels that seem to change as often as a child's shoe size.*

In another article in the series, "Proof Is Scant on Psychiatric Drug Mix for the Young," Gardiner Harris describes a contemporary reliance upon symptom-relieving pills.

> *Stephen and Jacob Meszaros seem like typical teenagers until their mother offers a glimpse into the family's medicine cabinet.*

> *Bottles of psychiatric medications fill the shelves. Ste-phen, fifteen, takes the antidepressants Zoloft and Desyrel for depression, the anticonvulsant Lamictal to moderate his moods, and the stimulant Focalin XR to improve concentra-tion. Jacob, fourteen, takes Focalin XR for concentration, the anticonvulsant Depakote to moderate his moods, the anti-psychotic Risperdal to reduce anger, and the antihypertensive Catapres to induce sleep.*
>
> *Over the last three years, each boy has been prescribed twenty-eight different psychiatric drugs.* [8]

This dubiety about symptom-based diagnosis in teenagers, this skepticism about the wisdom of a reflexive attempt to relieve symptoms with pills, which is an uneasiness we have come to share, has also been expressed publicly by academic psychiatrists. For instance, Jerome Groopman, MD, in a recent article in *The New Yorker*—whose title begs the question "What's Normal?"—described the essential problem with diagnosis of bipolar disorder in children and teenagers. By extension he is also describing the larger problem with psychiatry's nomenclature (*DSM-IV*), which relies upon the diagnostic concept of a *disorder*, which turns out merely to be a cluster of symptoms and signs that lacks (in almost every *DSM-IV* diagnosis) a demonstrated underlying etiology. A disorder is a trouble without a cause.

This clinical preoccupation is like treating only the symptoms of "fever and cough disorder" in ignorance of any underlying cause of fever and cough. It is like prescribing medications that can lower a fever or soothe a cough without yet having discovered the bacteria that causes pneumonia, the thrombophlebitis that is the basis for a pulmonary embolus, the human immunodeficiency virus that causes AIDs, or the viral basis for the common cold. Psychiatric pharmacology is all too much like treating all of these causes of fever and cough with aspirin and cough syrup.

It is no one's fault that we do not know, as yet, what causes most of the disorders listed in the diagnostic manual. But this lack of knowledge is worrisome when these syndrome diagnoses are the sole justification for prescriptions for children and teenagers of vast quantities of potent psychotropic drugs. For these psychoactive medications are prescribed to relieve symptoms, not to attack specific causes of well-understood diseases. Groopman underlines the unknown risk in this practice, given that those prescriptions are written for children and adolescents whose neural circuitry is still actively under construction. He quotes Steven Hyman, MD, recently the director of the National Institute of Mental Health, who shares his uneasiness:

> The problem with describing a kid who is up-and-down and irritable and sullen and wild and then grandiose is that he could indeed be [bipolar], but it could be an awful lot of other things, too… . Bipolar disorder in children represents the intersection of two great extremes of ignorance: how to best treat bipolar disorder and how to treat children for *anything*.[9]

This diagnostic ignorance brings me full circle—back to a remote ranch in Montana, where over the past ten years several hundred students have arrived, bringing with them (usually multiple) syndrome diagnoses and (usually multiple) psychotropic medications.

This diagnostic dilemma was our dilemma, too. If all those disparate symptoms and misbehaviors were incidental to an unknown underlying cause, what was that cause? If the long list of our students' enrollment diagnoses did not really explain the clinical common denominators among them, what was the explanation? And if their symptom clusters did not contain an essential insight to guide effective treatment—any more than fever and cough guided an effective treatment for those mere symptoms—then what ought to guide our treatment? And, given that most of the pills already prescribed on the basis of *DSM-IV* disorders already had failed to remedy their many problems, what should we do to help?

This was a puzzle for which we had no solution.

A Quest

Visiting parents already had struggled with these uncertainties. Most already had received for a son or daughter at least one *DSM-IV* syndrome diagnosis, already had tried prescriptions for pills that already had proved ineffective. As we met at the ranch with parents of prospective students, week after week, month after month, this uncertainty was always in the air.

Our interviews with visiting parents became a ranch ritual, which took a standard form: talk about the (absent) prospective student, discussion about the concept and the details of our program, tour the campus, and then lunch in the dining hall at one of the team tables. The prospective student was fully engaged elsewhere—usually in a wilderness program, or in a hospital. Typically, the parents had flown to Montana the night before—from Boston, Dallas, Chicago, Portland, or L.A.—and had rented an SUV to make the hour's drive west from Kalispell on a windy country highway. Beside a deep blue lake they had turned off the pavement and climbed a few more miles up a piney ridge, and then had descended into Lost Prairie. They asked questions, walked over the campus with us, and then, seated at our conference table, they rehearsed a son's academic collapse, a daughter's unseemly relationships, a boy's dalliance with drugs, or a girl's loneliness. They told of a teenager's troubles, and their own anxiety and grief.

Always parents arrive in Lost Prairie like knights on a quest. They have come a long way from home. What they hope to find may make all the difference in their lives, and so the stakes are very high. For they fear a son or daughter will not make it "like this" in a heartless world. They worry about what surely could happen to a son or daughter who fails to become competent, self-disciplined, motivated, and well-behaved. These parents are not blind—and so they can see the future coming, even if their children cannot. Time is running out. And so they are afraid. They arrive having tried everything else they knew to try to change that prognosis. Montana Academy is not their first try. It is their last hope.

In these encounters it touches me that these mothers and fathers have embarked upon a tireless quest for the solution to a problem they cannot name. They have already done their homework—consulted, read our Web-site, reviewed our resumes, mastered the jargon, talked to experts, googled *DSM-IV* disorder diagnoses. They have read up on medications, devoured self-help books, mastered the latest research about ADHD and non-verbal learning differences. Yet they are baffled. They cannot fathom why their highly honed academic skills and determined persistence have not yet yielded them the answer to the riddle. They are upset that they cannot even name the heart of the problem. They describe its aspects, recite all the explanations experts already have provided, but they sound unconvinced, their confidence in modern psychiatry shaken.

Out of my own curiosity, it has become my habit to ask what problem they think they are trying to solve. What do they think is the *cause* of all these symptoms and misbehaviors? Their lack of a theory galls them. After a sigh and a pause one father left me with a memorable reply: "I don't know, Doc, and thinking about it is like trying to bottle smoke." Occasionally a parent will cling to a *DSM-IV* diagnosis, hoping that it provides the answer. But this has been rare. Most parents already have dispensed with syndrome diagnosis. One exasperated mother was typical. After an expensive interview with an eminent psychiatrist, he told her that her son suffered from oppositional-defiant disorder. "Dammit," she said, "I knew *that* before my son walked into the man's office!"

Their anguish moved me, but it put us on the spot. Although parents could not demand that I provide a diagnosis, since I had never set eyes upon their daughter or son, the riddle hung suspended over those conversations, nevertheless. For its solution was what they had come to find. Like other pilgrims they had covered great distances, going on despite weariness. They had preserved the hope, despite disappointments, that in some remote, unlikely place they would discover what they longed to find, even if, like all knights errant, they had little idea what that grail would look like.

This was, of course, the riddle: treat *what*?

3   A Flawed Approach

ARRIVING STUDENTS immediately demonstrated at the ranch, just as they had done at home, the academic fecklessness, interpersonal boorishness, and unhappy choices that finally had provoked their parents to banish them to Montana. The repetitiousness of these troubles in the months prior to an individual student's arrival at the ranch—and the prevalence of repetitive academic and social failures among our student body—pushed us to notice the unsound "approach" with which most of them had tried (and failed) to negotiate the core challenges of a modern adolescence—at school, at home, and socially, among age-mates.

Such a global disarray suggested a faulty general strategy.

An Approach

Here I will coin a needed psychological term—an *approach*—to denote a person's general mind-set, or way of framing a problem, or style of thinking and feeling. This general mind-set is not the same as any particular idea, emotion, or specific decision.

A psychological approach, then, is a general point of view on any of life's challenges or problems, a general way of making sense of the world and gauging the prospects for taking action, a general mind-set that shapes a person's motives, influences his strategy, and guides his tactics. Partly cognitive but also emotional, a psychological approach frames a challenge, specifies what action might be called for, and arrays available options from which to choose. A characteristic approach tends to remain stable over time, although particular challenges or tasks come and go. In fact, a husband or a friend's general approach may be so familiar, albeit distinct from any specific act or choice, that knowing "how he thinks" permits a wife or friend, hearing about a new challenge or problem or situation, to anticipate "exactly what he will say (or do)."

An approach need not be pathological, of course. A person's approach is simply his general psychological style. Yet one person's approach may be much superior to another's—in terms of outcome. No doubt this diction has meaning only if one person's approach may differ from another's—if your approach can differ from my approach. The point is: for some people a characteristic approach tends to bring success, whereas for others a usual way of making sense of challenges repeatedly produces failure.

Most children and teenagers cannot define their own approaches, cannot even say what an approach is. Yet a teenager's approach can be inferred from the way she reasons about a problem, from actions she takes, from her explanations and excuses, from her attributions of blame. Repetitive behaviors, repeated comments, similar reactions to cognate events, reveal the shape of a psychological lens that repeatedly brings into focus her perception of her predicament. Her approach defines the options she can (or will not) consider. Her approach influences the choices she ultimately makes—and is implicit in them.

A person's characteristic approach seems as natural to him as his characteristic accent and diction. His approach seems to him to be automatic, reflexive, and right, even if to others that approach makes little sense, even seems harebrained. From a person's own point of view, that is, his approach seems internally consistent (assuming that, as a part of his general approach, he cares at all about consistency). It seems to be sensible and right, even if to others it appears illogical, nonsensical, self-defeating and just plain wrong. Human beings, particularly children and teenagers, perhaps, seem only exceptionally to have much insight about the approach they take to their problems. This blindness to the way one's characteristic style comes across is surely one source of comedy (and tragedy) in relations among the generations.

Finally, all parents discover (although many long remain incredulous) that an approach cannot be quickly altered—and, in particular, that a new and better approach to a teenager's life cannot be taught. An approach is not a skill, like cake baking or tent pitching, whose stepwise accomplishment quickly can be learned. Changing a teenager's approach is not a matter of education. Long before our students arrived at the ranch, most of their parents already had tried to persuade or coach or teach or elucidate a better way to reach good decisions. The failure of those teenagers "to learn" better "coping skills" or "decision making" had much to do with their parents' decisions to send them. Most parents have tried, and some have learned, that eloquent lectures do not promptly remedy a boy's or girl's persistent global disarray. Yet they may still employ the diction of teaching and learning even long after they themselves have demonstrated that teenagers cannot simply be taught to straighten out and fly right.

The obvious question—about how a person's approach *does* change—must wait. This will be another discussion (part 4). For now we merely note that a young person's psychological approach is not easily altered, although a teenager's flawed approach is precisely what worried parents hope that we can help them change. When this change in a son or daughter's approach does take place, it turns out to be precisely the transformation that parents hoped for.

A Flawed Approach

What so many visiting parents unhappily have observed across our conference table is that a flailing son's unsound approach to the challenges of adolescence differed in unsubtle ways from the much better approach taken by more successful siblings or classmates. They have described a son's repeated bad choices and contrasted them unfavorably to the good choices made by age-mates or sisters or brothers at the same age. Moreover, a son's *un*successful approach differed drastically also from the much better approach his mother and father say they would themselves have embraced. They would have perceived his academic or social predicament differently. They would have evaluated options differently. They would have made better choices.

Yet, try as they did, they could not change that son or daughter's flawed approach. Neither pointing to options a son had not considered, nor arguing the merits of better choices they would themselves have made, ever seemed to cut short a son's or daughter's string of bad choices.

This imperviousness to eloquent lectures and instructive experience may explain why a troubled teenager persists in coming to adolescent tasks, again and again, in the same futile ways. Because a sound approach is not simply a function of education, it is unsurprising that troubled young people "refuse" to learn a better approach despite all of their memorable failures. Because of this imperviousness to learning, young people persist in bad choices even while other teenagers demonstrate the superior results that a more effective approach tends to bring. Instruction and example do not quickly alter a teenager's flawed approach, and so troubled teenagers fail to learn promptly from unhappy experience. Parents regularly report with exasperation that failing sons and daughters keep on making the same bad choices, even though the obvious consequences are wretched fighting at home and serial humiliation at school.

At the ranch we saw this, too.

Moreover, we could see among our many students what parents of but one unhappy son or daughter usually could not see: that there are only a limited number of ways in which teenagers flounder. Usually parents have experienced only one version of this dysfunctional approach. At the ranch over the years our sample grew into the hundreds. And among all those floridly failing young people were typical (that is, repetitive) ways in which they struggled and failed to make themselves at home—or resisted making themselves at home at all. Among them there were only a few typical (often repeated) ways in which our students tried to explain away a shameful history. There were only a few typical (repeated) ways that exiled teenagers failed to make or keep friends, or offended parents and alienated other adults. There were typical excuses, repeated efforts to blame others, characteristic ways to explain away a failure to accomplish a chore or do an equal share of a team's task. Despite the variety in parents' descriptions of their children, we noticed, as we saw all of their sons and daughters together, a number of common denominators. In our conferences we assembled what we knew, and gradually a picture emerged: of a typically flawed approach.

The first hint was that the impact of a flawed approach was *global*, affecting a teenager's performance across most or all venues of adolescent life. A flawed approach did not merely happen to be a different approach, an expression of personal idiosyncrasy. A *flawed* approach had unfavorable results across the board.

A second hint: a troubled teenager's flawed approach tended to be stable over time. It did not improve quickly despite angry parental exhortation, teachers' remonstrances, or therapists' interpretations. Students re-created at the ranch the troubles that had dogged them prior to their arrival—and these had been repetitive, intractable, and usually progressive. Over time the scope of their failures broadened, the consequences became more dire, and whole families came to be affected. And yet a son's or daughter's flawed approach continued, not remedied by negative consequences.

A third hint was that one student's flawed approach resembled another student's flawed approach. It was only in the specifics that one dysfunctional student differed from another. Specific misbehaviors, particular academic difficulties, a teenager's unique personal repertoire of social *faux pas*, differed among our students. This diversity explained why their symptoms were various, why their symptom-based diagnoses were scattershot, and why the pharmacological cocktails, aimed at those symptoms or clusters of symptoms, were also disparate. Yet each unsound approach, which we could infer from these disparate combinations of troubles, closely resembled the others. And so we realized that each new student's dysfunctional approach to the tasks and challenges of adolescence was a variation on that common theme. There were not many flawed approaches, but only one: *the* flawed approach of troubled teenagers.

Common Elements

This inference was unavoidable. For the elements in tens of parental descriptions of this flawed approach became repetitive—all but universal. Moreover, in living and working with their children, we experienced at the ranch precisely what parents had experienced at home. Our own experiences, combined with these hundreds of accounts from visiting parents describing what worried them the most, came down to a short list of complaints. We soon could tick off on the fingers of one hand the common elements of this flawed approach:

- Gross narcissism.
- Lack of true empathy.
- "Puppet" relationships.
- Magical thinking about the future.
- Selfish and concrete morals.

When these five core complaints became familiar, I began to test this inference—that there was but *one* flawed approach, that each of our students was a clinical variation upon that common theme.

This informal test was not difficult. Parents of prospective students visit the ranch without their children, and so there is ample time for grown-up conversation about their sons or daughters. After a tour and our collaborative review of the case, parents usually ask whether we think, after hearing about them, that their son or daughter will fit in with other young people at the ranch. Because we have not yet set eyes upon the teenager in question, I offer to describe a typical Montana Academy student, so that parents can draw their own conclusions. Always, visiting parents welcome this description.

Then I explain that our students are individuals who must be understood separately, each in a unique way. I remind them that our seventy students represent seventy different histories, seventy different families, seventy disparate clusters of symptoms and *DSM-IV* diagnostic profiles. I then say that there seem to be a few common denominators our students seem to share, at the outset, however. Ticking off these element on my fingers I explain that at home, before parents made the decision to take action, each of our students:

- Thought only of himself, his words and actions demonstrating little consideration for parents, siblings, teachers, or anyone else except his pals—and often not even his pals;
- Seemed incapable of empathy except for the close friends she considered to be "just like *me*"—and certainly not for anyone she considered to be *un*like herself;
- Treated parents and girlfriends like puppets whom he had a right to expect to do his bidding—to pay for him, to wait on him without thanks, to exercise no independent judgment, to take seriously no motive apart from his wants, to enjoy no right to separate wishes or a distinctive point of view—so that if a parent or sibling or girlfriend said "no" or tried to go her own way or to express a different opinion, he felt he had the right to throw a tantrum, argue, threaten, badger, or punish—or else felt entitled to sneak around or defy any prohibition;
- Considered it all about *now*, leaving the future a hazy, unimportant destination disconnected from the present, where (insofar as she bothered to imagine any goal) she expected to arrive by means of wishful thinking; and

- Was willing to manipulate or sneak around or to cheat or steal or dissemble or mislead so as to get his way or to get something he wanted; and, although also open to all available rewards, he was inwardly restrained from defying a prohibition only by virtue of his calculation of the odds of getting caught and punished.

The results of this informal poll have been remarkable. With numbing repetitiveness, mothers and fathers have expressed consternation that "you have described my son" or "you know my daughter"—although, of course, I have never met their children.

Yet all I have done was to read back to one teenager's parents what so many other parents have so frequently described. I am not describing their son or daughter, whom I have never seen. I am simply describing what seems to be: *the* flawed approach of a large population of troubled American teenagers.

Desired Outcomes

Always, at this moment in our discussion, parents cease to be ambivalent or vague, and they say clearly that in fact *this* is what worries them. Yes, a daughter's symptoms concerned them. Yes, a son's squirminess in class worried them. Yes, they had registered those diagnoses—of dysthymia, of ADHD, or oppositional defiant disorder, of bipolar disorder, of substance abuse. They had acquiesced in medication trials. But the elements of my description of a flawed approach were what truly scared them. This was what kept getting daughters and sons in trouble, repeatedly, progressively, disastrously. It was this flawed approach in their children that they hoped to find a way to change.

Once these elements of a teenager's flawed approach had been summarized, parents were entirely clear, and unambivalent about what a desirable remedy would look like, too. Immediately they could name the outcomes that would define a successful treatment. These desired results were implicit in their descriptions of their children's problems.

Put briefly, parents wanted their sons and daughters to embrace a new approach that was not flawed. Yes, they were upset about a son's specific bad decision, but they did not hope that we would coach him about particular decisions. They did not want us to teach him new facts or give him new skills. They wanted us to transform *him*—to change the decision maker—after which, they understood, good decisions would follow. They wanted his choices to take into account the law, wanted him to know and accept that all the laws applied to him. They wanted him to prepare for a fully anticipated future. They hoped that he might become considerate, so that he might be liked and have friends—and find love. They were concerned about a daughter's self-esteem, but were not asking that we "make nice" or prescribe a pill to make her feel better. Rather, they hoped we might help to transform *her*—to change her into a diligent student, an empathic friend, a chaste romantic, an attractive lover, who would legitimately respect herself.

Robert Kegan has described this parental wish for transformation—in a troubled boy he called Matty—in a passage I cannot improve upon:

> What kind of a thing is it Matty's parents want of him? One answer is that it is a behavior, a way of acting. They want him to stop doing certain things he does and start doing others. But…it is more than behavior…[His mother] wants him to "behave," but she wants him to do so out of his feeling for members of the family of which he sees he is a part… They want him to feel differently about them, about his willingness to put his own needs ahead of his agreements, about his responsibility to his family…
>
> But where do these inner feelings come from? Or, to put it another way, what would have to change in order for Matty's feelings to change? The answer, I believe, is that Matty's feelings come from the way he understands what the world is all about…What [they] want is for Matty to change…the *way* he knows… What [his parents] want…is for his mind to be different. They want him to…change his mind.[1]

This parental wish was *not* to make Matty a psychiatric dependent. They were not hoping to find a medication-for-a-lifetime. Rather, they wished they could transform an unacceptable, dysfunctional, annoying, and fundamentally flawed approach to his life and to his relationship with them—into a better approach. They hoped such a transformation would permit him to ride off into an adult horizon where he would be able to be loved and productive and happy, without further need for his parents or a shrink to ride behind his saddle, cleaning up his messes or counting out pills.

This much parents told us clearly—that they wanted teenaged daughters and sons to find a better approach. They even knew what this outcome should look like. The remedy would be "to change his mind," to alter her approach:

FROM:		TO:
Gross narcissism	⟹	Consideration for others
Lack of true empathy	⟹	Accurate true empathy
"Puppet" relationships	⟹	Separate relationships
Magical thinking about time	⟹	Goals, plans, disciplined follow-through
Selfish, concrete morals	⟹	Abstract, social ethics

The Solution to the Riddle

But what was this flawed approach?

Change what?

Where did an approach come from? What caused a teenager's approach to become flawed? How could that underlying cause be addressed directly, so as not merely to medicate symptoms? How could a dysfunctional adolescent approach be transformed into that more effective approach that parents hoped for?

As the ranch community elaborated a constructive culture, which required months, even years, some of these questions began to answer themselves. Even before we recognized what we needed to do to transform a troubled teenager's flawed approach, some senior students just did it. They demonstrated the desired transformation. Their approaches to their lives changed.

These remarkably transformed young people spontaneously developed consideration for others, besides themselves. They seemed less grandiose, less self-important. They spoke with new genuine empathy for parents, teachers, and fellow students, whose feelings they had not previously noticed or cared very much about. They began to imagine the future, to map goals, to make plans they then followed to completion. They startled us by speaking with affection about team, community, school, and family. They took offense at mean-spirited hazing, which other students kept trying. They railed against "shit talking" about other students, for they now could not ignore how hurtful it was to be talked about. They stopped having tantrums, ceased to argue when the answer was no, even if they were disappointed. They could argue without rancor. Their ethical diction changed, became abstract, and they talked about what was right and wrong, what was honorable and contemptible. They considered what affected, for better or worse, the team and the community and the family. Once-sneaky students made alliances with adults and stopped sneaking—and expressed contempt for lying and sneakiness among their fellow students.

In other words, the transformation happened before we knew what factors had contributed to that happy outcome. We realized that some of what we were doing might be right—or not entirely wrong—and we began to study what preceded this salutary progress. On the other hand, perhaps these shifts in viewpoint and behavior were spontaneous, or resulted from extraneous factors, so that we were merely studying how we had moved our feet before it rained, so as to learn to do the rain dance. But in the meantime parents became noisily grateful about the transformation of a daughter or a son, confirming that this often-remarkable sea change was precisely what they had hoped would happen at Montana Academy.

Yet, not knowing for sure what the causes of the presenting problems had been, much less what exactly we might have done, if anything, to bring about these radical improvements, we simply tried to keep doing whatever it was that we had done in these cases. And we kept reviewing our successes and failures, comparing them. For even in the presence of these sporadic successes, we were still in the presence of the riddle.

What was the problem? Certainly there were implicit theories. To parents and teachers these transformations seemed the unexpected arrival of academic and interpersonal virtue. Program staff thought that their stern consequences had induced good (and discouraged bad) behavior. Others implied that these startling changes might be the result of a shift in intelligence, for they noticed that these exemplary students had begun to make clever and smart (good) choices, rather than stupid and foolhardy (bad) decisions.

Then, all at once, we tripped over the answer. It turned out neither to be the sudden arrival of virtue nor a spontaneous mid-adolescent rise in IQ. During a staff conference about one student's annoying, repetitively dysfunctional behavior, my wife, who had trained at the Yale Child Study Center, pointed out that every element in the boy's flawed approach to every challenge and task at Montana Academy was perfectly normal—in a three-year-old. We laughed—good line.

And then we thought about it. She was right. One could tick those elements off on the fingers of one hand. It was, after all, perfectly normal for a toddler

- To think it's "all about me";
- Not to be able to imagine the world from an adult vantage, not to have any idea at all how an adult (parent) thinks or feels;
- To have no long-term goal, no plan, and no self-discipline to stick to a plan;
- To have no close relationship that was separate—and so to treat parents and siblings as puppets who ought to acquiesce in whatever he wanted to do—or else he would throw a tantrum; and
- To have no inner ethical constraint, when it came to what he wanted to do, even if that wish had been prohibited, other than to worry about whether he might get caught and punished.

This review made it obvious. A troubled, dysfunctional teenager is not bad, not a psychopath (yet), even if sneaky. A globally failing teenager is not stupid, not even illogical. When she misbehaves, she is *childish*.

From this developmental vantage, a troubled teenager's many troubles—his bad decisions, her lack of empathy, his puppet relationships, her primitive ethics, his crude manners and her inconsiderate social *faux pas*—all came into focus. In that moment we had a theory of cause. And once we said it aloud, it already sounded like a firm grasp of the obvious.

That flawed approach was *immaturity*.

A Remedy

We have come to accept this hypothesis—that much of the trouble of troubled teenagers results from immaturity. Over this decade we have had many opportunities to test this hypothesis by informal means.

Certainly, our clinical experience supports it. We have watched this shift in maturation time and again, although its occurrence is not inevitable, not a sure thing. We have begun to study this recovery process, to develop our own instrument to measure that progress in a systematic way (chapter 10). We have developed a practical theory about what moves the tectonic plates of character, and a brief discussion of this "parental" approach comes later in this book (part 4) and will be described in detail in a second book to be published (in press, 2008). On the basis of this understanding of adolescent developmental delay, we have shaped the evolution of Montana Academy.

Parents also support this developmental hypothesis. During this decade, parents often have spoken at our graduation exercises, usually tearfully. They confirm that a developmental transformation has taken place—or has begun to. They tell us repeatedly that the changes that have occurred were precisely the transformations they hardly dared to hope for. In thirty years of psychiatry I have never before experience this kind of enthusiastic response to my clinical work. My experienced partners say the same. And to parents this maturational transformation, when (and if) it happens, is an unsubtle outcome that they often describe as miraculous.

Furthermore, we have noted repeatedly a correlation between this recovery of developmental momentum, on the one hand, and a radical improvement in academic and interpersonal functioning on the other. Those among our graduates who became exemplary students, who restored warm affiliations with parents, who made friends and found lovers, all have changed that initial flawed approach in obvious, substantial, and predictable ways. At graduation, our successful students no longer appear childish. And the exceptions (e.g., when an unsuccessful student leaves the ranch prematurely) prove the rule. In short, these appear not to be independent variables. Positive major changes in function—at school, at home, among friends—coincide with positive shifts in maturation. The one seems not to occur without the other.

Variables other than maturation surely influence a teenager's prospects. Maturity is not all there is to an adolescent's coming of age. Yet among troubled teenagers we have known at the ranch, a recovered developmental momentum (or lack thereof) seems to be the most reliable predictor of future success.

To make sense of a developmental explanation for the problems of troubled teenagers, we must briefly review normal development—the purpose of part 2. Having traced normal stages of development, we will be able to make sense of what delayed development looks like. To predict the elements of that flawed approach, we need only locate where in the sequence a step has been blocked, and from this vantage a troubled teenager's struggles clearly make sense. Also, once we recognize at what point in development a delay occurred, we can infer from the history what event or disturbance or equipment problem turned into an obstacle. We will cover these matters in part 3.

Finally, we will consider in part 4 a two-step approach to diagnosis and treatment, which makes sense of the role *DSM-IV* legitimately plays—as a description of potential intrinsic obstacles to normal maturation. Removing or mitigating the impact of these obstacles is the first step in treatment. The second step is to restore momentum to a stalled maturation. In the end, if and when parents, clinicians, and troubled teenagers themselves can accomplish these steps, the result is a remarkable remedy.

That remedy, of course, is simply to grow up.

Part 2
Normal Maturation

4 · Thought & Time

To UNDERSTAND a *lack* of maturity, we must start with normal development. We need to have in mind a vivid portrait of a thriving adolescence before asking about a troubled teenager, "What's wrong with this picture?"

Yet psychological development is as complex as anything we might try to describe. We need a way to clarify the process of development by slowing the action, so that we can follow the sequence, which tends to become a blur. To do this I break the sequence into its parts the way a Julia Child would demonstrate *haute cuisine* by laying out along the counter, in sequence, the sliced vegetables, the segmented fowl, and all the makings for the sauce. Then, having displayed them in the coming sequence, she would put them together in real time—and *voilà!*

In psychology, the component parts are *developmental lines*. In this chapter, I first consider the steps in the maturation of *thinking*, and describe the sequence by which a child's sense of time unfolds. In chapter 5, I rehearse the stages of psychological *separation*, as an infant grows up to become an adult—and so explain the bases for *empathy* and for *ethical reasoning*. Just as John Madden explained a complex third-down pass play, we will rehearse the steps in slo-mo, and I will provide a chalk-board diagram. Then in chapter 6 all of these component parts are put together to make sense of the stages of development from infancy to incipient adult maturity.

A developmental line is a sequence of steps that carries a child toward maturity. It is a sequence of psychological milestones. To illustrate, the stages of the life cycle can be thought about as a developmental line, the steps of which we might name: infant ⚬ toddler ⚬ schoolchild ⚬ adolescent ⚬ adult.

Here is a chalkboard diagram:

AGE	LIFE STAGES
0-18 mo	Infant
18 mo-5 yrs	Toddler
6-12 yrs	Schoolboy/Schoolgirl
13 -18 yrs	Adolescent
18+ yrs	Adult

These age ranges are approximate, of course. These stages are not bounded by precisely the same chronological ages for every child. The arrow points in the direction of passing time and maturation. This is straightforward.

This listing of life stages **is** a proper developmental line. *Why?* Because its steps follow a *chronological order* and *each step is distinctive*. No one mistakes a schoolgirl for an infant. Moreover, the sequence is invariable. Each step is a necessary preparation for the next step, each step emerges organically from the fullness of the preceding stages. No infant becomes an adult without passing through each prior stage, and always in this same order. That is to say, these stages are logically linked in one continuous process. No normal schoolboy can navigate third grade without having already achieved spoken language in the previous (toddler) stage.

Yet not every list of life events is a developmental line, even when those events are arrayed in chronological order. As a counterexample, this sequence of events in a man's life is *not* a legitimate developmental line: *marry ⚬ conceive children ⚬ wake up worried in the night ⚬ go bald.* Some of us will insist that this sequence is plausible, but yet it is not a proper developmental line. For there is no organic linkage among its steps. The sequence is not fixed. These events could occur in any order.

Some descriptions of developmental lines are classic, and students of developmental psychology should master them. Some of them will prove to be very helpful in making sense of the maturation of children and teenagers.

- Sigmund Freud inferred from the symptoms of his adult patients the symbolic reverberations of childhood's *psychosexual* stages.[1]
- Decades later Jean Piaget stayed home with his own children and,

by careful observation, defined the normative stages in a child's *cognitive* development.[2]

- Margaret Mahler studied the sequential steps in an infant's and toddler's *separation* and *individuation* from his parents.[3]
- Heinz Kohut, who worked with adults in psychoanalysis, described narcissistic character pathology that he thought the result of an arrested development in interpersonal relationships. This developmental line got an obscure name—*object relations*.[4]
- Robert Kohlberg, who also managed to make a career of playing with children, told the same stories to children at various ages, so as to figure out how they thought about ethical dilemmas. In these encounters he discerned the sequential stages in the development of *moral reasoning*.[5]

Each of the above writers described sequences that play out in the first two decades of life. I should mention two students of development who staged the entire human life cycle.

- Erik Erikson mapped eight sequential psychosocial crises that mark the way from infancy to senescence. These crises occur at the boundary between a developing person, as an individual, and the society in which he is reared.[6]
- Robert Kegan, in his brilliant synthesis of all these developmental lines (and others, too), described the evolution of the self.[7]

These developmental lines simplify and clarify. Each does not happen separately in the lives of children. Rather, they are to developmental psychology what freeze-action and slo-mo are on *Monday Night Football*. They provide instructive camera angles from which to review the progressive developmental stages of a child's life. For example, Freud's "anal" stage is but one viewpoint on a toddler's psychology. In the same toddler (at the same age), Piaget noted a typical "preoperational" way of thinking. Or again, in that same preschooler (at the same age), Erikson saw an inevitable psychosocial struggle between a toddler and his family (society) over "autonomy." That toddler, of course, is not any one of these partial descriptions, but the sum of many developmental contributions— each developmental line contributing its peculiar perspective upon, let us say, the "toddler." In this sense, a two- to three-year old child struggles with the developmental task and psychosexual themes of toilet training, doing so by means of a peculiar preoperational thinking, and in doing so, sounds for the first time a lifelong leitmotif—autonomy. Considered together, in short, various developmental lines contribute to a composite portrait of one maturational stage—*voilà!*

Thought

Let's start with *thinking*.

That is, let's pay attention to *how* children think, as they grow up—not *what* they might happen to be thinking. As children mature, the structure of their thinking changes. Every Christmas, for example, American children get reminded that a portly bearded man in a red suit will sneak down chimneys into every home on the planet. As we know, four-year-olds and ten-year-olds are not equally inclined to believe this—for developmental reasons. A four-year-old does not think about this proposition in the same way that a ten-year-old can.

The idea that we see the world through the prism of mind is not new. Immanuel Kant suggested that we cannot experience "reality" directly, because we can only know the world beyond ourselves through innate mental categories that shape our grasp of that world.[8] He said we cannot see a "thing-in-itself" (*ding an sich*) as it truly exists, beyond our ken. We register only a world reflected in the fun-house mirrors of our minds.

To this venerable philosophical idea, Jean Piaget offered a modern twist.[9] He agreed that we are imprisoned within the psychological structures of our thoughts. But in his brilliant studies with his own children he demonstrated that those mental structures are not fixed. They change as a child's capacity to think matures. As she grows up, as her thinking matures, so too do the ways in which she makes sense of the world. The refractive mirror of her mind undergoes predictable changes, which alter what she can be taught, can learn, can know. That is to say, a child's cognitive approach to her experience passes through predictable stages—a *cognitive* developmental line.

THINKING[10]

Infant	Sensorimotor
Toddler	Magical [Protean Categories][11]
School Child	Concrete Logic [Durable Categories]
Adolescent	Abstract Logic [Cross-Contextual]

This chalkboard looks a little formidable. But stay tuned; it is not arcane or unfamiliar. After all, we have all been through all of these stage, ourselves. We have all thought all these various ways ourselves. And if we are parents, we have watched our children pass through these stages of thinking. This will be familiar, and it will help to make sense of what exasperates and charms us about adolescence.

Let's consider these stages, one at a time.

An *infant* seems (to us) hardly to be thinking at all. Babies during this **sensorimotor** stage appear to feel and react automatically, like a bundle of reflexes. Stimulated by the "outer" world, an infant seems to react with programmed responses. We can only imagine how it seems to him as he floats helplessly in a sensory chowder thick with faces, noises, colors, and feelings that arise from he-knows-not-where, attached to he-knows-not-what. He can have little idea what is his and not his; what is inside and what outside; what is attached and what disconnected. His voluntary repertoire, however charming, remains rudimentary. He sucks any nubbin; he smiles at digestive sensations or a sister's grinning mug; he sleeps when tired, pees when his bladder fills, cries in pain or hunger or boredom. He does not have reflexes, in Robert Kegan's formulation. He *is* his reflexes.[11]

Genetics propel him onward. Experience fills his sensorium and paints his dreams with portentous spectacle long before he understands a single word or organizes his experience in culturally-defined categories. As the months pass, he imposes control over his hands and legs in efforts that appear to require fierce concentration. Waking and sleeping he is engrossed in some mix of sensation and motor effort.

This effort, and his growing strength and coordination, gradually transform him into a *toddler*, who is no longer immobile. In those first few years a once-helpless bambina becomes a little girl. Now she rolls over, sits up, crawls, stands, walks, then climbs and runs through the toddler's gate into the **magical** garden of her thoughts. What has changed is not merely strength. A dialectic of assimilation and accommodation propels her mentally, too.[11] As she enters childhood's garden standing up, she also can talk. By the end of two years she can express her thoughts in short sentences. At three, her syntax reveals a complex, whimsical train of thought. Ever firmer motor control lets her peek around, open up, crawl into, and creep under tight places—and so explore that garden. Ever firmer control over her sphincters and a new interpersonal negotiation promote continence. Her ever more agile mobility propels her toward trouble, and so her words now must mediate her first social interactions with strangers and the frustrations of her first encounter with the parental *No*.

What is she thinking?

A toddler is a dreamy playmate described so well by Selma H. Fraiberg in her classic *The Magic Years*. She is an alert, articulate, proudly dry pal capable of make-believe and dress-up. Her costumes, like her thoughts, mix pretend with real. For she *is* Alice in Wonderland. When she plays she now thinks differently from the way infants do. She employs a capricious logic that Piaget demonstrated in his own children. When, for instance, he poured water from a short wide cup into a taller narrower glass, and asked whether the "amount" of water had changed, toddlers usually said yes. The essence of this childish logic, Piaget came to think, was subjectivity, a confusion of fact with perception, a mixing up of perception with feeling, a blending of reality with wish. The world's properties and categories are, for a toddler, as protean as her whims.

Magical thinking makes toddlers gullible and charming. It is OK with them that water expands when poured from cup to glass. It is fine with them that when a girl sips from a bottle labeled "Drink Me," she shrinks to thumb size. It is all right with them that a tornado sweeps Dorothy and Toto all the way to Oz uninjured. It is all right, too, if Mary Poppins flies with an umbrella and Peter Pan can fly merely by wanting to. Toddlers make imaginary friends and believe in the Tooth Fairy. It is plausible to them that a red-suited fat man flies a sleigh drawn by reindeer and slips down chimneys to visit every child and to nibble every cookie on every saucer beside every Christmas tree on the planet.

It is sad for us, if not for them, when our small-fry leave this Eden. The classroom is less enchanted.[12] For *school-children* think differently from the way toddlers do. This new kind of thinking—**concrete logic**— exiles them from the garden. They do not seem to mind. Schoolboys and schoolgirls put two and two together and know the sum is *always* four. How do they know this? *Durable categories* tell them so. Unlike toddlers, schoolkids realize that qualities and properties remain stable in space and time. Once properties stay put, a schoolboy can apply logic to them and to their stable properties, an application that otherwise would be pointless. He rushes to learn about mechanical toys and tools and stamps and rocks, to master facts, to figure out the logic of inner workings. For what is a fact, after all, but a property or measurement that persists and so remains true over time? Equipped with durable categories, schoolchildren rush from the dappled leafy paths of Eden into the sunny meadows of reason. Equipped with concrete logic they accumulate facts, make lists, figure out how, locate where, and measure how long.

Schoolboys and schoolgirls now can apply this new logic to persons and roles. If volume is conserved, so are dispositions and traits. If a mom likes golf and pizza today, she will like them tomorrow. The role of teacher persists, even though the woman calls in sick and must be replaced by a "substitute." A dad can be a neighbor, a coach, and policeman all at once.

Mastery has its own appeal. Boy and Girl Scouts aspire to skills, knowledge, mastery. Reciprocally, they embrace adults as teachers, mentors, helpers, and coaches. School children welcome adult help to learn *how*—to put together a model airplane, to bake a cake, to pitch a tent, to play Chopsticks with two fingers. They are pleased if allowed to light a fire, to build a coop, to ride a horse or sew on a button. As always, when they leave behind an old milestone, schoolchildren are disdainful about the gullibility of toddlers. They scoff at the very idea that a paunchy adult can slide down a flue or that a reindeer can fly. They cannot be fooled by Santa wearing daddy's slippers. They chortle, and barely contain their contempt for small-fry who actually believe those fairy tales.

Yet schoolchildren miss Eden. This is plain, for so long as it is labeled "magic," and distinguished with a code word, that world of whim is a place that schoolboys and schoolgirls like to visit. Harry Potter loves to go there, too, just so long as the distinction remains clear: magic is one thing, the natural logic of the real world another. For diapered little sisters and brothers, no such distinction exists.

Testing schoolchildren, Piaget demonstrated that they were logical but concrete. They sorted and counted colored beads with accuracy, but had difficulty with imaginary or improbable categories, even if the improbable category remained constant. Jerome Kagen (1972) demonstrated this concreteness with a test syllogism:

> *All purple snakes have four legs.*
> *I am hiding a purple snake.*
> *How many legs does it have?*

Ten-year-olds quibble about "the very idea of there being a purple or four-legged snake," because purple or four-legged snakes "are not found in the concrete world." Reasoning about them "is problematic," Kagen discovered. Schoolage children enjoy little capacity to lift off from the mundane facts, to reason about imaginary creatures. For schoolaged kids, he reported, the "notion of truthfulness . . . is tied to the domain of correspondence to observed phenomena."[13]

The thought of schoolchildren is concrete, but logical. This kind of thinking provides a sound basis for reasoning about tangible items: stamps, hems, baseball cards, matches, knitting, saddles, knives, papier-mâché, wiring, model airplanes, photographs, and coins. The leitmotif for concrete logic, of course, is the list, whether the ingredients in a recipe for cookies or the checksheet for the Cooking Merit Badge. Group memberships get marked by uniforms, flags, trophies, badges, and passwords. Academic projects, short on prose and long on props, contain demos, models, maps, collages, and lists. Schoolchildren can be fun, but not very funny in the way an adolescent can be funny. For they remain too concrete for metaphor or irony.

The thinking that comes in *adolescence—**abstract thought**—*is the crown jewel of cognitive development. Abstraction applies logic to ideas that are not immediate, to objects not present, to qualities not tangible—and so permits reasoning about non-citizens, even non-ducks. Abstraction generalizes from particulars, grouping them under a "higher" category on the basis of a common denominator. Abstraction subsumes pals and playmates under an overarching concept of Friend. It lumps exemplary actions and ideals under the rubric of Honor. Compared to concrete logic, abstract thinking permits an adolescent to hold in mind any number of particulars—so that a bridge term can embrace them all.

Kegan called this capacity to think *across* categories or contexts "cross-categorical" thinking.[14] This term sounds more complicated than it is. Let's say that as a teacher you describe (a) Galileo's recantation, (b) the martyrdom of Jordano Bruno, and (c) the arrival of the first pilgrims at Plymouth, Massachusetts. If you then were to ask your students, "What do you suppose these three events were all *about*?" you would get different answers depending upon the maturity of your students. For maturity would make them think differently. If you asked that question in a fourth-grade classroom, your students might draw you a picture or paste cutouts to render each (concrete) historical *tableau*: a bullied astronomer; a burning heretic; three ships docked upon a very special and particular rock. A ten-year-old in that classroom could recite the story of Galileo, conjure the first Thanksgiving, and tell how to start a fire with two sticks. But grade school girls and boys would have trouble grouping events by a common abstract theme.

You would have to drive across town to find high school sophomores ready to think *across* those three contexts, to link them abstractly, and so discover a theme—e.g., religious oppression. In this sense the achievement of abstract thinking opens for exploration previously undiscovered continents. Once his students have arrived on this abstract shore, a math teacher can write an equation defining a logical relationship between variables x and y, and an adolescent can solve for the "unknown." Provided with experimental facts, adolescent students can infer whether those data confirm or fail to confirm an hypothesis. Thinking abstractly, a teenager can leave the concrete here and now—our town, our culture, our era—to join in imagination an anthropological tribe of the not-us, to travel in literature to the not-real, and to visit a utopian not-yet. Teenagers can hold multiple historical events in mind, put them into temporal sequence, and compare or contrast: the Peloponnesian War, the Middle Ages, the End of the Frontier, and the Sixties.

Adolescence also changes a teenager's capacity for social understanding. The adolescent capacity to think across categories opens up new social continents to be explored. For example, a teenager can hold in mind, simultaneously, both her own desires and her mother's enduring values, and so anticipate how her own misbehavior might alter their warm *relationship*. A teenager can anticipate whether a particular act, such as his staying out past his curfew, will injure the *trust* he enjoys with his parents.

In the context of a maturing adolescent society, abstract thought provides a relative social advantage—and soon becomes necessary to social acceptance. Conversely, a lack of abstract thinking becomes a social handicap. For if abstract logic boosts a teenager's social performance, its absence reduces a teenager's ability to converse about anything his age-mates consider important.[15] Once others acquire this mature capacity to think, a teenager who cannot think abstractly becomes exceptional, a childish anomaly. For this reason, abstract thinking transforms peer relationships. It shifts the diction and subject matter considered cool in conversation. It promotes new relationships, gives new shape to ethical ideas, and transforms an adolescent's social viewpoint. Thinking abstractly, teenagers make new kinds of friends and new enemies on the basis of abstract groupings of Us and Them. At first the links of friendship may remain concrete, e.g., we attend the same school. But to this concrete basis for affinity a mature teenager now adds abstract common predicates (e.g., shared political views). Romantic affiliations become nuanced (e.g., with subtle rules about "going" with).

Abstraction transforms a teenager's academic performance, too. High schools can teach abstract academic concepts, such as cause, contrast, comparison, principle, and theme. Cross-contextual discourse becomes the intellectual *lingua franca*. Mature teenagers energetically debate political, literary, religious, and economic ideas that, only recently, they could not have cared about. Political thinking (across categories) becomes so exciting that teenagers perennially imagine they have invented equity and the rules of romance. Ideals (e.g., democracy, or "our country") provoke loyalties so passionate that teenagers will risk dying for them. Surely it was no accident that when Socrates asked, "What is justice?", he was talking with teenagers.[16]

Time

Adolescents acquire "executive functions," which seem to be localized in the frontal lobes of the brain. These coordinating, directing, ordering capacities have been compared to the contributions a conductor makes to a symphony orchestra.[17] Among these executive capacities is an ability to conceptualize and orient pragmatically to the future and the past.

When it comes to academic performance in high school and college, few cognitive innovations matter more than future orientation, i.e., a capacity to define a goal, create a logical plan to reach that goal, and stick to it. When it comes to academic mastery in particular subjects, such as history, few cognitive innovations matter more than a capacity to relate to the past. The ability to manage time, to fix upon a goal and define the steps in a plan, and also the capacity to integrate the past with the present and the future, depend upon cross-contextual thinking. However, its importance warrants separate consideration of a developmental line—the mature sense of *time*.

Here's the chalkboard:

PERCEPTION OF TIME

Infant		Now (Futureless, Pastless)
Toddler		Magical Future (and Past)
Schoolchild		Clocks & Calendars
Adolescent		Pragmatic Future and Past

Again, let's briefly focus upon each stage.

We cannot ask an *infant* what she thinks of time. Yet all new parents soon learn that babies could care less what time it is. We infer from watching them that infants orient to what is happening **now**—to light or darkness, hunger or satiety, alertness or torpor, comfort or cold wet diapers. Because infants react to now, and cannot speak, we can make no promise of future solace that can provide any consolation to an infant who is unhappy now. Infants train parents to conjugate all their verbs in the present tense. Time *now* to feed her. Time *now* to burp her. Time *now* to change her shorts. Time *now* to sleep (before she wakes us up again). A full night of sleep becomes a fond memory.

Toddlers can communicate their ideas in words, and so we know they think about time in **magical** ways. The future is a destination to be reached by wishful thinking. Toddlers believe that they can someday reach Never-Never Land if they want to fly there badly enough. The past, like the future, remains fantastic—a realm where big events (e.g., his own birth) somehow transpired Once Upon a Time. A toddler still inhabits an island called Now whose shores extend only a short way in both directions, past and future, and vanish into Outer Darkness.

For toddlers, feelings seem to stretch or shorten spans of time. For toddlers, time is as subjective, as protean, and as plastic as that liquid Piaget poured from a squat glass to a skinny one. Hunger, for instance, stretches the span from now until food arrives into an eternity. Comfortable, warm, fun play passes the hours in an eye's twinkle. Stressed by hunger or other discomfort, a toddler can wait a little, but does not want to. Given his limited ability to imagine the future, he cannot console himself long with anticipated solace. He cannot tolerate for long the wait for food, company, warmth, or a changed diaper without emotional circuit overload, the damaging neuropsychological blown fuse we call trauma.

This is why we make it criminal to leave a toddler unattended. On the other hand, clever parents figure out what is "too long," and so they stretch the span a frustrated toddler can tolerate by providing suitable frustrations, which push this envelope. Such frustrations help children to grow up, so long as the wait does not overwhelm a child with anxiety. This titration is one of a parent's critical judgments.

A *schoolgirl's* (or schoolboy's) grasp upon time improves as soon as she can measure it. And she can measure it when she knows that units of time are durable categories, i.e., that each unit remains a stable span of time. Schoolgirls can use tools. Gadgets help to count units of time. Once a child can tell time on **clocks** and cross off the days on **calendars**, time loses its whimsical quality, its elastic tendency to expand with waiting. Adults help with bells to mark hours, chapter divisions to mark units a child has read, and calendars to mark off in anticipation of a holiday. All these divisions parcel out time in durable units.

Despite these tools and gadgets for measuring, a schoolchild's grasp of time remains concrete. At nine, my daughters could not hold in mind a sequence of key events or construct a rudimentary history of the world. At that age none of them could put the ancient Greeks, the Founding Fathers, and John Kennedy's election into chronological order—no matter how often or eloquently (or irritably) I rehearsed the sequence. On one memorable evening a 9-year-old daughter startled me, in the midst of a particularly cogent history lesson at dinner, by clapping her hands over both ears and fleeing from the table. She could not picture the sequence. She could not hold onto it, and trying made her head spin. Her older sisters kept shushing her—"Be quiet! We want to hear about when Dad saw the Rolling Stones!" But at nine all those remote events swam together in a temporal soup. She could not line up historical events in eras or by theme or by causality. Surely, this is why wiser teachers refrain from lecturing about world history to third-graders.

This conceptual incapacity is also why distant goals mean little to schoolchildren. Anticipating when you will apply to college or evoking that future grown-up era in which you will make a living for *your* family—means little to school children. A nine-year-old cannot pursue an extended papier-mâché project all the way to completion without a persistent adult's sustaining help. This is why it is always sweetly ambiguous who truly earned the Wolf Badge—Johnny or his mommy?

And I have learned that when a schoolgirl tells me she means to go to college someday, she might as well be anticipating her visit to Lilliput.

In *adolescence* comes abstract thinking—and a paradigm shift. This new capacity to think across disparate contexts alters the relationship, in a boy's mind, between time-present and time-future. When a boy can connect present and **future** in this pragmatic sense, he holds now and then simultaneously in mind, and he can picture the logical *relationship* between them.[18] He can consider alternative futures, pick one version as a goal. When he can map the steps from here to there, and can alter his present behavior so as to move closer to that goal, he has created *a plan*.

Abstract thought makes it possible to connect the present with the **past**. Once able to hold present and past in mind, a teenager faces a staggering inference: that the planet may have been inhabited before he arrived.[20] Adolescents can imagine that adults once were children. It occurs to them other actors long strutted and fretted their hours upon the stage before they themselves made their star entrances. This new historical perspective helps to sort out the jumbled memories accumulated in earlier, less time-bound eras in their lives ("Oh, *that* must have happened in Cleveland, because I remember the swing set behind the house.") Teenagers can sort the past much as they might sift the family clutter in an attic. Holding in mind both now and then, they discover *relationships* among remembered puzzle pieces, whose fit they had never before anticipated. Putting memory fragments together, adolescents and young adults find themselves wanting again to visit that old house with the swing set, to travel to the Old Country, or to track down a lost biological parent.

This is to say, adolescents can learn history. They can, because they can hold in mind past events and yet maintain a contemporary mental set. They can reason about reasons, consider alternatives. They can segregate fact from theory, debate alternative explanations, learn about various eras—the Golden Age of Athens, the American Civil War, the Sixties— and keep the chronology straight. Moreover, they can discern abstract themes (e.g., women's rights) that connect disparate happenings, so as to bring to contemporary events a historical resonance.

In short, both the past and future begin to haunt the present.

5   Me, Myself,…and *You*

The grown-up concept of *you*, as distinct and separate from *me*, comes to children and teenagers in step-wise fashion—and with difficulty over most of two decades. The idea that an important separate you might have rights that I ought to take seriously is a late milestone.

I, me, my, myself, and mine. These pronouns come readily to very small children's lips, even as the inner representation of the creature to whom they refer changes over time and becomes more substantial as development takes place. The concept of *you* evolves, too, and during adolescence normally acquires a new, complex, reciprocal meaning—of you, as separate from me. As normal psychological separation takes place and a distinct self arises in the mind of a young person, the emerging *other* becomes more alluring, more elusive.

A distinctive, fully-detached, fully-imagined *you* normally is an adolescent achievement, but a precarious one. As we will see, this successful, albeit tentative, differentiation—of *self* from *other*—has a profound transformative influence upon his relationships and his capacity for moral reasoning.

Separateness

In the absence of a separate *you*, a child cannot be expected not to be *self-ish*—for the *you* of the small-fry remains attached conceptually to *me*, and gets all tangled up with what *I* want. In this sense *self-ishness* results from a lack of *separate-ness*. These self-ish terms—*self-*preoccupied, *self-*indulgent, *self-*referential, *self-*important—all properly belong to normal children in whom we expect a lack of separateness—e.g., in toddlers. In this sense they belong to toddlers without the negative connotations.[1] After all, selfishness and egotism are natural in small children. Fully *separate* relationships are later developmental achievements.

This distinction—of *me* from *you*, of *I* from *thou*, of *self* from *other*—may seem obscure. But all of it is familiar, for all of us have been through these stages. Moreover, as we define these stages, you will notice echoes of them all around in daily life. For they define the terms of relationships as commonplace as marriage, employment, military service, and religious or political hierarchies. We see these forms of relationships also in the day-to-day behavior of our children—with us, with their friends, and with their romantic others. The degree of separate-ness, of one*self* from an*other*, defines the alignment of forces so fundamental in our relationships that separateness makes sense of powerful feelings that are tied up in the chemistry of those bonds. These forces may not be obvious under normal circumstances, but become apparent when they are released explosively, if tight bonds are broken—whether in a high school cafeteria, a bar, a bedroom, or a court of law.

To understand the psychology of separate-ness, we have to begin with an infant, who is *not* psychologically separate. Although an infant has left the engulfment of his mother's body, he still has little or no capacity to distinguish himself from an engulfing world. As an infant grows into a toddler, a schoolboy, and then an adolescent and an adult, his capacity to frame a relationship between *self* and *other* changes considerably. From the regular sequence of these innovations we can assemble a developmental line for *separateness*.

Here is the chalkboard:

SEPARATENESS (IN RELATIONSHIPS)

Infant	Fused
Toddler	Puppet (Magical)
School Child	Puppet (Practical)
Adolescent	Separate

Let's take these steps in turn.

Insofar as we can know, an *infant* experiences little or no separation of self from other. Watching a newborn we sense that she is psychologically *fused* with her surround. We infer that her experience of herself embraces all that she perceives—and so she does not conceive of an other beyond herself.

Put yourself in her booties and imagine her world. There in your crib, flat on your back, unable to roll over or sit up or move your arms or legs to any purpose, you cannot know that those floating fingers belong to you, or know that your mother's smiling face does not. You have no categories or words for "face" or "hand" or any body part. You have no concept for "belongs to" or "is attached to," so that, when you feel a colicky cramp, you can feel it but cannot locate it, let alone know why or wherefore. When you smell an odor you cannot imagine wherefrom or why. When touched, picked up, hugged, kissed, fed, or changed, you cannot know which body part has been caressed or kissed or wiped or bundled up except that you feel what you feel. For you have no way to know that you have a body, let alone body parts. In the hours since you left the womb you have been afloat in an engulfing soup of images, smells, tastes, sounds, and sensations. For you all the world is One—all *me*.

This psychological approach is not volitional. An infant does not choose his vantage. He has none of an adult's ways of making sense of his cosmos. His perspective and thinking are functions of his limited maturation, his baby strength and baby balance, his infantile coordination and infantile mind.

When an infant grows bigger and stronger, when his brain takes charge of his limbs, and he can coordinate his hands and legs with his eyes and ears, he learns to roll over and crawl, to stand and walk—and we call him a *toddler*. This neuromuscular progress prods a child to distinguish *me* from *not-me*. Once he can crawl and walk, he can crawl or walk out of the kitchen where his mother works at the sink. He experiences (a tentative) separation, for suddenly, he cannot see her. Yet he registers, again and again, that his toes stick with him when he crawls into the hall—and so they must be parts of him*self*. He registers that the sink and refrigerator do not come along wherever he goes—and so must be *other*.

His relationship with his mother, at this stage, becomes partly separate. When he crawls out of the kitchen she is not with him. But as soon as he cries she *is* with him. He seems to be alone when she is gone, but when he pokes his head back into the kitchen, there she is, and she looks up and calls to him. When he toddles out of a room he cannot see her for that moment. Yet there is no important event in his life—eating, drinking milk, getting his diaper changed, going down for a nap, riding in the car—when she is not there. Is she separate from him—or not? If he gets into mischief the refrigerator does not show up, but *she* does. When he falls down and wails his crib does not come to find him in the back yard, but *she* does. When he is hungry, she shows up with a sandwich. When he is tired, she figures it out and puts him down for a nap. When he wants a story, she reads one. Is she separate? She seems to be *partially* separate.[2] To a toddler she is an other person, whose sole reason for existing seems to be as an extension of himself. I call this a **puppet** relationship.[3]

The structure of this relationship gets repeated all across the life cycle.[4] For this reason let's digress to consider a puppet relationship. To a three-year-old his mother might as well be a hand puppet—out of sight but never out of mind, separate but still attached to him, expected to come when he calls, to dance to his song, to be, in short, the reciprocal to his desire. She is the one who, when he needs something, is supposed to get it for him right now. She is his fairy godmother, whose wand responds to *his* wishes (certainly not her own!). She is Tinkerbell to his Peter Pan. Her task, her only *raison d'être* insofar as he is concerned, is to provide what he needs and wants, to give him what he wants, without his having to ask.

Puppet relationships are partly separate, but never equal. A three-year-old can do little for his mother except to *be*. He is incapable of understanding what it might be like to be an adult. He has no idea what it means to her to be his mother. Moreover, in her he recognizes no legitimate volition apart from her duty to meet his every want and need—to which he is entitled and for which he need not be grateful. He grants her no capacity to think or feel or want anything for herself. He expects her to concentrate entirely upon him. She has no rights, no privileges, no time off for good behavior. Were a brother or sister to come along, he would feel enraged about having to share his small solar system. But his concept of a plausible adjustment does not include her emancipation from her proper orbit—around *him*.

This egocentrism is not his fault, of course. His *self*-ishness is normal. For a three-year-old there are no other kinds of relationships. How could he imagine anything else? From the moment he came to conscious awareness that there was anyone on the planet besides himself, she has been his puppet, willingly wiggling whenever he moves the finger of his will. She has been a beloved puppet—insofar as she speaks and sings only for his ears, and insofar as her song is really ventriloquism, her talk his soliloquy.

How does this puppet relationship look to a toddler's mother? She had some idea what to expect. She knew that for a time she would have to provide for an infant's every need. By his toddler stage, however, she wishes for some control. She weans him from her breast and urges him to use the potty-chair, so that she does not forever have to attend to his backside. Of course small-fry do not ask to be toilet trained. This is the stage at which a baby first encounters the parental *No*—and toddlers usually do not like to hear the word. A modern toddler also may resent his mother's attempts to limit his scope of action, to curtail his right to pee whenever and wherever he likes.

From an adult point of view, a small-fry's puppet relationship is a brief tyranny. From an adult point of view, a parent is a more or less willing slave. When she weans him, his mother only asserts a reasonable ambition not to go on nursing until he can drive a car. She wishes not forever to be awakened in the night, not always to be interrupted peremptorily no matter what else she might be doing, like a servant. She considers these constraints to be modest proposals. She did not mind her time as puppet, but now would like, some fraction of the time, to be the puppeteer.

The toddler's relationship to his puppet is **magical**. He imagines his mother connected to him as by an emotional umbilical cord, so that she can reasonably be expected to provide whatever he wants without his even having to ask. To a toddler, his mother is an all-purpose sprite, the reciprocal to his every desire.

This puppet duet continues through the school years, but in a different key. For *schoolchildren*, the important adults become **practical puppets**. Teachers, scoutmasters, coaches, and parents help school children strive for mastery. A schoolgirl expects her teacher to correct her math, but not to tuck her into bed. She expects her ballet instructor to teach her to pirouette, but not to wash her underwear. She assimilates her mother to these more formal mentor roles. Her mother becomes a teacher, too— e.g., a baking expert, who can instruct her in the production of cookies. A schoolboy expects his 4-H mentor to help doctor his pig, his coach to raise his batting average, his dad to throw him the ball. But the puppet's role becomes task-oriented, practical, and the goal is to help a schoolboy or schoolgirl to achieve mastery in the world.

The puppet roles turn out to be reciprocal. Parents are puppets for children. But our children are their parents' puppets, too. When a three-year-old plays an angel in the preschool play, parents consider that stunning public achievement to be representative of themselves, a social extension of the family. They feel as proud about a daughter's performance as if they had done something praiseworthy themselves. The crowd's applause is for them, too. And when a five-year-old wing forward approaches the goal, and his parents begin to shout detailed instructions, who is the puppet, and who the puppeteer?

❧

For an *adolescent*, the advent of cross-contextual thinking makes possible a new kind of close relationship—one that is **separate** and equal. What is novel is a shared expectation that neither party's need or wish will enjoy a primary claim. No difference in power subordinates one to the other. Nor does either party owe the other anything, or bully the other for a yes. Each acknowledges that the other is free to grant a request or offer any favor. Neither is obliged, however. One may ask and hope the other will agree. But in a separate relationship, the answer may be yes *or* no without an argument, without a battle. In a separate relationship, there is no puppet, no puppeteer—only free agents whose preferences and decisions get treated with respect.

To participate in a separate relationship requires cross-contextual thinking. For it is necessary that there be two contexts, not one. This is why parents can treat toddlers as separate, giving them scope to make some of their own decisions, but toddlers cannot reciprocate. To the extent that children cannot yet see their parents as separate, they can only treat them as fingers, as extensions of themselves, which they expect to wiggle when they want them to. When teenagers acquire the capacity to think abstractly, they acquire the potential, but not yet the developmental achievement, of separate relations. The achievement of separate relations is not automatic, and does not happen without practice. Experience must push him to this more mature relationship. That is, when abstract thought becomes available, an adolescent *can* hold in mind at once both his wishes and an other's desire. He can imagine a relationship between two separate and equal human beings, who can want different results. Taking this idea of a reciprocal relationship into account, he can recognize that bullying might cost him the abstract thing we call a *relationship*.

The emergence of separate relationships, then, is the emotional equivalent of the cognitive achievement of abstract thought. In fact, the one depends upon the other. Cross-contextual (abstract) thinking is the necessary, primary acquisition. It makes possible a teenager's grasp of the laws of physics, but he must be pushed to use his able mind to master these ideas. It also makes possible separate relationships, but he must be pushed, by apt experience, to use his able mind to this end.

When separate relationships arrive they startle parents, who have long been used to puppet relations. A teenager who treats parents as separate begins to pay his share, to notice their feelings and wishes, to take his parents' plans into account. This achieved milestone is a radical step away from selfish narcissism. It is the cure. And when it comes, a teenager's request is a request, not merely a demand backed by pouts or tantrums. When it arrives, a reasonable parent's undisputed answer can be yes—or no.

Narcissism

In this discussion of perceptions of self and other, we are talking about *narcissism*—the developmental line that sequentially transforms a child's capacity for relationships. This can be a complex subject. Many books have discussed its abstractions, many words have been coined to define its fun-house mutual mirrorings. For our purposes, the critical developmental line is the one that starts with an infant fused with his mother and results, at the close of adolescence, in a young adult capable, albeit fleetingly, of separate relationships. We call this the *narcissistic* developmental line. Its drama—of separation and individuation—is the sequential disentanglement of *me* from *you*.

As I have already suggested, a separate world appears not to exist in the mind of a newborn baby. Among his perceptions there appear to be no distinctions between those that belong to himself and those that belong to separate objects and persons. During toddler and childhood and adolescent stages, separation (e.g., from mother and father) creates a world of separate *others*, who come to exist in his mind but separate from his own *self*. As he matures and defines what belongs to him, and so discovers himself, he sheds those elements of the world that once were confused with him, as a snake sheds its skin.[5] And so he creates a world (of distinct representations) of *others*.

The narcissistic developmental line, then, is a series of such sheddings, which leave behind a "self" standing more alone, more clearly distinct from an "outside" world that she can see as separate. At each stage, then, the important *other* in a child's life will change in character. He may always call her "mom," for example. But what he means will change as he matures. What he perceives her to be will change, for his capacity to imagine what goes on inside her will change. What he thinks he is entitled to expect of her will change. And so, in this sense, an infant's "mom," is not a toddler's "mom," is not a schoolboy's "mom," is not a teenager's "mom."

- For an *infant*, mom doesn't exist—she's fused with me.
- For a *toddler*, mom is that other, an extension-of-me, who magically knows when I'm hungry and makes me a sandwich.
- For a *schoolboy*, mom is that other, that extension-of-me, who has skills to teach me, who helps me make a drum for my merit badge.
- For a mature *teenager*—not yet firmly an adult—mom is sometimes separate-from-me and sometimes her-own-person. In his new mature self, he can ask her for help and she can say yes or no, and that has to be all right with him. She has her own point of view, her own motives, her own needs. (And of course some of the time when he is not at his most grown-up, she does not seem separate, and his attitude and behavior may more resemble a *toddler's*—cf. chapter 6.)
- For a mature *adult*, mom is her own separate person, who may help me if I ask for it, but may also be busy with other things. Sometimes, of course, she needs me to help her.

Because their capacity for a separate relationship changes as her children grow up, a mother's experience of parenting changes too. To be an infant's omniscient-omnipresent-mom does not feel the same as to be a toddler's watchful-servant-mommy, and this is very different from a teenager's confidante-mom. As an adult, to be married should not routinely have to feel like one of these juvenile relationships. It ought instead (at least some of the time) to feel like a stable partnership with another separate adult.

Along this developmental line, much is at stake. The normal outcome of this final shift in adolescence, if all goes well, is a young person who grasps the presence and the rights of others. The desired outcome is a teenager who concedes, even in the most intimate relationships, that there is a separate *you*—and not just a puppet-extension of me. When all goes well, teenagers mix it up—boy finding girl, Prep finding Goth, Montague falling for Capulet. An *I* looks for friends and romantic others, and finds *you*, not merely another version of *me*.

This is not an easy or obvious or automatic result, however. Puberty's transformations turn moody teenagers in upon themselves, normally making them *self*-conscious. It is not hard to see *self*-preoccupation in their common costumes, clubby idiom, and shared affinities for musicians. In homogenous groupings each self discovers a carbon copy. In adolescence there is a natural tendency to seek as friends only those who do, and to shun—as dorks, dweebs, jerks, or lesser mortals—those who do not provide at least a warped fun-house mirror of self. The quest beyond planet self for an *other* to love, for someone who is not a stand-in for one*self*, must lift off against the powerful pull of narcissistic gravity. The symbol for this danger for two millennia has been a mythic Narcissus, enthralled only by the image of himself, who spurns Echo (and all others), and drowns in his own reflection.

Empathy

Empathy is a related milestone, which must rely upon the achievement of separate relations. For empathy, and the considerate behavior which is empathy's courteous expression, can only have meaning when it involves a distinctly separate person. There can be no empathy for puppets, for puppets are not permitted to have their own separate feelings. We do not think it empathy when we merely pity a stand-in for ourselves—a sympathy I call mirror-empathy or pseudo-empathy. True *empathy* has its own developmental line.

By empathy we mean the capacity to imagine oneself in another person's position. Said this way, empathy sounds like a geometrical manipulation in virtual space. To feel empathy requires that a person transport himself, in imagination, into the heart and mind of another person. He then experiences the feelings he would experience in the other person's place. The word suggests a generosity of spirit. Empathy goes beyond kindness.

Empathy does not reduce to pity or sympathy. For pity leaves us safely laced into our own shoes. Empathy requires that we hold our own point of view while also simultaneously stepping into someone else's shoes. The result is a viewpoint: our own and another's vantage. We remain ourselves and still can think in our own way, but we also feel what another person feels, too—in *his* circumstances.

True empathy, as an Israeli psychiatrist once taught me, is not necessarily pleasant, particularly when it is most needed. Empathy can be painful, which is why some prefer a blissfully oblivious narcissism. For to feel empathy we have to let ourselves imagine what it might feel like to be that other person in a time when something awful, frightening, or painful has occurred. We, too, experience a loss, an illness, a rape. To feel true empathy in the presence of a survivor of the Holocaust, that Israeli psychiatrist explained, requires that in imagination we board that packed boxcar with our own children. To experience true empathy is not merely to wave at a passing train or merely to pity its passengers, but to imagine ourselves reading the sign *Arbeit Macht Frei* and disembarking on a platform to make Sophie's choice—and then to have to watch a shrieking daughter led away to the ovens. "True empathy," he said, "can be difficult."

But true empathy is not merely difficult. It is also a developmental achievement, a capacity for which we are not equipped at birth. We become capable of empathy only much later, usually in adolescence. This being so, it is not a fault when a toddler cannot imagine what it might be like to be his mom, or when a schoolgirl cannot guess what it is like for a father to work too hard and get too little sleep. A child cannot give what she does not have. She cannot imagine what she is not yet able to imagine.

At each stage of development, a child's capacity to make sense of another creature differs. A toddler's capacity for empathy is not the same as an adult's—but how? Let's take these stages one at a time. Here's the chalkboard:

EMPATHY

Infant	-----
Toddler	Self-Preoccupation
Schoolchild	Mirror- (Pseudo-) Empathy
Adolescent	True Empathy

An infant depends upon parental empathy, but can offer **none** in return. A newborn depends completely upon adults to guess what she needs, to provide it without having to be asked in explicit terms. An infant's signal amounts to a squawk of dysphoria that caregivers have to decipher conscientiously, around the clock. Fortunately, a baby's needs are rudimentary and few in number, and usually can be inferred by an attentive adult. But the converse is not true. Babies do not know who is attached to what, much less what an adult might think or feel or need.

As babies mature they learn to talk, and they may listen, but they cannot feel true empathy. By nature, a *toddler* is self-referential, **self-preoccupied**, entirely concerned with getting from adults or other children what he wants or needs. He feels entitled to this. He is not capable of feeling any other way. Conceding the point, parents devote themselves to figuring out what a cranky toddler needs—A snack? A fresh diaper? A hug? A nap? However cuddly, funny, tender, and brave a toddler can be, however, he cannot return the favor. A toddler has no idea how his weary mother feels at the end of the day. He cannot guess the career sacrifice she makes to stay home with him. He cannot imagine the grief or rage or angst she might feel, or understand the hope that sustains her in her adult life. All empathy flows in one direction. Rewarding, in other ways, as taking care of a toddler may be, in this sense it is a lonely job.

Schoolchildren express a sweetness that resembles empathy. *Schoolboys* and *schoolgirls* experience the first part of empathy, which I call **mirror-** or **pseudo-empathy**, a child's self-referential fellow feeling with another creature—e.g., a younger sibling or the family spaniel or a captured frog. The premise is, "You feel like *me!*" This certainly is not a bad start. Kindness and loyalty often accompany mirror empathy. But the range of fellow feeling is limited to what a schoolchild has experienced. A young boy's kindness to a cocker spaniel is predicated upon this assumption of fellow feeling. A schoolgirl may console her weary dad, as schoolgirls do. But it is unlikely that her assumption—that he feels "like *me*" —is close to the mark.

For schoolchildren, pseudo-empathy divides the living world into creatures "like me," who deserve the compassion of fellow feeling, and those beings who are "*not* like me," who deserve none. Inside this self-referential circle—the clan, clique, tribe, or gang—a boy or girl may recoil from harming one of *us*. But the circle divides those who should receive a friendly nod from those other alien creatures who, without his feeling shame or guilt, can be hacked, fried, smashed, or dissected. Boys hug their pets, but will also pull the wings from flies. In junior high school corridors, girls taunt to suicidal despair a girl they perceive to be *not like us*. Early teenagers may inflict all cruelties upon those beyond the pale—the nerds, preps, dorks—who are *not-us*. A delicious fellow feeling born of pseudo-empathy among *us* may justify a paranoid, hateful assault on *them*. It can startle adults to find that children and teenagers can readily be drafted for wars, pogroms, witchhunts, lynchings, or jihad.

Where that line gets drawn—between *us* and *them*—takes on great importance. In wars, which are usually fought by armed adolescents, military leaders draw firm circles to exclude from compassion those called *enemies*. We dress children in uniforms to mark *ours*, who must be spared, from *theirs*, for whom the taboo against fratricide has been suspended. Governments, in time of war, do all they can to emphasize, even fictionalize, what makes *them* different from *us*, to dehumanize *them* so that they may be slaughtered. To do so, nations and tribes rely upon the concrete logic of schoolboys, the hallmark of pseudo-empathy, by providing distinctive uniforms and flags for *us* and by pointing to concrete disparities—of language, physiognomy, language, religion, or race—to sustain the murderous argument that the *other* is different. To *them* the Golden Rule need not apply.

Given the power of such symbols, given the delicious social cohesion formed by mirror-empathy, it is striking that, when they develop true empathy, adolescents are capable of erasing the concrete circle that separates *us* from *them*. During the Vietnam War both pseudo-empathy and true empathy were at odds: a cold war hatred for "communists" and a racial derogation of "gooks" and "dinks," on the one hand, and an inclusive Peace Movement, on the other, responsive to a sense of common humanity and universal love.

The developmental acquisition of the ability to think across categories makes possible **true empathy**, an achievement that is not inevitable. Once a teenager can hold in mind at once both her own and another's heart and mind, she can enlarge the social or family circle to include both—of *us*. An abstract redefinition permits that circle to include those not just concretely like us, but also those who share in a generalized humanity. It permits, for instance, a boy to feel empathy for a girl, an Asian for a Caucasian, a straight for a gay, a white for a black, a Catholic for a Protestant, a Christian for a Muslim. It is true empathy that permits a young Wasp male senator from an affluent family to imagine how it might feel to be old, or to be poor, or to be an immigrant, or a woman, or a Muslim or a Jew. Empathy permits a therapist to understand experiences (e.g., childbirth, or the loss of a child) that he has never had. It permits parents to put themselves (back) into the shoes of teenagers.

It is hard to exaggerate the civilizing significance of true empathy. With it, enemies end feuds, alienated parents reconcile with children, husbands and wives stay married. True empathy inspired the Sermon on the Mount. Empathy does not require a teenager to surrender his point of view or give up an opinion. Yet true empathy becomes the basis for a tolerant adult's ability to see both sides.

Moral Reasoning

Finally, let's talk about right and wrong. A child's capacity for ethical reasoning also passes through predictable developmental stages. It stands to reason, after all, that a young person, who generally thinks differently as he grows up, would think differently as he matures about ethical matters. It stands to reason that a person who conceptualizes his relationships in novel ways, as he matures, would also conceptualize in novel ways the duties and obligations that are entailed by those relationships. In short, the moral meaning a child or teenager attaches to his own behavior and to the behavior of others usually changes as he grows up. These stages in his moral maturation constitute an *ethical* developmental line.

ETHICAL MOTIVES[6]

Infant	-----
Toddler	Avoid Punishment
School Child	Win Rewards
Adolescent	Social Ethic (Concrete)
	Social Ethic (Abstract)

We reasonably surmise that an *infant*, helplessly afloat in her sensory amnion, cares little about ethical ideas. Recognizing no separate person in her universe, aside from herself, she can have **no moral ideals**. Inasmuch as she cannot grasp our words or speak to us about her ethical ideas, or demonstrate their implications, moral reasoning remains a moot point. Infants remain blissfully oblivious to our most eloquent moral lectures.

A *toddler*, on the other hand, encounters social constraints. His rapidly achieved mobility propels him into collisions with the parental *No!* With his exciting new motor skills, he inevitably crawls, climbs, walks, and runs into trouble. Toddlers don't like this word: *No*. It curtails a hard-won autonomy. Yet they must hear it and take it seriously, to be safe, and so parents have to do what they have to do to get a toddler's attention. When children wander into potential catastrophes, oblivious to warnings, parents must yank them back from danger, exile them to their bedrooms or spank their bottoms. Even indulgent parents are forced to shout or otherwise admonish oblivious toddlers. For in a toddler's world there are mortal risks— hot stoves, scalding tubs, bottles of pills, razors, knives, fan blades, ovens, open doors, rushing traffic—that kids must be kept from if they are to survive.

This is our human fate. Inevitably, there will be a *No*. Even if incompetent parents never manage to say it, eventually someone will say *No* and mean it—a babysitter, a teacher, a coach, a cop. Every small-fry eventually discovers there are consequences that follow from attempts to ignore that *No*, whether merely mommy's annoyed look, or daddy's loud words, or the shock and awe of a parental spanking. If parents fail to provide sanctions, then civil society later will have to marshal policemen, prosecutors, courts, and prisons to provide a sterner version of rough parental hands. Its price is the social cost we pay for lax parenting—a huge tax to support a "corrections" system for adults, which has to intervene when parents have failed to provide the basis for a toddler's first moral imperative: to **avoid punishment.**

By grade school, if not before, *schoolchildren* respond favorably to **rewards** for desirable behavior. Parents and other adults willingly provide them. Grandparents consider gifts and treats their prerogative. And teachers, scout leaders, ballet instructors, coaches, pastors, and nuns all offer prizes to draw youngsters toward virtuous behavior.

These moral principles organize the first decade of a child's life. At home, at school, on playing fields, in Girl Scout troop meetings and youth groups, the culture of childhood is organized around two motives: (a) to avoid punishment for "bad" behavior—by avoiding making dad angry; by avoiding the humiliation of a poor grade on a spelling test; by avoiding being sent to the principal's office; by avoiding a docked allowance or a spanking; and (b) to gain pleasure in rewards for "good" behavior—by winning mom's praise; by earning an "A" on a math quiz; by scoring a basket and hearing the cheering. The public lives of children are organized around incentives—the school's award assembly: certificates of merit, prizes, scholarships—for diligence, cooperation, and good manners. Coaches and dance teachers preside over public contests and performances that bring accolades to those who perform well. Throughout childhood, adults punish misbehavior with sanctions and reward compliance and cooperation and learning—with allowances, gold stars, merit badges, prize ribbons, and gold-rimmed certificates suitable for framing.

Normal *adolescent* development offers two new dimensions to moral thinking: a social standard, and abstract ethical ideals. In general, adolescents attend to opinions of peers, even as adult moralizing loses its valence. The peer group exerts a new, potent social influence upon a teenager's moral thinking. This **social ethic** is, at first, concrete—not generalized or abstract. Whatever the moral dilemma, the resolution will not be with reference to cosmic ideals about justice, or moral principles. It will not emerge from theoretical analysis, nor have necessarily to do with what the entire nation's teenagers think. Rather, a young teenager first worries about what her particular friends—Sara, Jessica, Ted, and Jack—think. This is a teenager's first social ethic.

Over a surprising range of moral topics, this concrete social reference point will serve—whether the issue is the snubbing of a new girl; passing notes in algebra; copying another student's homework; bullying a gay (or Korean or Muslim) boy; cheating on an exam; giving a date a blow job; shoplifting at the mall; drinking at parties; snorting cocaine; driving intoxicated or fast. Whatever *it* is, the rules may not much matter. Nor will the language of the statute or rule, nor the opinion of parents, cops or parsons. What *does* matter, in early adolescence, is whether Jack, Sara, Ted, and Jessica think *it* is all right to do.

This is normal. It is what a vulnerability to "peer pressure" refers to. This concrete social ethic is not merely to do with a girl's getting talked into sex or a boy's getting pressed to inhale, however. At this stage of development, teenagers normally check with their friends about everything. In an earlier generation, this impulse to share perceptions, compare tastes, and assay social opinion was stunted by our technological backwardness. We had to rely upon pencils and scraps of binder paper, or a busy, shared family phone. Now teenagers have been equipped with cellphones and IM. A lovely fourteen-year-old daughter in my home, who once had been attuned in a flattering way to her dad's wisdom, began to float through the house with a cell phone pressed to her ear, oblivious to adult conversation, murmuring, "Do you think I *should* call him?" From across the room her expression of solemn moral deliberation suggested she and Sara might be discussing *The Brothers Karamazov* until I heard her ask, "Do you *really* like these pants?" For teenagers at this stage, the moral imperative is social and concrete: *what we think.*

As adolescence progresses, normal teenagers continue to think with a ***social*** standard of reference. They also begin to think in ***abstract*** ethical terms. Once a teenager can think cross-categorically, she can apply principles to specific dilemmas. Teenagers can be challenged to think beyond what a pal wants, and beyond the mindless concrete maxim, "Don't rat on a friend," if pushed to consider whether it *always* makes sense to protect another teenager from getting caught and punished. Is it possible, they can be asked, that what a friend wants (e.g., cocaine) is not what he needs? Once they can generalize, they can be challenged to consider general questions that reach beyond their particular clique at the high school, e.g., if a friend wants to drive drunk, what would a true friend do? Is there ever a time when a friend *should* rat? Once teenagers begin to think abstractly, they can be asked what honor requires, or what duty they owe to a family? to a girlfriend? To a teacher? To a team? To a school?

Thinking cross-categorically, a teenager can orient to less concrete affiliations—and feel a part of a religious faith, a political party, or a country. No longer constrained by opinions of particular friends, she may begin to respect the expressions of a communal will, e.g., a religious tradition, a law, a platform, an international treaty. Able to recognize others' needs, she now can act against her own interests—e.g., for the good of the family, or to serve what's best for all. She is ready for Plato's question.

This capacity for abstract ethical debate was why Socrates liked to talk with adolescents. For teenagers are excited by the novelty and hope this new, abstract moral capacity inspires. When they become able to think cross-categorically, they discover abstract ideals and, never having considered life in that way before, imagine they invented them. When it occurs to them that they are not the first to discover these larger questions of justice and morality, they may feel disgusted at world-weary adults, who seem relatively complacent about the world's badness. With delicious moral superiority teenagers realize that they are the ones riled about universal ethics—and may want to lecture adults about what is right and wrong with the world. Watching CNN, they are shocked to discover all the imperfections from which, inexplicably, their parents have not yet rescued the planet.

6   Gear Shift & Guitar

IN THE PRECEDING TWO chapters we have assembled the key ingredients for a mature adolescent personality. Now let's bring these developmental lines together by arraying them side by side. The arrows in fig. 6a indicate the normal sequence in which a child acquires new capacities. The horizontal line marks the point of arrival at the adolescent goal—a pre-adult maturity.

Figure 6A

KEY DEVELOPMENTAL LINES

DEV. STAGE	THINKING	TIME	EMPATHY	SEPARATENESS	ETHICS
Infant	Sensori-motor	Now	Self-Aware Only	No Other	None
Toddler	Magical	Magical	Self-Preoccupied	Puppet [Magical]	Avoid
Schoolgirl & Schoolboy	Concrete Logic	Clocks & Calendars	Pseudo-Empathy ["Like Me!]	Puppet [Practical]	Win Rewards
Adolescent	Abstract	Pragmatic	True Empathy	Separate	Abstract & Social

Developmental Stage

Now we must shift our perspective from developmental lines to the stages of maturation. We found it useful to concentrate upon discrete lines, so as to take note of the sequence in which new capacities are achieved. But we meet a child or teenager whole, not one sector of her personality at a time. At the breakfast table or in the classroom we encounter a toddler, a schoolgirl or an adolescent—a young person, not an abstract sequence of

89

milestones in a developmental line. To see that young person whole, we must reorient our vantage upon fig. 6a from vertical to horizontal—to look *across* the page, rather than downward—and so grasp (as does the circle in fig. 6b) a *stage* of development. For it is across the page that the appropriate elements in each developmental line fit together into a coherent *stage* in personality development. For example, it makes sense that a toddler's plastic perception of *time* is congruent with her *magical thinking.* A toddler's lack of true empathy makes sense at a stage in which close relationships have a puppet quality, and the important other is not yet conceptually separated from self. To reason about the expected achievements at any of the major stages of maturation—infant, toddler, schoolgirl and adolescent—we need only to orient to fig. 6b left-to-right, rather than up-down.

Figure 6B

DEVELOPMENTAL STAGES—INFANT TO ADOLESCENT

DEV. STAGE	THINKING	TIME	EMPATHY	SEPARATENESS	ETHICS
Infant	Sensori-motor	Now	Self-Aware Only	No Other	None
Toddler	Magical	Magical	Self-Preoccupied	Puppet [Magical]	Avoid Punishment
Schoolgirl & Schoolboy	Concrete Logic	Clocks & Calendars	Pseudo-Empathy ["Like Me!]	Puppet [Practical]	Win Rewards
Adolescent	Abstract	Pragmatic (Goals, Plans)	True Empathy	Separate Relationships	Abstract & Social

Referring to fig. 6b in this fashion, we can reconstitute each stage from its component elements and so—as a child grows up from infant to toddler to school-girl to adolescent—we can picture, looking across the table, the changes that can be expected to occur at each stage in a child's most mature *approach* to life's challenges.[1]

Briefly, then, let us consider each developmental stage, one at a time. To provide an example, a mother will describe her daughter's more or less normal maturation. As she recalls what happened as Jane grew up, she makes it plain that to speak of a normal development in adolescence is not to imply a road without potholes.

Infant

In the beginning, a fetal babe in the womb starts in cocoon darkness—and then there is light. The world of the newborn is an emancipation from intrauterine life—more spacious, roomy enough to move her arms and legs, even if not to any purpose. Sensory perceptions bombard her with information she has no schema to organize. She cannot separate self from other. In that brave new world that must seem One, her sensations are unmodulated. She cannot choose what to perceive. Her movements are reflexive, not deliberate. She cannot decide what to do. She does not have perceptions and reflexes—she is her perceptions and reflexes. "*Thinking* … begins in its own form at birth with the moving hand and the sensing eye, the newborn's body being its mind."[2] An infant's mental experience is *sensorimotor.*[3]

In Kegan's phrase, an infant has an *incorporative self*[4] that merely takes in what is given and "acts" only in pre-wired ways. She can only experience herself, at the start, as fused with her surround, a consciousness afloat in a sensory bath from which ego will, in time, emerge. She sees, hears, touches, and is touched—and has internal sensations she cannot locate.

Each of the infantile elements of the various developmental lines (fig. 6b) fits into this description of an infant's psychology. There can as yet be no sense of distinctive self, no other—only *selfother*. She floats in *now*—with no past or future. Her sense of duration can only be the experience of an inchoate urge that gets sated sooner or later—a warmth that comes, a wet cold that goes, sound vibrations, complex images that appear and vanish. Days come and go. She can know only darkness and then the light. In utter helplessness, an infant waits to see what happens. Then, as her nervous system matures, she registers—when hungry, cold, or bored—whether relief arrives sooner or later. If she has to wait long without relief she reflexively fusses, then becomes upset, red-faced, noisy in protest—and then she freaks out. If this distress persists very long, there will follow an ominous listless silence.

She cannot solve her problems for herself. Repeated relief or repetitive frustrations, even panic, will reflect the attentiveness of parents. A pattern defines what she can expect, and in this pattern, of solace or neglect, she first discerns whether she can *trust* the world to respond to her cries—or whether, in need, she can only mistrust—whether anyone will come, and, if they do, whether the response will be accurate or inaccurate, gentle or harsh.[5]

This is where parents come in. Parents preside over this early experience. In the face of hunger or cold, boredom or exhaustion, an infant can only cry out. Either an adult shows up to resolve the problem or does not. For most infants, parents routinely provide good-enough attentiveness, reasonable patience, obvious affection, and pleasure in an infant's existence. As a result, a growing baby's response is a trusting one. On the other hand, for some of the wretched of the earth, a cry provokes a shout or a blow, or else mom has left for the bar, or has passed out, too intoxicated to hear or respond. Infants reasonably well cared for will come to approach the world with a general trust, which becomes the basis for an enduring *faith* in life—that when there is a need, there will be a way.[6] Infants neglected or abused come to the contrary conclusion—and approach challenges and relationships, all of their lives, with a reflexive mistrust. Her mother recalls the welcome *Jane* received:

> My pregnancy with Jane seemed easy. My husband attended Lamaze classes with me, even though he insisted he had mastered puffing and blowing the first two times out. Jane arrived without mishap after a six-hour labor. She made it all look easy—Apgar 9 and 10, pretty pink cheeks, fingers and toes all present and accounted for. She was lovely—and we both fell for her.
>
> I nursed Jane. These were our special times together until, at ten months, she seemed ready to stop, and we just did. She was intrigued with solids, had a good appetite, wasn't fussy. We fed her when she was hungry—no arbitrary times or limits. She was alert and curious, and her brother and sister loved to play with her. She had trouble sleeping those first weeks, however, and did not care as much as we did what time it was. I got tired out. Then, at about three months, she began to sleep through, and I recovered my sense of humor.
>
> Her brother and sister liked to change her diapers—happily grossed out! They got down on the rug with her eye to eye, helped her roll over, and crawled all over the house with her. All motor milestones were on time. She made "mah" and "dah" noises, prompted by her siblings, at about thirteen months.

I was luckier than some mothers in my generation. I could close down my journalism career as each child came along. I write freelance, so I could control the flow of work, the amount of travel. My agent helped me, so I could go back to work part-time when Jane was six months old, but I only had to go into my den, next door to her bedroom, and write while she napped or played with her brother. We were lucky, too, that my husband could almost carry us financially. I could work as little or as much as Jane was ready for me to do.

When Jane was eleven months old our pediatrician heard a systolic "creaking" with her heartbeat, and he un- hinged me by talking promptly about open-heart surgery, the chances for survival, the prevalence of various kinds of valve deformities and septal defects. For a month, I put my ear to Jane's little chest every hour to listen for this "murmur." I don't think I ever was sure I heard it. And I suppose this pediatri- cian meant well, but I kept waking up dreaming Jane was in surgery, hearing her shrieking, and I could not break through the locked door to the operating room. We waited three weeks for an appointment with a specialist, so there was no diagno- sis. And when we finally saw the woman she ordered an echo- cardiogram and said it was mitral valve prolapse—"a normal finding in 10 percent of Stanford women." It took me a month to calm down, and, God help me, I changed pediatricians. Probably that wasn't fair. But I no longer trusted him. We were so scared—needlessly.

I knew then that Jane would end up at Stanford. That's what we do, don't we?—read later events back into childhood. I think Jane's sunny disposition started in childhood, too. She greeted the world as an opportunity to play. She liked nursing, liked pabulum, liked peek-a-boo, liked her sister changing her diaper, liked rocking on her haunches, liked naps. She loved her family.

Only that one small cloud shadowed her sunny days— that abnormal heart sound. I knew I would remember. I never dreamed that she would. I suppose we mentioned it from time to time, out of relief. We should have let it drop, but we were still upset. I often wonder whether our terror left a pre-verbal scar, or whether she just heard us talking, years later. In any case, when Jane started preschool and was given colored chalk to draw, she kept making a peculiar many-colored squiggle, which floated around in her pictures—a rainbow? A bird? A cloud? When asked, she confided solemnly that they were "murmurs."

Toddler

The infant's narrow scope becomes confining. As a function of neurology, of motor strength and coordination, he rolls over, crawls, sits up, stands, and walks out of infancy. Soon he can climb, run, and jump. He speaks words, phrases, then sentences—and parents no longer need to guess, because he *says* he is hungry, bored, or cold. He asks for help or demands it. He understands a parental command and acquiesces—or does *not*. This is new, a toddler who can say *No*. During what is commonly called "the terrible twos," a small-fry is no longer a passive, receptive creature who has to take what the world offers lying down.

A toddler becomes an active, deliberate child, who wants to do, to say, to make up his *own* mind. There is a hint of coming separateness in this. He has wishes, and will travel. No longer merely a recipient of sensations, no longer confined to motor reflexes, he now *has* them and, having them, he wants to act on them. Yet this phrase suggests deliberation, and so falsifies a toddler's experience. For him the gap between wish and act is so fluid and brief that we must speak of an impulse to act, not a decision. A toddler does not *have* a wish. He *is* his impulse. In toddlers, Kegan describes an *impulsive self*.[7]

Each of the toddler elements of the various developmental lines (fig. 6b) fits into this description of a toddler's psychology. He thinks like a toddler. He has sensations, but his perceptions remain slippery. A toddler thinks in terms of the qualities of his desire—more, bigger, faster—and yet the qualities that define his world will not hold still. Physical properties remain protean, categories fluid, dimensions changeable. Properties of things and persons are subject to feelings and desires. This mutability of properties gives a toddler's world its magical character—its reliance upon emotion.[8] For persons and objects appear to be shaped in his mind by what he wants, needs, believes, or feels.

Time expands or contracts for Alice, because she lives in Wonderland. A toddler's minute passes quickly or lasts an eternity. He is not good at waiting, because the distance between now and then is indeterminate, expanding with frustration or need. Past and future events such as "when my brother was born" or "when I am big" amount to vague Once-Upon-a-Time locations where spaniels and little brothers and sisters have their mystical origins. These are Over-the-Rainbow sorts of places—to which a child may go merely by strenuously wishing. In this world of whimsy, a toddler offers no objection to a trip to Never Land, has no problem with children flying if they believe they can, and it is all right with him if a wish makes dreams come true.

There is a selfish dimension to this enchantment. There begins to be an active self, distinct from others. A toddler expects parents to comply with *his* wishes, to be willing to do pretty much what *he* wants to do, to follow *his* impulses, or else he gets cranky. He may *not* want to do what others ask—as Freud famously pointed out about toilet training. His resistance is not sick or wrong. It is a predictable bid for autonomy, for the power to do *what* a toddler wants to do *when* he wants to do it. Toddlers typically demand the right to tie their own shoes, to be spared unwanted help.

This struggle for control is a bid for separateness, but only partial separateness. For a well-attended infant, whose cries were answered, it is not unreasonable to expect parents to continue to wait on him. A toddler is a small-fry Sun King. He thinks his potty seat is a throne. He is an unrepentant tyrant who thinks, *L'état, c'est moi.* He expects his wishes to be taken for commands. He cannot fathom that others presume to be independent of his desire. He cannot imagine that others are separate, that they have a right to their own motives. He *can* only be self-referential— and this is not his fault. He *can* only be preoccupied with *his* impulses, *his* desires. It is natural for him to expect parents to be his puppets.

Finally there is an ethical dimension to his self-preoccupation. Prior to preschool, a toddler already has achieved knowledge of *disobedience*— and its consequences. He has encountered the parental *No*. He probably has experienced the parental loud shout, and he may even have encountered the parental spanking. And so his ethical grasp extends as far as knowing that he impulsively may grab what he wants, if it is within his reach, but only so long as he does not get caught and punished.

There is a related moral idea that, by the time a toddler is old enough for kindergarten, he has taken seriously. Preschoolers know about rivalry, may well have experienced at home the The Eternal Triangle. By age five a boy usually knows others may covet what he wants, that he might be punished for taking what is forbidden, that he competes with rivals. He has learned that it takes *initiative* to pursue the object of desire, and to defeat rivals.[9] But he also encounters the dark knowledge of his reciprocal wish to harm those he resents. This rival may be a beloved father—and so he encounters guilt. Sophocles understood this oedipal dilemma more than two millenia ago.

Some adults find it difficult to take seriously the idea that preschool children know about rivalry and may imagine a mortal competition with adults. But they do. Consider how enthralled they are by fairy tales—about ogres and witches who devour children they catch stealing the treasure trove. Children understand that Jack climbs the beanstalk to impress his mommy, and it is just fine with them if Jack takes the ogre's Boodle while he sleeps and snores. They are not bothered by the ethics of his theft. They identify with his antagonism toward the ugly old giant. They are thrilled when he comes home undevoured to his grateful mommy. They know that Jack had better be nimble and quick, too. Because they sense that, for his attempt to challenge the old one, there is a terrible doom that awaits a boy who gives himself away and awakens the giant.

Inevitably toddlers, who want so badly to make up their own minds, run smack into the parental prohibition. There comes a time when young Adam and young Eve are told *No* in no uncertain terms—and have to choose. The toddler's infuriating knowledge is of the parental *No*, and the choice. To be a toddler is not to be an infant, for if toddlers still enjoy the cooing of mothers, they also hear in Eden the voice of dad saying *No!* like a clap of thunder. Toddlers learn what thou shalt not do. More precisely, they learn that it is not nice to get caught doing what thou shalt better not be doing. Having transgressed, they must leave the Garden. In the Land of Nod, east of Eden, No means No.[10]

Jane went from crawling to walking at a year. She liked to be on her feet, heading off in her own direction. She did not want to be thwarted. So her sister and brother became expert at heading her off, distracting her, so that she changed direc-tion. They thought this was funny, and it was. Her clumsy little-kid gait amused them, and so she learned to run early to please them. Jane was fun as a toddler—a sunny explorer. We lived in a house with a fenced yard, and when her sister got pushed on the swing, Jane wanted to be pushed, too. By two years she could hold on pretty well, although I had to keep her brother from pushing her too high.

She spoke in phrases at twenty months. At two years she could speak in short complete sentences, such as

Can I have a glass of water?

No, I don't want to! and,

Push me on the swing, Daddy!

She seemed precocious. Her fluency charmed her father, who teaches English at our high school. Between two and three years Jane greeted him at the door every night with a new word, as if already she knew how to wow him. He didn't disappoint. She was "daddy's girl" and "Ms. Shakespeare." They took long walks when he came home and held long serious conversations. He read her a bedtime story every night— sometimes two.

For all the fuss about "toilet training," Jane just sort of did it herself—because she wanted to "sit on the thrown" and "make pee-pee" like her big sister. Her father told her we would all be proud of her when she could make her bm "like a Princess." So she did.

But it wasn't all easy. She resisted if pushed too hard. She was slow to dress herself and to tie her own bows and shoelaces. Her sister did all that for her, as she might have dressed a doll. Her sister liked doing it for Jane, and Jane liked to be fussed over—but this help made it take Jane longer to tie her own shoes. Once she did learn something on her own, however—e.g., flushing the toilet—she wanted no one to take away her chance to do it for herself.

I was home so much of the time, during those preschool years, she could always find me at my desk or in the kitchen. Perhaps for this reason she had difficulty starting preschool at age four. The teacher called me back the first day to say Jane was so upset that I left her there—I had better take her home. When she got the drill, however, when she realized that I would come back at the end of the morning, she was fine.

Those were the last enchanted years—when we had a little girl around, wide-eyed at every holiday. When she was four her sister was seven and her brother ten. So they thought it great that Jane could be talked into believing that bunnies hatched from Easter eggs or talked into helping them collect lawn clippings for Rudolf the Red-Nosed Reindeer. The older two crept into our bedroom to help their dad dress up as Santa Claus—always wearing his favorite slippers, which he wore to read her bedtime story. The older kids giggled behind their hands when Jane didn't spot the socks, or see her dad's wedding ring or watch, either. They loved how Jane kept calling to him, "Daddy, come quickly! Santa is here." Every time Santa said "Ho, ho, ho," Jane's brother and sister rolled on the floor, giggling.

School-Age

Stepping beyond Never Land, school children leave behind the Garden where they learned hard lessons about No.[11] Despite the enchantment of those years, first-grade students are also excited to get beyond fairy tales. There is little choice, because schoolboys and schoolgirls think differently, and so the world appears different to them. Accordingly, they set out to master the academic lessons of grade-school and the skills of the Scout troop. They can now think with *durable categories* and *concrete logic*. With a little help from adults, they can master the practical world and experiences themselves as *imperial selves*.[12]

Each of the schoolgirl elements of the various developmental lines (fig. 6a and 6b) fits into this description of a schoolgirl's psychology. She thinks like a schoolgirl. For a schoolgirl sorts her experiences by common properties, figures out how things work, and she counts on stable persons, things, places, and roles. Logic modifies social categories. A schoolgirl continues to have puppet relations, but she limits her expectations of adults. She understands that a coach is not (literally) a father or mother, that the relationship is about the team and the game. To a schoolgirl, the role limits the relationship—the coach is a coach. Relationships among schoolchildren share a concrete affinity, an engagement in common pursuits, e.g., by a shared classroom; common riding lessons; an equivalent enthusiasm for model airplanes; joint membership on the Little League team or Scout troop; residence on the same block. Until Eros overwhelms a natural revulsion, girls avoid boys and hang out with other girls, boys with other boys. Within groups defined by doing the same activities, there is a friendly acquaintance. But schoolchildren remain oblivious, unaware of subjective differences, and do not yet think about erotic love.

What are schoolchildren to *do*? Adults expect school-age children to learn. This makes sense, for durable categories and concrete logic allow them (as magical thinking did not) to apply complex logic to practical problems. Their new capacities—to think logically and organize and remember facts—permit them to absorb factual knowledge. For what is a "fact," after all, but an attribute or category that remains durable over time? Schoolchildren research concrete problems, put blocks together, take a clock apart and put it back together, make collections (e.g., stamps, bugs, bottlecaps), and discover taxonomic orderings.

Durable categories and concrete logic underlie the acquired skills and creative output of this prolific stage—school reports on pilgrims, words spelled correctly, looped cursive, repeated summersaults, properly hit baseballs, collections of marbles, realistic sketches and paintings, model airplanes, Halloween masks, and lists of accomplishments to earn Scout badges or sports awards. In the course of these activities, schoolchildren inevitably discover whether *industry* produces knowledge or a product that is worthwhile—so that they themselves, like their creations, seem worthwhile. The psychological risk to a boy at this stage is a discovery that, however sincere his effort, his result is not up to snuff, that he is inferior, a disappointment. The practical consequence of this discovery can be a child who ceases to try.

Schoolgirls master time in concrete and logical fashion. They learn to tell time and read a calendar. They read a clock and calculate how long, and so can wait for the end of a school day. They count backward and know how many weeks since last Christmas, and count the days to the next holiday. This capacity for anticipation has social and ethical consequences. A toddler anticipates punishment, but a schoolgirl learns the rules and can picture punitive consequences in concrete terms. Schoolgirls don't expect consequences to be influenced by wishes. But more to the point, they can also can be motivated by future rewards. They can wait for promised gratifications, escape the shackles of Now. They can save nickels and dimes, calculate the interest, and learn the logical relationship among cash, interest, and time.

Starting from school-age, we orient, in our civic lives, to punishment and rewards. From grade school on we face social sanctions: dad's shout, exile to a corner, early bedtime, spankings, staying-in-at-recess, report card F's, docked allowance, confiscated car keys, parking fines, academic expulsion, lost stripes, IRS audits, speeding tickets, and jail. From grade school on, we orient to rewards: a cookie, a hug, an encouraging word, a gold star, an A, a ribbon, a badge, a place on the team, a higher wage, a Phi Beta Kappa key, a scholarship, a trophy, a diploma, college admission, a degree, a bonus, a dividend, tenure, and the Pulitzer Prize. Sanctions discourage crime. Rewards promote enterprise. There is a limit to the effectiveness of rewards and consequences, however. They apply only when behavior is seen. They may not constrain misbehavior when no one is standing watch.

It seems odd to recall, now that she has grown past these stages, that Jane was a funny girl with a quirky intelligence. She was left-handed, like her grandmother. She read early, but for a long time she got letters and gloves and place settings backward. She was a skinny, sweet schoolgirl, who struggled persistently with homework, even when mistakes and misspelled words discouraged her. She was very bright, particularly when it came to her sizing up others. In this, as in so many other things, she mimicked her adored sister and brother. Perhaps for this reason her apparent empathy seemed precocious when, really, she merely assumed that others felt the same way she did. Sometimes this assumption proved wrong. She got curious, earlier than her siblings had, about what the cat or dog or rabbit or neighbor boy (who had Down syndrome) might be feeling.

She was always interested. Already by sixth grade, when she first encountered adult feelings and behavior she couldn't grasp (e.g., when good friends fell out of love and filed for divorce), her reflex was to join in with consolation, to pay attention to the feelings of those she loved—starting, of course, with a not-very-smart retriever and some bunnies, but extending to friends and their parents. Her misconceptions produced cute remarks, e.g., "My bunny wants a hot dog, too!" They also led to memorable misunderstandings. She really had not yet mastered that boundary between herself and others. And so when she began to write a story, pecking it out on her sister's computer, seated happily beside her father, she found that she had put into it what she knew to be serious misbehavior—a girl who got pregnant, boys using drugs, sneaky thefts, lying to parents—and panicked to think this "badness" on paper had come from her.

Her thinking was so concrete she got up from the key-board and refused to be consoled. If those "thoughts" were hers, then so was the badness her words described. She couldn't rise above that concrete logic. She refused to return to her fic-tion—until she reached a creative writing class in high school, when she was ready to try again.

Adolescent

With puberty, the adolescent makes his laughing, angry, sarcastic, or brooding entrance. What is most striking, Aristotle thought, as did Piaget, is his new capacity to think abstractly. From this capacity to think across categories, an adolescent (guided by adults) fashions a new understanding of his practical, academic and social world. He entertains abstract and social ideas about how to behave.

This process, for all its risk and slapstick, culminates in something new, which we refer to as fully formed character. When its developmental warp and woof come together, we call it an adult *identity*.[13] In this process all previous threads, all prior selves, present themselves again to be woven into whole cloth.[14]

And so *trust* once again becomes an issue—as teenagers wonder whether to trust their parents, teachers, friends, erotic partners, or their unpredictable bodies. Equally, adolescents find out whether they can be trusted—as sons or daughters, as students, as friends, as lovers, and as citizens. This question continues, even beyond adolescence, to hang in suspense. Can we be trusted as husbands or wives, as parents, as employees, as friends, as taxpayers, or as the responsible adult children of elderly parents? And teenagers struggle again with *autonomy*—as they debate, among themselves, who gets to decide what I wear; what I eat; how I do my hair; who will be my friends; where and when and with whom I go out or stay in; when I come back; whether I drive; whether I drink; whether I use drugs; whether and where I go to college. With urgency, teenagers have to figure out—or try to ignore—sex. They again become enchanted by romance—and (try to) take *initiative* in erotic love, and deal with guilt and murderous rivalry, and struggle not to behave childishly about the risks of pregnancy. And, if that were not enough, academic *industry* remains an issue; we expect teenagers to attend school and to learn and to prepare for a career.

When all goes well in adolescence, all these threads may get woven together into strong, durable, and coherent cloth—and then we speak of an *identity*. However, when this weaving does *not* go well, adolescence offers its own risk: *confusion*.[15] This is a grave risk. For instead of launching young men and women into coherent careers where, as adults, they can commit to sustained excellence in creative work, a confused adolescence leads to wasted motion, lack of commitment, and incoherent effort. Instead of launching young women and young men into committed, intimate relationships where, as adults, they can be loyal friends and lovers and parents, adolescent confusion produces ephemeral relationships and marital breakdown, and an unstable basis for parenting the next generation.

Each of the adolescent elements of the various developmental lines (fig. 6b) fits into this description of adolescent psychology. Abstract thought seems to be the design in the cloth. Certainly it is abstract thinking that permits teenagers to generalize from particulars, to soar among cloudy concepts. Thinking across contexts brings sophistication to humor, for adolescents now can hold in mind at once two ironically-related contexts, as humor requires, and grasp the double-edged significance of metaphor, sarcasm, and irony. They can take the literal as a sign for the figurative. They can construct (and respond to) symbols. Across the warp of an abstract conceit, rhythm, or rhyme, adolescents can weave concrete nouns and vivid images—and so make poetry. They can hold in mind the theme of a novel through pages and pages of action and description, and so appreciate a work of art, not just a yarn. In all these ways teenagers become *ready* for apt experience to prod them to feel empathy, to grope for separateness, to embrace social and abstract moral values. Teenagers become ready, as schoolchildren never are, for secondary or college curricula, for adolescents can read a symbolic text, reason from history, solve for x, even imagine y as an asymptotic curve that closes in upon, but never reaches, a set value—in the limit, as x approaches infinity.

Abstract reasoning across contexts prepares a teenager—makes him ready for apt experience—to hold now and a future goal simultaneously in mind, and so see the logical intervening steps that make a plan. This same abstract reasoning makes a teenager ready for experience to integrate abstract social ethics that mark maturity. Generalizing across "my friends" brings a social dimension to moral reasoning. Beyond selfish interest in what suits me, a teenager wonders what we think is all right to do. Generalizing across instances of admired and ugly behavior, a teenager can, with prodding, bring to moral ideas an abstract dimension, and so may consider what is right, not merely what is expedient, and wonder what friendship, honor, or duty require. He can be pushed to consider, beyond individuals, how society can be organized, why nations fight wars, and what social order might plausibly bring justice. He can join abstract debates about economics, or master the arcane arguments for and against globalization.

And the complex new weave of adolescent psychology makes *empathy* possible. That is, it constitutes a readiness for empathy, if experience proves apt. Cross-contextual thinking makes empathy plausible, for to feel it a teenager must put himself at once into another person's shoes while remaining firmly situated in his own, a complex geometrical maneuver that younger children cannot quite do. It is to feel what it would be like *if I* were *you*. Empathy is cross-contextual thinking applied to the inner worlds of separate human beings.

And so, if experience is apt, a teenager also may rise to *separate relationships*. To separate (say, from his mother), a young man has to experience himself vis-à-vis his mother—and still know how he feels, what he thinks. He must countenance (listen to, accept) his mother's different point of view, and respect her decisions, her preferences, her opinions, even her refusal to agree to a request, and yet not demand she be him, or be connected by an umbilical cord—and partially fused. She must be allowed to make up her own mind, and he must think across contexts (his and hers), while tolerating the difference—so as to recognize the relationship between two independent persons. Separateness is cross-contextual logic applied to relationships.

These interpersonal innovations—empathy and separateness—emerge during a teenager's entry into a complex social system. For an adolescent is a social creature, and has an *interpersonal self*.[16] His interpersonal achievement is contradictory, for it is an acquisition of separateness, but also a passion for membership in a group. Teenagers become close, making a break from the Apollonian play of the grade-school playground, but they also want to feel one, to be part of the crowd. They want to join a sexy, co-ed circle of "my friends" and break down barriers to make lasting relationships and feel intimate. They cross *terra incognita* of gender to develop co-ed empathy. Yet, as I say, they also become ready for separateness.

There is an irony in this. Teenagers work at both paradigms. To participate in a clique requires that they think first of the group, consider themselves part of a unity, and submerge a separate *me* within the group's *we*. This is a powerful bond and a remarkable source of altruism. Teenagers can love the group (clique, team, platoon) more than themselves, more than life itself. In close military units, teenagers behave with startling unselfishness—or with a self-regard that becomes entirely identified with the group. They move us with a selfless willingness to risk themselves, even die for one another.

As in other sectors of adolescent development, in short, there is a constructive tension between this wish to fuse with a group and the need to differentiate, to achieve separateness, an independent sense of self. Kegan suggests it's first the one, then the other. As school-children move solidly into adolescence we can say that, although ready for apt experience to teach them separateness in relationships, what comes first is a psychological fusion with the group. Much of the time during this evolution of the interpersonal self, adolescents don't have their friends—they *are* their friends.[17]

> Given our closeness during her childhood, we were star-
> tled when puberty arrived and Jane dropped us like hot rocks
> in favor of her friends, who took on what seemed an engross-
> ing, even exaggerated importance. Amused, her father called
> her "Ms. Telephone," for at fourteen she became a sylph float-

ing through a dinner party crowd of adults, oblivious to any of them unless addressed (in which case, of course, she would be sweetly polite). She conducted what appeared to be a somber conversation, perhaps about Dostoyevsky or the nation's trade deficit, until, as she passed close by, her free hand pushing from her eyes her long hair, she murmured audibly, "Do you think he's cute?" or, regarding her extremities, "Do you really like these pants?" She was fused with her friends, so that it was doubtful that she knew anymore what she thought or wanted, or whom she liked or didn't like, without checking with her friends to discover what we thought, what we felt, what we did or didn't like.

Despite these social preoccupations, she also became fully engaged and busy during high school. She played in the orchestra—and led the flute section her senior year. She ran with the cross-country team—and her loyalty to the whole team made her so supportive, so self-effacing about her own athletic ambitions, that I believe she genuinely hoped for a teammate's victory just as passionately as she wished for her own. I don't think she entirely gave up what she wanted, but she wanted so much for her team to get their wishes that sometimes she seemed to forget her own.

In the context of her friends, Jane had difficulty saying No—and when this led her into mischief, it seemed not so much her own naughtiness that was at issue as her wish not to disappoint her friends by not joining in. I may be making excuses for her misdemeanors. However, I saw this fusion in another context when she first fell in love. She became infatuated with an older boy, who, frankly, seemed more interested in himself than in her. I worried about this "love," for she lost all track of where she ended and the boy began. I did not much mind when he dumped her—as kids bluntly put it. But she was not glad. She looked as if she'd lost an arm. She walked around like a sad somnambulist. For two weeks she seemed to have forgotten her name.

Then, sophomore year, perhaps inevitably, this abject loyalty put her in conflict with our rules. Jane told us she would stay overnight at a girls' team slumber party. But the supposed parent-hostess called at 9 P.M. to ask when to come over in the morning to fetch her daughter—and we both realized we had been snookered. We went to work on the phone, and a few calls later we knew where the girls had gone. I went along with Jane's very angry father when he drove over to knock on the door of a home in which we discovered some cute boys, some older girls, a cooler of beer, dim lights, and no adults. I won't ever forget Jane's face when she looked up from necking with a young man to register, through the loud music and smoky murk, that her father was beside her, and that he had just said, "Get your purse and keys Jane—you're coming home, and I mean now." I doubt she ever will, either.

So I don't mean it was easy. That lie was not her last sneaky behavior. Once, when we were out of town, she lied to adult friends to escape their home, where she was supposed to stay the weekend. She left the friend's home with some lame excuse and threw a party at our home, while we were not there to supervise. When caught, she tried to blame her friends—they wanted to party; they suggested the subterfuge; they bought the beer. This was another memorable midnight—the police called our friends to say they'd broken up a noisy party and had arrested Jane, who at seventeen was sitting on the porch with a friend, drinking a beer, as they arrived. Would our friends like to come down to the station to pick her up?

These crises had consequences—tangible privations— calculated for maximal inconvenience to her. For weeks she lost her car keys except to drive back and forth to school. For weeks she lost her right to go out on weeknights or weekends. But I don't really think it was the grounding or the extra chores that stopped her attempts to fool us or evade our rules. It was what happened between us—to our relationship. There were blunt, no-nonsense talks with both of us about her betrayal of our family. We called her behavior "rude" and "nasty" and "low"—so as to make it clear we held it in contempt, even if we didn't (yet) hold her in contempt. Her wish to think the rules didn't apply to her was predictable in teenagers, I think we said, but it was not nice, we didn't like it, and we wanted it to stop. Nor would we put up for a moment with her blaming anyone else for her misbehavior. We made unambiguous our expectation that she take all responsibility for her own words and actions. I found it painful to watch her squirm, but I know that what got to her was not the punishment, and not even the angry chewing out her father gave her, so much as what it meant between us. Her misbehavior made her squirm because she knew we loved her and she loved us, and she knew she had disappointed us. She squirmed because she realized she had damaged our relationship. She could see, in our eyes, that we saw something in her we didn't like. This was what kept her awake in the night.

These painful encounters petered out during her last year in high school. This was great. I was grateful for a peaceful interlude of a few months, prior to her departure for college, when she behaved with sweet consideration for us, almost without exception. She was thoughtful about us. She always had been affectionate as a small child, too, but now she accurately could anticipate, most of the time, how her adult parents would think or feel. That is, she ceased to assume we would behave or think as she wished we would, or as she hoped to badger us into thinking or feeling. She began to take seriously the proposition that others, including her parents, when asked, legitimately might say No—and that this was their right, and had to be all right with her. There were no longer strenuous efforts to debate a point with us, to browbeat or persuade us, beyond a reasonable rhetoric, or to sneak past a clear No. This consideration produced a warm closeness among us again, just before she left home.

By the time she graduated from high school and departed for the frosh dorms at the university, we worried about all the ways the world might harm her or break her heart, but we no longer worried that, if she were out late at night, she wouldn't be where she said she'd gone, or that she would climb into a car with an intoxicated driver, or that she'd get drunk and try to drive a car herself. We knew she'd tell us the truth—insofar as the truth was any of our business. She'd be considerate enough to come home before her curfew, or else call when she would be delayed. She would admit her errors, and there would be no fatuous excuses. And although Jane does not agree with all of our moral ideas, we know she can say no—to sex, to drugs, to alcohol, to cheating, to cruelty. This is to say that, whatever she chooses to do, it will be her idea.

Beyond Adolescence

One sees signs of readiness earlier, but only late in adolescence can young people treat important others as fully separate. By then they normally become capable of relationships that, some of the time, do not confuse self and other. During this stage there is a tension between more familiar "puppet" relations of childhood and the young adult novelty of separateness. Often both are at play. As in adult life, a young person oscillates within the same relationship between irritable demands that the other be reciprocal to his desires and a relaxed willingness to let the beloved be, and choose for herself.

This tension is not odd. It is a tension seen in every other aspect of emerging maturity. To feel empathy, for example, requires separateness and also a capacity to cross the gap to imagine being "in" the other's mind. Or again, to act upon abstract and social ethics, as opposed to selfish motives, requires that a teenager consider the point of view and the needs of the larger group beyond himself, to be mindful of *us*, not just me. Yet to act upon his own principles, e.g., to find his own sense of honor, he also has to be able to depart from the group's consensus, to refuse to conform.

Robert Kegan framed this more mature autonomy—of late adolescence and early adult life—as the *institutional* self, a stage in the evolution of self (beginning around seventeen) when young men and women become capable of affiliations, opinions, and ambitions not validated by the group. Younger teenagers play at this kind of autonomy from the group. For example, they pair off in tenuous "couples," making pledges of eternal fidelity, and becoming romantic items within the clique. But these differentiations from the group don't last. In short order there are equally melodramatic partings. When the mature form of autonomy arrives, it is no longer puppy love, nor is it mere posturing upon the group's stage. When it arrives, a young man can leave the fraternity and a young woman can leave the consoling herd-warmth of the sorority. They become capable of pairing with private intensity, personal commitment, and an enduring loyalty. In doing so, they leave behind the club, team, platoon, gaggle or flock to set an autonomous adult course.[18]

This differentiation from the group is a step toward the next developmental stage—toward the first adult crisis—of *intimacy*. Erik Erikson famously suggested that this fidelity, which can join fully separate adults, rests upon an adolescent achievement of coherent identity. In the absence of this sense of self—in the context of confusion—young men and women may take their vows, but have no solid basis for the lasting commitment required to found a solid family. Without this basis for intimacy, the risk to young adults is *isolation*—and precarious, merely transitory attempts at marriage.

ℭ

For our purpose, we don't need this summary to proceed further. Its glimpse of the incipient adult capacity to leave "the crowd" for the intimacy of marriage brings to a close a rehearsal of normal maturation through adolescence. We end it properly, however, by noting that adolescence is not the end, but the prelude to adult life. Ahead, during later stages of all those same developmental lines, more advanced forms of thinking and ethical reasoning will emerge. Adolescence is a ripeness, but it is not all.

Surely this is obvious, that much of a full adult life remains. Adolescence spans but two decades out of an expected span of seven. At twenty we have passsed through only five of eight of the Eriksonian stages in the full cycle of life. At the end of adolescence we have only begun to play at intimacy—the basis for marriage. When marriage and family stages arrive, we still have to negotiate career and parenting. Midlife tasks center upon *generativity*—giving birth to, raising, shaping, paying for, and helping the next generation. This is what parents do, or fail to do. When development goes awry, failure in midlife amounts to a failure to reach back a hand to the next generation To fail at midlife is to live only for oneself. Erikson called this flat outcome *stagnation*.

In modern mass culture it can be hard to keep in mind that adolescence is not life's goal or final opportunity for happiness. When all goes well, adolescence leaves mature children physically ripe and mentally ready for adult tasks. If teenagers are fortunate in the neuro-psychological readiness they inherit, and in the experience their parents provide for them, and are lucky about all those catastrophes parents cannot entirely prevent, they may arrive upon the cusp of adult life fully prepared to think abstractly, to find goals and carry out plans, to form close but separate relationships, to think ethically, and to behave responsibly in human society.

This preparation does not necessarily make them mature adults—only young men and women ready to become adults. This is no small distinction. For surely in the decades after puberty, many men and women function well and contribute greatly—as fine adults. Many of us manage to cross from childhood into productive, satisfying adult lives. Yet a cursory reading of any good newspaper demonstrates also that, at a heavy cost to our society, many others have not.

Gear Shift

After all of this, what *is* maturity? And when a teenagers behaves playfully, does that suggest immaturity?

What a piece of work is a young man or woman! At best they resemble gods—in beauty, allure, dignity, wit, social grace, and moral reasoning. We glimpse the ideal when we watch them debate, run a race, dress for a prom, or walk to the podium in cap and gown. We enjoy polite talks with them, admire their essays, laugh at their ironies. What we recognize in mature young people is the best in ourselves. We see the ghosts of our once-youthful idealism, hope, and ambition. We like to think we once resembled them.

But is mature behavior *all* you ever see in normal teenagers? Once a teenager *can* behave like an adult, does he? Always? If not, how can a teenager be mature, and also not be mature? Is maturity an on-again/off-again sort of thing?

We must ask, because this is what we see—a bright teenaged "A"-student who sometimes procrastinates getting his homework done; a girl applying for college who forgets all about her physics exam because she's jabbering on the telephone with a boyfriend; a considerate boy, an exemplary student, who one day tells his teacher Fido ate his algebra homework.

Do we not know of a highway trooper pulling over a speeding honor student? Or a speeding physician? Or PTA President? Do we never hear of considerate young people who sometimes gossip? Do we all not know about a Rhodes Scholar elected to the highest office in the land, who risked it all for a blow job in the Oval Office? Do we not know another President (*not* a Rhodes Scholar), who sent an army into another nation's capital without a plan for what would follow? What about the college sophomore who, in a single day, wrote a good essay, brought roses to a roommate's mother in hospital, joined a demonstration calling for justice in Outer Zambezi—and then, after midnight, hoping to be elected to a frat, sang nonsense lyrics on a crowded subway platform and then swallowed a goldfish? Can you be mature and not mature? Is it not true that *all* of us—long after achieving all the milestones of mature adolescent or young adult personalities—can shift temporarily into less-adult levels of academic, interpersonal, or ethical functioning?

We must revise our "gearshift" model of psychological development to accommodate this observed flexibility. We have noted, along with many classic observers (Piaget, Erikson, Kohlberg, and others), that psychological development adds, at each stage, a new gear to ever more sophisticated transmission. But with each "higher" (more mature) gear, we do not discard all the earlier gears.

Here's what is missing from our model. A maturing psychological transmission must have a gear shift. To describe day-to-day functioning in an adolescent or young adult, we must put heads at both ends of those arrows—so that it is understood that, hour to hour, a teenager's level of functioning can shift up or down the continuum on any developmental line. Without a gear shift, we would mean that mature adults have entirely rigid, unidimentional personalities—the equivalent of using one gear under all road conditions. The truth of our experience is otherwise. So if, for example, we put up a chalkboard diagram for motor development— the obvious truth is that the arrow points both ways.

MOTOR FUNCTION

Infant	Crawl
Toddler	Walk
School Child	Sprint
Adolescent, Adult	Run a marathon

It is true enough that an infant can only crawl, that a toddler can only walk or crawl. But a mature adolescent athlete can run a marathon—and he can still sprint, walk or crawl. Just because he is mature enough to run a long race does not mean that this is all that he does. So for this purpose, to describe the full repertoire of a mature teenager, we have to draw the arrows pointing both ways. In the complex gearbox of the mature adolescent, all of those previously acquired "gears" remain accessible.

Figure 6C
FULL REPERTOIRE OF THE *MATURE* ADOLESCENT

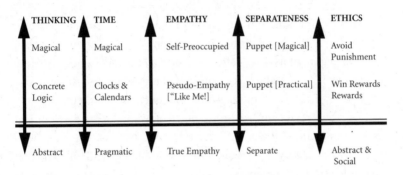

THINKING	TIME	EMPATHY	SEPARATENESS	ETHICS
Magical	Magical	Self-Preoccupied	Puppet [Magical]	Avoid Punishment
Concrete Logic	Clocks & Calendars	Pseudo-Empathy ["Like Me!]	Puppet [Practical]	Win Rewards Rewards
Abstract	Pragmatic	True Empathy	Separate	Abstract & Social

This revision suggests a flexible repertoire for a mature teenager. Perhaps you will think it too flexible, inasmuch as it suggests that, depending upon the context, a normal teenager can act like a two year-old. But that is true, is it not? This "gear shift" model is much more realistic. For at times, depending upon context, mature teenagers can and do act like two-year-olds. Moreover, if we point the arrows in both directions, we correctly imply that normal teenagers can use abstract logic, but do not always have to think abstractly—or even logically. We imply that they *can* fully imagine a goal and make a plan, but that at times they may skip the goals and plans, and leave hours or days entirely unscheduled. Normal teenagers may not stick to every plan they make, either. This model implies correctly that mature teenagers can read clocks but don't always arrive on time; that they can feel empathy, but do not invariably treat parents, boyfriends, or girlfriends with consideration.

This is an important revision, which warrants repetition. As young people become fully mature, at each stage, they add gears to their transmissions. But they do not give up the gears that came before. A mature teenager can integrate the new and old, shifting fluidly among them. They can, when the occasion calls for it, shift into the most advanced gears, but, under stress or when a different stretch of the road calls for another gear ratio, they may shift down. What makes a fully developed teenager mature, then, is his access to the full repertoire that is normally available at his stage of development.

Guitar

The "gearbox" model is simple, effective, but clunky. It usefully captures essential aspects of normal development—and the flexible "shifting" that human beings do in their daily lives. But to capture the remarkable capacity of mature human beings to function at various levels at once, in effect to shift into three different gears at once, I now want to mix metaphors, referring to the full repertoire as a five-stringed guitar.

I have suggested that the fully mature adolescent (or adult) enjoys a broad range of psychological modes and can employ them all, not only the latest milestones. The most grown-up capacities in that adolescent repertoire—to think abstractly, to set goals and carry out plans, to behave with consideration, to treat others as separate and equal, to act upon abstract social ethical principles—are not necessarily always on display. We agreed that in a mature adolescent or young adult, they are simply available—and can be called upon when the occasion warrants them.

What we admire in mature teenagers, then, is the ability to suit a psychological mode to its occasion—to behave like a banker when adult decorum and discipline are called for, but to be able to fool around like a toddler when playing on the rug with a younger cousin. Mature teenagers attentively take notes during math lectures, flirt on the lunch hour, move with suitable gravity at a requiem mass, and dance with abandon in fright-masks at the Halloween hop. Maturity, for an adolescent, we now would say, is a flexible access to the full psychological repertoire of adolescence.

However, this capacity to move up and down the developmental arpeggio is not a case of multiple personalities. When a mature teenager (or adult) makes use of his earlier, more childish approaches, he does not become a child. When a ten-year-old turns the pages of a Harry Potter novel, he does not become a fatuous four-year-old. He may exult in the powers of the magician, imagine himself flying in a jalopy with Harry, who's casting spells. But he does not forget the concretely logical worldview of a ten-year-old. A toddler *lives* in that enchanted world, but ten-year-olds only visit—in books, dreams, or movies. To go there requires a suspension of a ten-year-old's disbelief. This is what magic "spells" accomplish, marking a suspension of the logical natural world that Harry never ceases also to understand.

Or again, when a mature college student goofs off, or cuts a class, perhaps because he is just too tired or stressed, he suspends his plans, flops onto the couch to watch football, but does not forget himself entirely. He has not *become* a toddler, even when he lets himself behave like one. He may not be worrying about his goals or plans, but he still *can* create a plan if he wants to. And a traffic ticket may snap him out of a period of magical invulnerability. But he comes back to a mature reality that he still has access to.

This mental flexibility is remarkable and, in the elegance of its subtle integration, it resembles a guitar more than a gearbox. Through childhood and adolescence, a teenager acquires those strings (milestones) one at a time, but once he has acquired and tuned them, he can play them together—in chords. To demonstrate the way, for example, a brilliant artist can integrate a toddler's magical thinking, a schoolboy's mastery of the concrete particulars of the practical world, and an adolescent capacity to grasp the abstract relationship between such particulars, here is an elegant adult example of a "chord" played on this guitar.

Seamus Heaney, the Irish Nobel Laureate, began "Digging" with the image of his own hand at work in the writing of the poem:

> *Between my fingers and my thumb*
> *The squat pen rests…*

and a few lines later, recalling his father, shoveling peat, he described the concrete particulars of a man using a spade:

> *The coarse boot nestled on the lug, the shaft*
> *Against the inside knee … levered firmly.* [19]

The poet, as he wrote—and the reader, hearing these words— pictures both images at once: a *pen* wedged against fingers and thumb; and a *spade* wedged between boot and knee. Both images come at once. We recognize, as Heaney did, the relationship between them—in an example of the cross-contextual thinking we have discussed. Wedged tools (pen and spade) set into a metaphorical equivalence two kinds of excavation: peat from the earth and images from memory. In the final lines, Heaney makes this conceit explicit:

> *Between my finger and my thumb*
> *The squat pen rests.*
> *I'll dig with it.*

Yet this poem is not only abstract. It is not merely a cross-contextual idea. It turns upon concrete logic, tangible images. To say "It occurs to me I'm like my father" would be to say that abstract idea; but a simile is not a poem. "Digging" required also, for its artistic impact, the assembled nouns of excavation: boot, lug, shaft, tops, potatoes, and hands, which all belong together like sorted beads.

Moreover, there is magic here. When Heaney glances out his window in the first lines, he "sees" his father digging in the garden, describing him as if he were down there digging below the poet's window. This is magical realism, the assertion of an enchanted idea: that a dead man is presently spading peat, just outside.

In short, Heaney's poem conjoins the magical thinking of a toddler, the concrete logic of a schoolboy and the abstract generalization of an adolescent—and yet Heaney seems to have put all these modes of thinking together simultaneously, in one integrated work of art. One cannot hear any gear-shifting; all these ways of thinking work together, like strumming a guitar, so as to use all the strings at once in a chord.

This is why "Digging," for all its magic, could not have been written by a four-year-old. It is why, for all its sorted concrete images, the poem could not have been written by a schoolboy. This is the synthesis of an adult who commands the full repertoire and the flexibility of mind, which come to us for the first time during adolescence.

Part 3
Immaturity

7   Delay

Immaturity

A relative immaturity is a failure, within the expected span, to achieve an expected developmental milestone—or a stage-specific set of milestones.[1] By definition, immaturity is a blocked development, a thwarted progress in growing up. Immaturity suggests that there has been an obstruction, and so a *delay*, which has left a teenager with a less-than-mature psychological repertoire. Now, having recapped normal mature pre adolescent and adolescent stages, we ought to be able to picture how an immature teenager will think, feel, and behave. We need only remind ourselves what it means, relative to age-mates, for an immature teenager's psychological transmission to be missing those mature "gears" that normally arrive last, and have not yet been achieved.

Here's the chalkboard:

Figure 7
REPERTOIRE OF AN *IMMATURE* ADOLESCENT

THINKING	TIME	EMPATHY	SEPARATENESS	ETHICS
Sensorimotor	Now	Only Self	No Other	None
Magical	Magical	Self-Preoccupied	Puppet [magical]	Avoid Punishment
Concrete Logic	Clocks & Calendars	Pseudo-Empathy ["like me!]	Puppet [practical]	Win Rewards

OBSTACLE   OBSTACLE

? Abstract thinking

Missing Developmental Milestones

An immature teenager posesseses few capacities beyond the repertoire of a normal schoolchild or toddler. His childish psychology *is* the troubled teenager's *flawed approach* (described in chapter 3). To see that this is so (in light of fig. 7) we need only tick off on our fingers the familiar elements. For the the repertoire of an immature teenager can be described in these same terms.

- Gross narcissism
- Lack of (true) empathy
- Magical thinking about time (past and future);
- "Puppet" relationships
- Selfish, concrete moral reasoning

Most troubled teenagers who come to Montana Academy can already think abstractly, but in key social domains they fail to do so. They are capable of cross-contextual thinking, and so they can generalize from particulars; they can understand member and class; they can let x equal the unknown and solve an equation. However, in key interpersonal, pragmatic, and ethical domains, they do not put this capacity for abstract thinking to mature use. In this sense, growing up requires both neuro-readiness and the apt experience that transforms readiness into a developmental achievement.

Childish teenagers are floridly *narcissistic*. Although it is expected that normal young people will be somewhat preoccupied with their own style of clothing, their favorite music, and their own pretty faces in any mirror, childish teenagers are so egotistical, self-referential, self-preoccupied, entitled, and selfish that other teenagers take offense. Even among friends a noisy insistence that others go along with her opinions and do only what she feels like doing wears thin.

This self-preoccupation fits with an immature teenager's *lack of true empathy*, which shows itself, for example, in mean-spirited social hurtfulness, which mature teenagers begin to dislike and shun. The achievement of true empathy allows a mature teenager to enlarge the circle of creatures she can "feel for" and befriend—in contrast to the childish teenager's constricted category of fellow feeling, which is limited to those who (concretely) appear to be "just like *me*." It is this lack of true empathy that explains the otherwise puzzling observation that an immature teenager can be kind and loyal to "friends," but callous with siblings, parents, teachers, and other teenagers relegated to alien categories, such as "dorks" or "preps," whom he considers *not* like himself. Such mean-spirited contempt is not entirely volitional. A childish teenager has little choice, for he cannot exercise a fellow feeling he simply does not experience. There is no empathy to regress from, for he never had it to begin with. The immature adolescent's limited transmission does not have the higher "gears" that permit tolerance or affection for those not like himself.

An immature teenager also approaches *time* with a child's magical thinking. The future and past shimmer at the opposite horizons like mirages, not to be taken seriously. The childish teenager lacks a stable concept of a practical goal connected to the present by a sequence of logical steps. She cannot map those steps to make a plan. She cannot anticipate consequences of present actions or words, or lack of action, or lack of tact. Ambitions remain wishful, for an immature adolescent lives in a perpetual now. Therefore, sincere promises of sustained, disciplined action remain vaporous, fantasies that blow away on the first distracting breeze. Such plans for the future can never be as pressing or as important as the prospect of immediate gratification. This upsets her parents, of course, who can see the future coming. And her childishness alienates her from her more mature acquaintances, who begin to discern their own goals and begin to make and follow their own plans—and so must leave her behind, marooned in the land of the lotus-eaters.

This parting of ways between onetime friends looks like a disparity in motivation, one trying, working, hoping, sticking to the task. And of course, it is. Parents could keep both children on course when they were toddlers and schoolmates, making plans for them, getting their lives organized, helping them accomplish the Cub Scout badge requirements—and so orienting both children to goals that they could not see for themselves. When teenagers become mobile, often absent from home, attached to other teenagers rather than to their parents, then parents cannot sustain the momentum. Halfway through high school a mature honor student no longer needs parental guidance or policing. At the same mile marker, the immature teenager has fallen behind. The mature and immature teenagers have begun to look very different, the mature student already a self-starter, acquiring his own ambitions, working to add to his resume in class and in extracurricular activities, the floundering immature onetime friend now lacking any plan or effort for the future.

This lack of ambition can be misconstrued. When a failing adolescent stops doing his homework, stops reading, stops raising his hand, stops showing up for school or for practice, it is common to conclude that he needs better study habits or coping skills or needs to make better choices. In a drifting teenager the adults may miss the lack of an imagined, plausible future. This lack takes two forms. One is a future that is merely a childish fantasy—a fairy tale afloat in virtual space, disconnected from any present effort, unanchored to a plausible plan, unlikely ever to happen. Such a teenager may refuse to learn algebra but dream someday that he may "be" an astronaut. In this situation, vigorous parents may be tempted to accept the "goal" at face value and rush in to provide the push and the missing plan—and to prod a reluctant son or daughter to join in this parental project. The second is an absence of any goal, the lack of any ambition—no pictured future at all. In neglected and underprivileged children this void may reflect the lack of parental resources, an economic and family reality. Yet the utter absence of ambition also can be found in teenagers whose parents provide every advantage. When I talk to troubled teenagers who have been making no effort in school I ask where they hope schooling will take them, what they hope to be doing in five years. If the answer is, "The Nobel Prize in astrophysics," I know I am listening to the first vaporous kind of magical thinking. If the answer is a shrug or "Whatever, dude," I know one reason this young person is not trying is that other kind of futurelessness. Who works without a goal?

Socially, immature teenagers cannot get far beyond *puppet relationships* (described in chapter 4). This partly differentiated, controlling form of relationship is normal in toddlers and common among adolescents, even when they become capable of more mature, separate relationships. If separate relationships have never been achieved, however, the lack suggests a persistent, gross narcissism. A lack of true empathy and self-referential ethics are usually part of this mix.[2]

Childish teenagers have yet to achieve separateness in *any* relationship and cannot treat important others any other way than as puppets. Lacking empathy, they cannot figure out why their old friends pull away. Even when they discover painfully that they are not liked, they are unable to learn. And, as time goes on, the reception becomes more hostile. In brief, adult reactions to insistant puppet relations depend upon the age of the puppeteer—and how aggressively and presumptuously that controlling relationship gets pushed. A mother ordered around and treated like a marionette by a toddler may feel exasperated, weary of endless thankless feedings, bathings, entertainments, supervisory hours, room-cleanings and read stories, and she may weary of having to say No to a small tyrant. But parents experience a toddler as funny, too. In small doses parents find a toddler's bossiness endearing. When precisely the same words come from the mouth of a defiant teenager, this presumptuous puppetry begins to make adults angry. And when a nineteen-year-old stranger breaks into the family home to steal, adults respond with fury. For one person treating another as a slave is, at the extreme, enraging. What is rape, after all, but a violent assertion of a spurious right to force another person to be a puppet?

Finally, there is an ethical dimension to immaturity—a *selfish, concrete moral reasoning*. Immature teenagers' ethics are self-interested. In their egotism they are oblivious to the needs of others. The other elements of an adolescent immaturity get mixed up in this childish ethic, too. For immature teenagers may embrace a magical view of the future ("They will not catch me!"), and so doubt there will be future consequences. In their narcissism they do not believe that the rules that apply to others also apply to them. This is not to say that childish teenagers are not nice, that they cannot also be well-meaning. Yet they are tempted to break any rule that is inconvenient to self-gratification, assuming they calculate that they can get away without getting caught. When tempted, they will obey a prohibition if they believe they will get caught and punished. Their moral logic leads to the key question: What's in it for *me*?

What is missing in immature teenagers, as annoyed parents and teachers know, is an empathic concern for others who are not members of the immediate peer group. What is missing is a an abstract recognition of other people's rights, of a social duty owed to the collective. What is lacking is compelling respect for social rules, laws, or ideals. Immature teenagers resent and fear getting "busted," and will avoid this outcome if they can, but this does not mean giving up selfish aspirations. It means calculating the risks of getting caught and the enormity of the consequences. Such childish teenagers can be moved by baubles, discouraged by threats, but no inner compass guides them toward an onerous, principled duty. They lack an internal self-denying social ethic.

A delayed ethical maturation alienates childish teenagers from more mature age-mates. For the latter come to resent a selfish ethic that permits lying, cheating, stealing, and other "sketchy" misbehavior. Why? Because as normal adolescents mature they consider what *duty* they owe to others, beyond self-gratification, and they respect universal constraints embodied in laws. They can imagine what others feel, and recognize the hurtful or offensive consequences of their own behavior. They can conceptualize a group, even if they are not personal friends with every member, and take seriously the harm that criminal misbehavior does to *society*. In short, they become capable of a social and abstract ethic, and in these terms a childish teenager's (or an immature adult's) selfish, sneaky misbehavior seems disgraceful.

Inevitable Troubles

For immature teenagers, what are normally pre adolescent milestones constitute their own highest developmental capacities. Relative to age-mates, this immaturity leaves them with a limited psychological repertoire, which proves inadequate to the challenges and tasks of a demanding, modern adolescence. Relative immaturity virtually guarantees that a teenager will fail across the board—at the academic, domestic, and social tasks of adolescence.

This unsound adolescent approach becomes the more problematic the longer a teenager remains developmentally stuck. This makes sense, for immaturity is relative to the task at hand and also relative to classmates and age-mates, who continue to grow up. The gap widens, and over time the academic and social challenges of high school become more daunting. An immature teenager's predicament becomes increasingly untenable, for the very capacities he needs to avoid trouble and make himself a success remain unavailable. As other adolescents mature they surpass him academically, and as they mature socially, they shun his childishness. Crises become inevitable.

Beyond its proper moment, an immature approach looks more and more like an egregious narcissism. This is because it is childish narcissism, which becomes egregious. It ceases to be tolerated by adults or by mature teenagers. Both recoil from evasions and infantile posturing. Both revile pouting and tantrums. Affectionate relatives weary of inconsiderate behavior. Parents grow anxious about a lazy failure to do homework or chores without nagging, and alarmed at an obliviousness about the SATs and college applications. Sneaky misbehavior puts off adults and mature teenagers, particularly when it comes at their expense. When underhanded selfish behavior persists, it becomes criminal.

From an immature teenager's own vantage point, these results are unhappy. In school, on social occasions, mature adolescents leave him behind. However noisily he insists he does not care, he suffers from loneliness, shame, and the humiliating company of other childish failures or younger children. Unable to manage anything else, childish teenagers offer one another pushy puppet relationships or the parallel play of pre-adolescence. Moreover, given what they lack, struggling teenagers can only regard these failures as perplexing, for they lack the means to remedy them. A childish young man cannot fathom why he cannot make or keep friends. A childish girl cannot understand why she no longer belongs to the in-crowd, why she no longer gets invited, why she has to stay home or put up with awkward unpopular peers in order to go out in company at all. For such teenagers, the social register becomes a slippery slope. Yet given their own skewed perceptions, they cannot readily be taught to do better. This bafflement, this inability to learn, makes sense. For it requires maturity to understand immaturity. It requires a mature point of view to recognize a mature approach to teen life. It requires the very maturity that is lacking to recognize what is missing. For these reasons struggling teenagers are puzzled and ashamed. They blame others, including their parents, but their accusations do not rescue them from feeling bad about themselves. Immaturity undermines their self-esteem and saps their confidence. The irony is circular. For a teenager's immaturity makes it impossible to see how to remedy the academic, familial, and social failures that immaturity makes inevitable. For this reason, advice is ineffective.

The way out, of course, is to grow up. But troubled teenagers do not know they need to. They sense that they are falling behind, but it does not seem to them so much a matter of getting left behind as being left out, and this omission simply feels undeserved and unfair. Immature teenagers do not know what blocks their progress, what makes them fall behind. They have no idea how to catch up. They cannot readily be taught, even if others can see plainly what they are blind to.

This being so, parents and other adults must recognize the obstacles and discover a way to remove them. Adults have to figure, because they cannot do it for themselves, how to prod stuck teenagers to get on with growing up. We adults have to help, because we can understand, and we can see the options. We can anticipate the dangers, and recognize the consequences, even if immature teenagers cannot.

A Case: Helen (Part A)

This is a case of delayed maturation. As she approached the end of high school, Helen was failing across the board in all the usual venues of adolescence: at school, at home, and among her peers. She tried to surmount the challenges of her adolescence with the flawed approach of an immature teenager. And she was unhappy enough about the results—and about herself, her family, and her life—to try to end it all.

1.

When she entered high school, Helen aroused no immediate adult concern. She might have, and she could have, and no doubt she should. have, but she did not. The change over the summer, since she finished in junior high school, was noticeable, but only to those who knew her in eighth grade. There, in junior high, her teachers liked her hard work and gave her straight A's. They appreciated her courtesy and quick smile.

But they were not there in the fall to see her get off the bus looking as if her ponytail had been cinched down too tight. She kept her head down, and made no fuss. Had her new teachers had time for a girl who made no noise or trouble, they might themselves have wondered about her deer-in-the-headlights immobility, her unwillingness to laugh when the class appreciated a wisecrack. She looked wooden and did not raise a hand or catch a teacher's eye—as though afraid to provoke an unpredictable deity. Her junior high volleyball coach would have been startled when the captain of the junior high team did not try out for the frosh team. But the frosh coach, never having met her, failed to notice when, on the day of the tryouts, Helen quietly climbed back on the bus after school.

After Christmas, the vice-principal did notice. He upbraided Helen in the spring when he saw that her algebra grade had dropped to a C- and after she was said to be "rude" to her algebra teacher. She had not been turning in her problem sets. Called to his office, she was defensive. She bitterly complained that her teacher made little effort, that she wasn't "doing her job." The vice-principal sent a letter home explaining Helen's suspension, but received no reply. Then again in the weeks before summer, he called to let Helen's parents know she was not always showing up at school—and her excuse notes looked like forgeries. Helen herself answered the phone, and told him her mother was asleep. She promised to give her mother the message to call, but he never heard from her. Hearing this, teachers shrugged and recorded zeros for her missing work. At the end of the year she failed algebra and civics. The vice-principal never received any reply to his voicemail messages and e-mails, and suspected that Helen was intercepting them. However, he was doing what procedure called for. He resolved to watch her in the new school year.

From the start of sophomore year Helen began again to cut classes. In December she was called back in to see the vice-principal. He chewed her out in a friendly way about her lack of work, her overdone make-up, her coming late and leaving early. In the spring he called her back in to warn her about hanging around with "irresponsible" seniors he suspected of drug use and "wild parties," whose parents often seemed to be out of town. This discussion lost its friendly tone. Helen bristled when he called her friends "trouble." Then she looked wooden. He mentioned that he had hoped to "get her to fly right" before leaving to take a new job as principal at another high school. Helen never saw him again.

In the fall of her junior year she was arrested at a mall for shop-lifting. A month late, a police officer showed up at the high school with a dog and a warrant to search Helen's locker—and removed a plastic bag for "evidence." In a week, the juvenile court sent a notice of arraignment. Helen arrived before the judge with her father and another attorney, who got her off the drug charge on a search warrant technicality and got her a small fine for shoplifting—on the basis of her father's promise to the judge he would have her consult a psychiatrist.

When she showed up to begin junior year, her home-room teacher thought she "looked like a basket case"—tired, irritable, expressionless. He wondered about drugs, about whether this girl was getting any sleep. But he was busy. He left a note for the new vice-principal: "I'm worried about this girl—she looks unhappy!" It was weeks before the busy new vice-principal got around to calling her into his office, however, and by that time she had vanished from the high school. He learned from other

127

students that the rumor was Helen had been "snatched by goons," who had taken her to "lockdown."

Helen arrived at the ranch in the third year after we opened Montana Academy—about the time we came up for air long enough to wonder what might be the source of the flawed approach that Helen's parents complained about. Helen's predicament demonstrated the heart of the problem in so many obvious ways we could not miss the point. She was assigned to one of my teams. I spent many hours with her. We liked each other. I saw her in my office often, because she came to knock on my door. She had a wonderful therapist, a warm young woman. Yet her avid interest in talking with me, too, suggested how much she also was looking for an older man. This thought, even if we had not taken a thorough history at enrollment, would have sent me back to her history to figure out why this girl was so hungry for a dad.

But I am getting ahead of myself.

So far I have presented an external account of Helen's signs, symptoms, and misbehaviors. It is an account I presented from the objective point of view—the sort of vantage upon her that would have been shared by her teachers, a vice-principal, an arresting officer, a juvenile judge—and a psychiatrist who saw her. These adults did not have a close relationship with her. She did not willingly tell them much about herself. And so all of them saw her "from the outside," noting her wooden face, her tension, her barely camouflaged anger, her averted gaze. This was a girl who looked unhappy, but kept the lid on. She did not rush to let anyone know what the trouble might be. And her parents were not very much in evidence.

When I met her at the ranch there was about her a self-sufficiency, almost an adult assertion: "I can take care of myself." She joined a team at the ranch and was always ready to listen to others, to offer advice, to defend new teammates if they seemed bullied or stressed. But she was not ready to ask anyone to help her. She did not wish to acknowledge that she needed help, much less wanted it—and seemed not even to know that she needed it. I guessed that she was determined not to depend on anyone, not to let herself be let down again.

Her defensive self-sufficiency changed, in time. We discovered she was scratching her forearms, hiding a series of tidy, parallel cuts under a sweatshirt or sweater sleeve. But she hid them badly, so carelessly at times that her new friends spotted them when she undressed. Our staff noticed them, too, when she let a sleeve slip "by mistake." We insisted on checking her body, once we knew, and worried with her about the meaning of this self-laceration. But I knew from the start that, whatever else was meant, Helen in this way forced her team leader and therapist to stop, look, and listen—to pay attention, to be alert.

This turned out to be the point. Over those first weeks, we noticed that she cut herself during times when she felt unwatched, unchecked, unnoticed, as when staffing changes or illness, or staff vacation days off-campus or some noisy distraction prevented our staff's close attention to Helen's well-being. Then she got found out or confessed. In this process, which she initiated, she forced us to become better acquainted with her. Her therapist and team leader then made it clear that they saw her competence, her independence, her ability to take care of others, her stoic uncomplaining—but that they also saw that this was not the whole story about her. They pushed her gingerly to let us hear about that other, sadder side of her. We all made it clear we already knew some of the story. We knew some of what she had endured. Yet we were having to wait patiently for her to tell us about her own experience—about herself.

It was as if we had lifted away that fixed mask. She began to hover outside her therapist's door, eager to talk. She seemed less and less to mind that others saw that she wanted to connect. She began to knock on my door to schedule times to talk. She began to let me know how much she longed for a little adult help, how much she wanted the adults to pay attention, to "get it" about her. She asked about my schedule, wanted to know what time I arrived and went home. I gathered she did not want to wait for me in suspense about whether or not I would be coming back.

This turned out to be no small matter, but rather a major leitmotif in her life. This became apparent when the past intruded upon the present, when we reenacted together an old theme. One winter day when I had scheduled to meet her early in the morning, I got caught in a blizzard and arrived on campus two hours late. The time for our meeting came and went, and she had gone on to school. I knew I owed her an apology and made a note to find her at lunch. When she came back to the lodge at noon, she sat in the midst of a gaggle of girls at her team table. I approached, tried to get her attention. Something under the table required her full attention. She pretended not to hear me, and so I had to take her by the shoulder and ask her to come up to my office, because "I owe you an apology."

She still looked unimpressed, but came with me. I did apologize— not for the blizzard, but for failing to call to let her know. Still she looked unimpressed. I told her I could see how upset she was. But she did not relent until I said that I had not missed the point, had not missed her letting me know how important it was to her that I be reliable. I wondered whether I was really the first man to let her down and make what might sound like an empty apology—and she began to weep. I said I could not stop a blizzard, but I certainly would try not to stand her up—and let her down.

So far, as I say, I have presented only an external account—of a girl's global breakdown. I have described a competent middle-school girl who began to struggle—across all venues of an adolescent life—at school, at home, among friends, and personally. Of course something had happened to her, or had not happened. Her performance dramatically changed. She had begun shoplifting, changed friends, began to use marijuana. Something must have gone wrong at home. Her parents had not responded to a vice-principal's explicit warning or calls for meetings. Helen was no longer captain of the volleyball team, had not even tried out for the team.

Those externals were apparent, but none of the adults in her life knew what any of this meant to Helen. Yet these objective facts about a young patient who refused to cooperate still permitted a psychiatrist, who saw Helen on the judge's order, to propose a tentative diagnostic profile:

I Cyclothymic Disorder
  Cannabis Abuse
  Rule Out Attention Deficit Hyperactivity Disorder
  R/O Conduct Disorder
  R/O Poly-substance Abuse
II No Diagnosis

I do not mean, in presenting this objective diagnostic profile, to treat this psychiatrist's evaluation with irony or contempt, but rather to emphasize how limited that diagnostic approach can only be. I had no trouble making sense of the diagnostic logic. Cyclothymic disorder reflected the account by Helen's father's of her mood instability, her apparent cheerfulness alternating with unhappiness, her late night sleeplessness, her collapsed academic effort, and withdrawal from sports. The psychiatrist knew (from the court ordered consultation notes) that Helen had been caught with marijuana. He would infer that her social and academic decline had to do with a depressed mood. He would wonder whether she had begun using other drugs, and would assume that she might not tell him if she had. He would worry that he was hearing the opening bars to a criminal swan-song. It would occur to him that she was developing an antisocial pattern that, at her age, might be called a conduct disorder.

So, trying to help within the few visits mandated for an "evaluation," knowing her parents' insurance did not cover any more, he prescribed Prozac, an antidepressant that might help her with a deflated mood and the anticonvulsant Depakote, a "mood stabilizer" that might stop her flip-flopping. The psychiatrist then would have urged her father to have Helen evaluated for outpatient drug treatment and suggested Helen see a therapist for brief cognitive-behavioral psychotherapy. He would have pointed out that she seemed to be dealing with low self-esteem in "self-defeating" ways.

However, Helen refused to go back to see him. She knew she only had to see him for a few meetings, and refused to go on any further. She took the pills, but only when her father watched her take them—and he was not reliably available to do so. Ted was upset about what had happened to his daughter, but tended to blame her mother. He could not bring himself to insist on a drug evaluation, and instead accepted her account of her merely "experimental" use and her assurances that "everyone" smoked.

Months later, when she was admitted to a psychiatric hospital, both her parents were shocked and scared, eager to help. They cooperated with the ward social worker to put together a much more comprehensive history, which included a detailed account of Helen's troubles—and her parents' own troubles. When Helen arrived at the ranch, this history came with her. In the hospital, she had been put on Paxil and Lamictal. As she settled in, she began to fill in a few details of her family's troubles—from her point of view.

2.

Linda, Helen's mother, remembered a cheerful toddler. Early milestones all had arrived on time. Helen was an outgoing, talkative preschooler, an energetic playmate on the swings, an avid artist at the finger painting easel. All went well until just after she turned four, when her mother's ankles and knuckles swelled up and became red and hot and painful. She could no longer stand at her drafting table for long. Although Linda improved over the next months so long as she took anti-inflammatories and steroids, her "hot" joints returned as soon as she tried to stand for long or to exercise to keep her weight down. In the end she had to give up her part-time job at a New Haven architectural firm, where she had been very happy. Her arthritis literally had knocked her off her feet.

*Both parents thought they handled this family crisis reasonably well. Ted, then a law student at Yale, took a leave of absence to come home to care for his wife and daughter. When Linda took to her bed with aching hands and feet, with migraine headaches and blues that the steroids exacerbated, Helen became "little mommy" and "daddy's girl." She was secretly guilty at her pleasure in helping Ted do the housework, the nursing, and the cooking. She asked him if he would "marry **me**, too?" and Ted laughed and said "Sure," when she was a big girl like her mommy, "if you still think that's a good idea."*

When Helen started grade school, Linda's illness improved—and she went into remission for a few years. Ted graduated from law school, joined a New York firm, and began putting in the long hours associates are expected to work. Helen did well in school. And Linda devoted herself to driving Helen to her various activities: soccer, flute lessons, Brownies, ballet. Linda waited up for her husband to come home, usually after midnight. While he ate a late dinner she told him what pleasure she took from watching Helen chase a ball or do a pirouette, now that she could appreciate what a remarkable thing it was to be able to do those things. During this long remission Linda began to plan to return to work. She woke up in the night dreaming about homes she wanted to design for people with disabilities. She was full of ideas again. She looked forward to an emancipation from her loneliness when Helen was at school. She dreamed of freedom from the static postures she assumed in her bedroom and in her Volvo.

Then she got worse again. Rapidly she slid backward. Her clinical course became an oscillation between sunny freedom from pain and incarceration in her bedroom. Her remissions filled the house with music and the smell of cookies, but these respites began to come further and further apart. As Helen reached puberty Linda sometimes had to stay in bed for weeks, waiting for a remission. Helen then tried to stay home from school to take care of her mother, although Linda tried to insist that she herself would "only be OK if you go on doing so well at all the things you do so well!" Helen pressed on through junior high school, secretly believing, in a series of magical fantasies that if she only could get straight A's...if she made first chair in the orchestra...if her team won the league championship ...**then** her mother would be cured. Each time, as success failed to make her wish come true, she made new, more challenging bargains with fate— as if this time maybe she could get it right.

As Linda became less able, Ted seemed to be busier. He hired a housekeeper to drive Helen to lessons and classes. When Linda felt up to it, the housekeeper also drove Linda to watch Helen scoop and spike. Freed from direct-care responsibilities, Ted came home later. Linda became too weary to stay up for dinner with him at 9 P.M. This conjugal ritual ended.

Over the summer before Helen started high school, her mother developed a "butterfly" rash over her cheek, which narrowed to pass over the bridge of her nose. She complained of new chest pains. Her headaches came often, and sometimes were so excruciating that all she could do was turn out the lights and lie with her eyes closed in the dark. She seemed more morose, irritable, unwilling to be "bothered." After another exhausting workup, Linda's doctors confided that this was not merely an atypical arthritis. It was lupus erythematosus, a waxing and waning, chronic autoimmune disease, which could affect any vital organ, even the brain. After this news Linda curled up upon herself. Her despair might have been the illness itself. She no longer wanted to talk much. She took less interest in what Helen and Ted were doing. She could not sleep without sedatives, and took her pills early. Often, she was snoring insensibly when Ted arrived home.

It frightened Helen that her mother seemed to be giving up. She felt her father's alienation from his own home, and this frightened her, too. In her first year of high school she tried to help them both. She came straight home from school and sent the housekeeper home early, thinking she was saving money, so that her father would not have to work so hard—and could come home earlier. She prepared her mother's dinner and made her own lunch for the coming day. She helped her mother to the table to eat or brought her a tray, if she refused to rise from her pillows, and sat beside the bed to make sure Linda ate something before she drifted back into stupor. As her mother slumbered, Helen waited up alone, still in her school clothes. Although not very interested in algebra sets or the Bill of Rights, she did her homework. Exhausted at the end of the day, she dosed on the cushions in the bay window until, coming up the drive, her father's headlights awakened her. Then she jumped up to warm his plate and open a beer.

When he came through the door, she threw herself into his arms. While he put down his briefcase in his study, she put his dinner on the table and brought him the beer. As he ate, she listened to him talk about his day—about "bond issues," "buy-outs," and "mergers" she did not understand or care much about. She cared about him, however, and she tried to cheer him up, even if she had no idea what he was thinking. She laughed at his jokes, celebrated his small victories, and silently felt more troubled that, ever more frequently, he forgot to ask about her mother's day. Then, according to ritual, she showed him all she had done—house-cleaning, shopping, sorting her mother's medications. He checked her math homework. When he looked up from her homework he gave her that special look she lived for, and she felt relieved when he outlined the next day's doings, and told her what time he would come home again. She carried out his instructions to the letter, anticipating his gratitude, whipping through housework and schoolwork, knowing he would see that she had done what he asked and would give her that special look, which told her they were in this together. "Here's looking at you, kid," he would say before staggering off to bed. For this she willingly sacrificed volleyball, after school activities and friends.

Her collaboration with both parents only upset her when she sensed friction between them. When her mother complained of pain, Helen tried to follow her father's careful instructions, dispensing Percocet and Valium from the egg carton where he had sorted out her mother's doses—"for every six hours, not less." Sometimes when her mother hurt, complained bitterly about Ted's rigid orders and the slow progress of the clock, she felt that she had fallen into the middle of her parents' unhappiness with one another. When he bitterly complained that her mother's aching joints recovered "way too slowly," when he wondered whether she was "really trying," or said her mother's stupors left him "alone," she felt squirmy. These were not problems she had any idea how to remedy. When he laid before his daughter a husband's erotic frustrations and marital loneliness, as if she were sharing in his sense of life's unfairness, as if she would be OK hearing about this, she felt a shudder of fear. For she sensed the truth—that her cheerful efforts were failing to make up for her mother's failings, that she was failing to make him happy.

In the spring of her freshman year her mother rallied—or roused herself to pretend that she was feeling better. Linda seemed stronger. She dragged herself out of bed to sit up in an easy chair, and she tried to do without pain medication for longer and longer. But Helen saw her pain. On those days Helen could hardly bear to leave her mother to go to school, and frequently she left campus to walk home during lunch hour. Irritable with pain, however, her mother could only talk about how angry she was about Ted's long hours. At night, when her parents sent her to bed, she heard her mother accuse her father of "working late on purpose," of "having other women." Slower to anger than her mother, her father could be even more enraged—in his indignation about Linda's "zoning out," her "avoiding sex," her "willingness to reduce our marriage to an empty shell." Beside himself with frustration he shouted in parting, "What use are you?"—and slammed the bedroom door. Helen knew he would sleep in the leather chair in his study and be gone by 6 A.M. Immobilized by her parents' pain, she lay awake listening to her mother's weeping. She awoke in the morning already tired before the day began.

Described from Helen's point of view, in this way (as a good therapist soon becomes able to do), Helen's troubles no longer reduce to symptoms or only to a syndrome diagnosis (dysthymia per *DSM-IV* 300.4). Moreover, once this history becomes clear, it seems less plausible that a pill (Prozac, Depakote) will remedy Helen's unhappiness or tame her "mood swings." Her symptoms ("deer-in-the-headlights" angst, "unwillingness to laugh"), her anomalous behavior (quitting the volleyball team), her academic sluggishness (homework not done, falling grades, truancy), and her cutting her arms, all take on a new significance. They arise comprehensibly in the context of an unhappy family. Now, clearly, they have a different source. With this history it is impossible to reduce her dysphoria or misbehavior to a biological-transmitter diathesis, as if merely the outward signs of a mental "disorder."

This appears instead to be a young girl in the midst of a protracted family crisis—and under great stress. She was the family member sent to the hospital and transferred to Montana Academy—the index patient. But long before her enrollment at the ranch, it was already obvious that she is not more stressed, or more disorganized or dysfunctional or unhappy, than her poor mother. And her father, who has behaved reasonably well, so far, and has done his best to provide his daughter enough parental attention and authority to compensate for his wife's disability, suffers also. He has begun to fray around the edges as his marriage has begun to unravel.

3.

As Helen entered her sophomore year, domestic matters got worse. Linda's remission required massive doses of steroids, which ballooned her face, thickened her figure, and deflated her mood. She began out loud to "wish I wouldn't wake up." Trying to right herself, she stopped the steroids, but then her pain and disability got worse. Her analgesics left her stuporous.

Frantic with worry, Helen rushed home each day, fearful of what she might find. Moreover, she was anxious knowing that her father had begun to accept defeat. Although he did not say so at first, she could feel that something had been decided, something she did not understand— and he was no longer was in suspense. He was slipping away. When he came home to find Linda comatose, he muttered in Helen's hearing, "We cannot go on like this." Helen tried ever more frantically to stand in for her mother, to change the subject, to cheer him up with accounts of her day, to surprise him with cookies.

In the winter of her sophomore year this suspense ended. When she came home to cook dinner for her mother, she found a note that he had left for her on the same kitchen table where she had served so many frugal repasts. The note was brief. In it she learned that her cooking and cleaning, her late nights and attentiveness, her sacrifice, had not been enough.

> *Dear Helen,*
>
> *I'm staying in the city for now. I'll be in touch in a few days. Your mother needs you, so hang in there.*
>
> *—Love, Dad*

She did not sleep that night, or the next night, or the next. She was waiting for his call. Unable to hold out, she finally called him at his office. He apologized for not calling sooner. He had been "very busy." For a moment his conspiratorial tone, which took her into his confidence and expected her to understand his needs, revived her strained loyalty and closeness. But she got off the telephone in a fog, and an hour after she hung up she realized that he had just informed her of his decision to separate and file for divorce.

He failed to call home for another three days. When he did, she begged him to come home. His tone had become distant, however. She was not reaching him. He did not agree to come home. He promised to visit often, but remained vague about what "often" meant. After she hung up she was furious. She felt angry, but less at him than at herself, for sounding so needy, for not pinning him down.

All that spring he did not come home—a gap in time that might not sound long to others. But to Helen it was a rent in the fabric of the universe. Sitting in the bay window, watching the barren driveway, she realized she was no longer near the top of his agenda. She began to guess that he had other people and problems on his mind. She was so let down she could not speak of it. She was, in a new way, all alone.

A stone seemed to form inside her and to begin to block the passageway to her soft feelings—a shift that took time. Helen did not immediately turn away from her parents. For weeks she simply endured the emptiness and grief. She spent her evenings, after her mother was asleep, parked on the cushions in the bay window, staring into middle distance, going over it all again and again. As her mother snored, she tried to figure out what she had done wrong, what she might have omitted. She tried to guess when he snapped, when he decided to cut his marriage loose. But she was too young to figure it out. And she could not put herself into her mother's slippers, either. She could not elude the conviction that this was her mother's fault. She was furious that her mom had driven her dad away.

For a while she made excuses for him, even while listening to her mother's rant on the theme of how right she had been "all along" about how her husband must have been "screwing around." For weeks Helen jumped when the telephone rang. Then, after many disappointments, she refused to answer at all. For weeks she rifled through the mail and scoured her inbox for e-mail messages. Doodling in algebra class, she pictured all the ways she might lure him home. When he left a breezy voicemail to say he "might be in the neighborhood" the next day, she stayed home from school, curled up in the cushions in the bay window, so as not to miss that moment, which she pictured over and over—her father climbing out of his Jetta, and Helen racing down the path to fling herself into his arms. As the day went by she imagined various alibis for him, that would make sense of his delay. And then he never showed up at all. The stone fell into place.

Her mother did not get a life, either. In the suspense of Ted's inaction, Linda did not file for divorce, but her anger became a broken record, unchanging but entirely absorbing, as if her recriminations had begun to substitute for a career and friends.

∽

*In the months that followed her father's failure to show up to visit, Helen's ties to both her parents gradually loosened. She began to feel numb about them. She had the conscious thought, "I'll divorce **them**, too." She lost interest in debating with her mother about who deserved more of the blame. She lost interest in cleaning and baking. She shopped for groceries only because she and her mother had to eat, but she ceased to care what food she put into her mother's mouth or into her own. She lost interest in the day's tasks, which floated off into space along with her math sets and history papers. She stopped going to class at all. She ceased to care about much of anything. She ceased to care whether she woke up in the morning.*

In time, Helen did get a life—and found enough excitement in risk, in naughty defiance, to keep from going totally numb. She had never before made up her mind for herself without her father's advice, but now she found any number of young men willing to make up her mind for her—about sex, about marijuana, about where to go and whom to hang with in the wee hours. She went with them, had sex with them if they wanted to, so long as they held her, and shared their weed, and did not leave her alone. Her jealous fights with rivals made her social life an exciting soap opera.

*She lost all respect for her mother, who clearly could not even hold onto a husband. It had been a long time since her mother was in any position to say no to her. Now her dad was gone—what was there to fear? Whom did she have to worry about disappointing? She began to treat her mother's nagging as ambient noise to be ignored. She answered with sarcasm: "You mean I should make the Honor Roll to impress **Dad**? You must be kidding!" She did as she liked, scathing about her mother's remonstrances about her "reputation." "You mean so I can have a brilliant marriage like **yours**?" She treated curfews as suggestions, lying without scruple about when she came in. She knew her mother would have no idea where she was when the Toyota turned into a pumpkin. Even if her mother woke up and noticed that Helen was not back, what would it matter? Helen could brazen it out. For she did all the shopping and errands. It wasn't as if her mother could just take her car keys. She faced down her mother with blunt irony: "What are you going to do to me—tell **Dad**?" She could tell him herself, but she did not. Angrily she wondered how long it would be before he noticed.*

*When Ted came up from New York on a warm summer evening to take her out for a hamburger and to dash away again, he seemed no longer to be interested in the fine details of her days, much less in her nights. He did not ask about friends or boyfriends. Instead, he wanted to talk about **his** social life. He had begun to work out at a gym. He wanted her to admire his reversed progress back down the worn holes in his belt. He encouraged her to press on, academically, but had not registered that she was not attending classes. He seemed oblivious to her failing grades, although he expected her to take an interest in what new car he wanted to buy, his prospects for making partner, and a "really good woman" he was seeing, about whom he promised, "You're really going to like her." He hugged her on the sidewalk before climbing back into his BMW. He said, "Here's lookin' at you, kid"—in such a way that she could not ignore the fact that he no longer saw her at all.*

In the fall of her junior year on her way home from school, Helen stopped at the mall. She wandered down an aisle at Nordstrom's, touching the glossy high heels, spritzing her wrists with a well-advertised scent, feeling unreal. She was lost in thought, still high from a joint she shared in the girls' bathroom at lunch.

She had started shoplifting, even though she had enough clothes. There was a thrill to it, some of the time, that punctured her ennui, her numbness. Getting away with it had been remarkably easy. Adults hardly seemed to be paying attention to her. It had been easy to elude them. At home she cut the price tags from silk scarves she found in her pockets. She left the cuttings in her wastebasket for her mother not to notice. She fished a display spray-vial of Ck One from her purse, feeling no remorse about an impersonal corporation her father probably had issued bonds for or helped to merge with some other corporation. It was not exactly that she did not know that stores mounted cameras to watch for thieves. But someone once had explained to her that security camcorders were installed solely for effect. It was all for show. No one actually watched the monitors. No one was really on duty. She had been misinformed, in this case.

Moreover, in the same week she was arrested at Nordstrom's, the vice-principal pulled her into his office because her Spanish teacher thought she was slurring her speech. In her purse the nurse found a vial of Vicodin with her mother's name on the label. The vice-principal called the police, and an officer arrived with a dog and a warrant to search her locker, where he found a baggie of marijuana. He read her her rights.

Even so, she did not worry too much. Her father was a lawyer. He and her mother would have to help her out. They would rescue her.

In this, she was right. She even managed to get her parents to talk to one another. Linda called Ted, who drove up to Connecticut to rescue her from both charges—shoplifting and possession. He brought along a litigator from his Manhattan law firm to get the possession charge quashed on a warrant technicality. Ted then paid off the store, but expressed to her his indignation that Nordstrom's "should have had more staff on the floor to prevent this kind of thing, not just grab a kid after she gets into trouble." He paid the fine when, as advised, she made a guilty plea and told the judge this had been her first outing. She was startled to notice that her father seemed not to be angry with her. He also did not seem to mind the lie his associate proposed. Oddly, this troubled her. For she felt disquieted to recognize that he seemed pleased, as if he thought that his defense of her wrong-doing made them complicit pals again. She sensed he thought her misbehavior canceled out his own—that they were both guilty, and so she had nothing on him.

Then, without saying good-bye to his wife, he went away again.

After those two days together Helen missed him all over again with an unbearable anguish. She did not go to school, and her mother did not have the gumption to make her go. She spent a few days and evenings, after her father's departure, dozing on the cushions in the bay window. She was stewing about him when she fell asleep, and she awoke to the ticking of the big clock on the mantel and her mother's steady snoring. She awoke angry, unable to bear it any longer. Abruptly, she stomped into the bathroom and noisily ransacked her mother's medicine cabinet, emptying child-proof bottles of pills into her father's baseball cap, swallowing them in fistfuls washed down with swigs of cough syrup.

She lay back on her pillows feeling oddly tranquil. She noted that her mother's snoring had never even shifted key, and she thought with a grim nod, "Of course not." Then she flopped back into the bay window, going fuzzy, thinking irrationally, as she passed out, that she would just doze awhile until awakened by the headlight beams of her father's Beamer—when he came up the driveway.

For a start, Helen's case demonstrates the flawed approach that, in a seventeen-year-old, marks an adolescent immaturity. At times she looked to be considerate, even empathic. Actually, she cannot imagine her mother's sick and lonely existence, what it meant to lose a promising career, what it was like to have her beloved family come apart. She cannot imagine what her father feels, either. She has no idea what it means to a hard-working man to feel stranded, alone, accused, the object of his bitter wife's envy and rage.

It is not empathy Helen feels, but an extension of what she herself feels. She imagines that her father needs only what she can provide— good cooking, housekeeping, a cold beer, and a friendly cheerfulness: a pal. Helen considers her mother to be a loser, because Linda fails to hold her husband at home, because her father might have "others" on his mind—and out of selfish need and to demonstrate that her mother is emotionally out of touch. Helen steals her mother's Vicodin. There is nothing wrong or bad about Helen's oedipal fantasy. It even seems brave that she tries to step into her mother's shoes and hold her father at home. There is a lot to admire about her hard work and heroic attempts to make the center hold. But it is not true empathy. It is fairy-tale fantasy and pseudo-empathy. She is not a young adult, only a very worried child.

Moreover, she has no pragmatic goals, no step-wise plan for her future. She is quick to duck out of homework when Ted is not there to hold her to it, and she is willing to play hooky as if there were no academic tomorrow. There surely was something generous about her sacrifices. There was something understandable in her skipping out on her academic tasks, extracurricular activities, work, and responsibilities, which ought to have provided the stepping-stones to get her to college and career. There was something sweetly pathetic about it, inasmuch as she hurried home to relieve her own frantic anxiety about her parents' marriage, about her mother's suicidal proclivity, about her father's drift down the road. But this is not future-mindedness. There was no plan— beyond getting home as quickly as she could to make sure her mother and father were still present and accounted for.

Her relationships were not yet separate—or respectful, as separate relationships can be. It is not that she tries to bully others in her relationships, but rather that she wishes to be the finger puppet on the hand of someone else who can make it all right—her father, later the boys who will exploit a scared, lonely girl. In early adolescence, she puts all her hopes into pleasing her father. She will do anything, make any sacrifice, if he would only just keep coming home. She is Cinderella, scrubbing pots and making dinner, hoping the Prince will show up with a glass slipper. There is nothing wrong, in its proper time, for this wish to be "daddy's girl." But there is as yet no trace of an independent, separate relationship. This is in no way, as yet, a young woman with her own goals and plans, her own ambitions or her own voice. No hint of it, as yet. And her suicide attempt suggests that, mired in her parents' marital debacle, she was "stuck" and saw no way past it—to an independent education and skill, to her own separate relationships, to a discovery of her own voice. Her suicide attempt, too, is potentially lethal, but yet has about it the wishful magical thinking of a child.

Finally, she demonstrates a still-concrete, still-childish moral reasoning. There has never been any evidence of an abstract ethical motive beyond pleasing and trying to take care of her parents, and getting the smile that was her reward. She has not been reluctant to blow off her homework assignments, to refuse to go to school—to see no "duty" that called her to make her best academic effort. She has not been in the least unwilling to lie, to cheat, to break her word, to forge a note, to sneak out and break her curfew. She thinks she is entitled to be rescued from her folly, to be magically freed from consequences. She has not ever acted or refrained from acting, insofar as we know, because of any concern about integrity or honor, about honesty, a sense of duty or any concern about "what's right" in itself.

∽

This, then, is an example of the global disarray which results from the flawed approach with which we began. The intervening chapters suggest that this flawed approach to life's challenges is not an arcane biological "disorder," but a developmental delay or arrest. This chapter on delay has urged that Helen's difficulty is not primarily a neurotransmitter problem, calling for serotonin, but a relative *immaturity*.

In Helen's case, and in general, perhaps, the next question is: *Why?* What is it that has disrupted Helen's maturation so as to leave her relatively immature? What has blocked her progress? What could have hindered her growing up? Helen's history provides a number of hints, a number of candidates. For to make sense of her immaturity, we are looking for an *obstacle* to her maturation.

8   Obstacles

A THEORY OF IMMATURITY implies that there must be obstacles to development. To consider what might impede maturation, it makes sense to start by noting the nature of the process that normally pushes development onward. Presumably an obstacle disrupts or prevents that constructive process—and so causes delay or arrested development.

A Model of Maturation

In the simplest terms, maturation results from the convergence of a neurological readiness and apt experience. Daniel Siegel puts it this way: "A wide range of studies has in fact now clarified that development is a product of the effect of experience on the unfolding of genetic potential."[1] In other words, development follows a genetic template, but does not result from an autonomous expression of genes. The process involves nature, surely, but also nurture. Experience is also key. *What* experience? Siegel writes: "The mind develops at the interface of neurophysiologic processes and interpersonal relationships."[2] That is, development happens within critical relationships—and does not properly take place without "parental" experience. Feral children do not develop normally.

In studies of his own children, Jean Piaget demonstrated that development results from an interaction between an unfolding neuro-readiness and apt experience over which, of course, adults preside. A child cannot be taught to read until she is ready. But neither can she learn to read unless she also has repeated mentored encounters with written texts.

This essential interaction—between readiness and apt experience—also produces other psychological milestones. In each case a neuro-readiness is necessary but not sufficient. Until he becomes ready, a teenager cannot advance beyond the "flawed approach" of a child, cannot embrace the point of view of a more mature adolescent. He cannot put others' needs before his own. He cannot achieve separate relationships. He cannot plan for a plausible, fully imagined future.

In each case, experience is also necessary but not sufficient. For each new step in maturation, an analogous parental experience is necessary, even decisive.[3] Without that experience, teenagers do not achieve empathy, cannot achieve separate relationships, or achieve a compelling ideal of honor. Children do not simply arrive at maturity, ready or not. They must be "reared." As Siegel puts it, "Genes do not act in isolation from experience."[4] The ripeness is *not* all.

An *obstacle* to maturation is anything that disrupts neuro-readiness or interferes with apt experience, or both. Accordingly, there are *intrinsic* obstacles, which disrupt neuro-readiness and extrinsic hindrances, which disrupt parenting. We may call a defect in brain functioning that prevents maturation an *intrinsic* obstacle, e.g., a defect in attentiveness and focus (ADHD), or chronic intoxication. An intrinsic obstacle is an equipment problem. Similarly, we may call disrupted parenting an *extrinsic* obstacle, e.g., the disrupted parental attentiveness that often occurs in the context of a divorce.

Because of the need for both, timing is critical. There is a window of readiness when apt experience readily produces a new milestone. Once that moment of readiness passes, the same experience may not produce the same result, and immaturity may become fixed. Florid egotism, lack of empathy, and selfish ethics, for example(s), describe the normal toddler stage. These childish aspects of character get subordinated in normal adolescent and adult personalities to more mature capacities for consideration, empathy, and altruism. When these later steps in maturation do not take place in the usual time frame, residual juvenile elements remain the highest capacities of a stunted personality.

In this sense there seems to be a season for every maturational purpose. There appears to be a period of readiness, when apt experience will prod a child to take the next step in growing up. If apt experience does not happen in that season, if ripeness ends without the requisite parenting, that lost innovation later becomes more difficult—or impossible—to achieve. Parenting cannot wait.

The stakes are high. The consequences of a failure to achieve an expected psychological milestones during adolescence and early adult life is an intractable character disorder. Once established, defective character pathology is, by definition, intractable. Immaturity can become a lifelong disability.

Arrested Adults

In jail, over the years, I came across compelling evidence that childishness can (and does) persist beyond adolescence. I came to suspect, in fact, that immaturity has much to do with incarceration.

At the time we opened Montana Academy, I regularly visited the Flathead County Detention Center to evaluate inmates for medication or to evaluate a defendant for the court—e.g., as to whether an inmate was presently competent to stand trial. At this time, our first students were arriving at the ranch. Sometimes I commuted from the one to the other. Coming from jail, I had an hour to reflect on the psychology of a fourteen-year-old boy accused of shooting his father. On the way back from the ranch, I had an hour to contemplate a sixteen-year-old student whose global breakdown had frightened his parents about the risks of his getting into more serious trouble.

What struck me then, so often, was the similarity of the approach of students and inmates. These teenagers differed very much in levels of privilege and parental education, in the resources that backed their play in life. They differed in class, in prospects. Usually the inmates had been brutalized, and our students almost never had been. Yet at both ends of my commute these teenagers were all failing in school, blowing out of their families, sliding down the adolescent social register, and keeping company with disreputables. In Lost Prairie and in Juvenile Detention, teenagers were deeply unhappy, angry at adults, indignantly innocent, and struggling with legitimate low self-esteem. At both ends of that pretty drive, students and jailed teenagers shared the same flawed approach.

All the same elements of a flawed approach were present in those young inmates, whose attitudes might be described as follows:

- **Florid Narcissism**: It is all about me—my need for money, drugs, or the things I steal or deal drugs for.
- **No Empathy**: I know nothing about "remorse" for those I

burglarize or rob or help to addict—those losers, who are not like me, and so remain beyond the radius of my concern and are not worth thinking about.

- **Magical Time:** It is now, always now—and my most important idea about the future, and the future consequences of present behavior, is, "They'll never catch *me*." My goals? To be a big shot, to have cash—now. I have no long-term plans. Drugs affect me *now*, sex is *now*, grabbing is *now*, fighting is *now*, and cash I want *now*. I am bored, and I cannot wait to *do* what I want—as soon as I get out of this jail, where all they do is make me wait.

- **Puppet Relationships:** Others are there to be used as cons, vamps, victims, jerks, punks, bitches—to be bullied, cheated, tricked, and beaten if they don't jump when I say jump. A girl is to be used, assaulted, expected to service me, and she'd better comply, and I mean *now*, or else.

- **Moral Reasoning:** I wanted it, and I wanted to do it—and there is nothing wrong with that, in my mind, so long as you don't get caught and end up here. I won't do it if I think I'm going to get busted, but otherwise—no problem.

Perhaps it is unsurprising that adolescent defendants and troubled students at the ranch had the same approach to life. But what surprised me at the time was that *adult* inmates also demonstrated the same flawed approach. From so limited a number of cases I cannot prove that criminal arrest always is associated with developmental arrest. Yet Stanton Samenow called this same flawed approach "the criminal mind," even if he did not at all understand that this flawed approach resulted from disrupted development.[5] Adult felons, more maltreated than any student who ever enrolled at Montana Academy, tend to have fully formed adult personality disorders, which seem clearly to be what adolescent developmental immaturity becomes. In tens of criminal evaluations over twenty years I cannot recall an adult felon who had yet achieved the full adolescent repertoire (fig. 6c). The adults I evaluated in prison were relatively immature, in this sense. Childishness appeared to be a risk factor for incarceration. A perpetual immaturity, you would think, made recidivism likely.[6]

The larger point is that a relative immaturity in adolescence does not inevitably resolve itself over time. These incarcerated men and women were in their twenties, thirties, and forties. Never having overcome obstacles to development, they remained stuck—stuck in prison, and stuck in psychological maturation. As a close reading of any newspaper teaches, relative immaturity is not only a problem for adolescents. For immaturity is not a problem teenagers inevitably get over. Childishness can become a lifelong disability.

Slow Normal Development

Before we consider specific obstacles, it is worth emphasizing that there is a broad span within which normal development can take place. The age at which a child achieves a particular milestone normally varies from one child to another. This variation makes diagnosis of delay or arrest tricky, for children normally do not all become ready at precisely the same age. For this reason, we must not be quick to pathologize a developmental pace that varies from the mean, particularly at the tortoise end of the curve. We must be patient, and careful in our diction not to humiliate the normal dawdler.

On the other hand, as adult inmates demonstrate, relative immaturity does not always reduce to slow-normal maturation. Slowed development may not merely be a variant of normal. Catching up is not inevitable. Time alone does not necessarily resolve a developmental delay or arrest.

Tentative Diagnosis

So how do we make the diagnosis?

Certainly one way to know for sure is to wait and see. Wise physicians have always known that, in the face of uncertainty, patience may be prudent. Time will tell—in the penitentiary, in divorce court, and in an adult mental health center. In the end, it becomes easy to recognize persistent immaturity and to be certain about the diagnosis.

On the other hand, certainty may come at great cost, assuming that something useful can be done to prevent the academic, personal, social, and economic debacles that immaturity makes probable. Certainty is elusive, at first, and early diagnosis must be tentative, given that immaturity is relative. And so the first diagnostic question about immaturity is relative to what? [7]

In practice, parents (and teachers, physicians, and therapists) compare a struggling teenager (a) to other teenagers, and (b) to social and academic and ethical norms. Most parents worry when a son or daughter lags behind socially, when former friends and other students seem less awkward, less socially clumsy, more gracious and considerate, more confident and sunny, than their own children. Parents and teachers worry when a teenager lags behind in academic skills, when siblings seem to make more of an effort, when other students appear to be more organized, more ambitious, more interested. This relative performance, which adults may or may not recognize to be a function of maturation, becomes explicit when a girl's grades begin to fall, when a boy quits the team, when someone else wins the races and the prizes, when fellow students are accepted to better colleges. To bourgeois American parents in particular, competitive academic hurdles make a child's psychological problems apparent, and may quantify the costs of a child's failure to grow up.

Relative immaturity presents as an insidious problem as teenagers who become relatively more mature leave behind those who remain relatively less mature. What gradually brings immaturity to parental (and school) awareness is a differential performance, academically, socially, and in the family. And as childish teenagers are shunned by more grown-up peers, as more mature classmates publicly outperform them in school and in extracurricular activities, as they drop behind and have to settle for less promising friends, too, they become personally unhappy and symptomatic: ashamed, withdrawn, sullen, angry, sad, baffled, resentful, envious, self-contemptuous, avoidant, explosive, intoxicated, or just hard-to-get-along-with.

In the absence of a biological illness, to medicate these problems generally is to miss the source. To do so only treats symptoms. Among our cohort of immature teenagers, medications do not effectively do even that.[8] After all, most of our students arrive after already having failed in one or more medication trials.

A tentative diagnosis can be made, first, by identifying the elements of a typical troubled adolescent's flawed approach, and second, by observing a teenager's diverging performance relative to average classmates—at the various academic and family and interpersonal tasks of adolescence. In the absence of any significant performance disparity, I would not assume that there was a relative immaturity to treat. However, as a teenager's performance in the various venues of adolescent life diverges further from the norm—as grades fall, as academic discipline flags, as social unhappiness reveals a social deviance—I would begin to suspect immaturity.

As this divergence persisted over time and worsened in degree, as secondary symptoms (unhappiness, pathological coping, substance abuse, cutting, risk-taking, defiance) appeared, I would become more sure of that diagnosis. At a certain point, even while the diagnosis of relative immaturity might still be tentative (i.e., while it still seemed possible that maturity might spontaneously supervene), I would act on that diagnosis. This decision would be a matter of relative risks, just as it is when an endocrinologist assesses a boy's relative physical immaturity, holding off long enough for the diagnosis to become certain and until a boy's unhappiness rises beyond a clinical threshold, and then offers growth hormone.

These reflections on diagnosis do not by any means suggest that every boy or girl who might be delayed in maturation ought to be treated, much less sent away from home to a program. Most of these problems are resolved at home or with competent local outpatient help. Most of the time, surely, a mild relative maturity gets resolved by attentive parents, helpful teachers, supportive coaches, and competent therapists. In fact, much of the time parents probably address these problems without even considering them to have anything to do with maturity.

However, to think of this diagnosis may help. Thinking about relative immaturity, suspecting it, even tentatively deciding that it may be the crux of the matter, does not cost much. It certainly does not mean that parents ought to rush to pathologize a child's difficulties, or rush to treatment, much less rush to send a troubled teenager away. It does not imply that pharmacology is warranted. It does not necessarily mean extended treatment, although psychotherapy could well become part of an effective plan. The only immediate implication, in contemplating this diagnosis, is that parents (or teachers, coaches, or therapists) might think about parenting differently. For a start, the possibility of a delayed or arrested development should initiate a search for something that could be hindering the progress of maturation: an obstacle.

Intrinsic Obstacles

Simply to organize this discussion, I have pointed out that developmental progress requires readiness and apt experience. I have not yet defined what that apt experience needs to be. Accordingly, I offered to divide potential obstacles into two categories: intrinsic obstacles, which disrupt neuro-readiness; and extrinsic obstacles, which disrupt or prevent apt experience.

An intrinsic obstacle is an "equipment" problem, a faulty brain function that prevents readiness. An intrinsic obstacle disrupts a teenager's capacity to use experience, including parenting, to achieve a developmental milestone. This makes intuitive sense—that brain dysfunction can hinder maturation. For if neuropsychological readiness is critical to a child's achievement of next developmental steps, it makes sense that a boy whose frontal lobes have been destroyed in a train accident might never develop empathy or frame meaningful goals, or learn to make and follow plans.[9] It is unsurprising that a teenager cannot make use of experience to grow up if he does not, or cannot, perceive his surroundings or interpret his relationships or communications properly—if he cannot think clearly, if he cannot feel his feelings. It is obvious that mothering and fathering will be less effective if a boy misperceives, or cannot hear, or cannot attend to, or cannot make sense of that parenting.

Moreover, neurology and experience interact in both directions. Any prolonged or repetitive disruption in brain function will change in reciprocal fashion the world's reaction to a girl's behavior—and so alter her experience. A student like Helen, who comes to school stoned, bringing an intoxicated brain, will be unable to digest or make use of her classroom experience. And her intoxication itself will change that experience, insofar as her teachers and fellow students surely react differently to a girl giggling at inanities than they would react to a sober classmate. Chronic intoxication disrupted Helen's brain's functioning, altered her experience in the classroom, and interfered with maturation.

A complete list of potential intrinsic obstacles would be long. I will not try to provide an exhaustive classification. Other books are devoted to intrinsic obstacles and to advanced techniques—e.g., psychotherapy, psychopharmacology, and substance-abuse treatment—which may ameliorate or eliminate an intrinsic hindrance. An encyclopedia of obstacles is not the goal. Yet it may help to list common intrinsic obstacles and to consider how they can disrupt development.

Here's the chalkboard:

Figure 8A
INTRINSIC OBSTACLES [10]

Faulty Equipment
> Brain Injury (E.g., Traumatic, Toxic, Infectious)
> Congenital Learning Disability (E.g., NVLD[11])
> Attention Deficit Hyperactivity Disorder (ADHD)
> Fetal Alcohol syndrome
> Asberger's syndrome
> Autism
> Mental Retardation (E.g., Down Syndrome)
> Schizophrenia

Disrupted Brain Function
> Psychological Trauma (in a Child)
> Bereavement (in a Child)
> Disrupted Mood (in a Child)
> Mood Instability (in a Child)
> Somatic Illness (in a Child)
> Substance Abuse (in a Child)
> Attachment Disorder
> Obsessive-Compulsive Disorder (OCD) (in a Child)
> Eating Disorder (in a Child)

Intrinsic obstacles presumably disrupt a young person's developmentally useful experience of the world. That experience, whether a parent's attempt to parent or a teacher's attempt to teach, may be shaped precisely to promote a normal child's maturation. But that skillful parenting or teaching may not be effective at promoting maturation when internal distortions nullify or distort that experience or prevent a child from attending to it or making sense of it. In the overland race to grow up, intrinsic obstacles are equipment malfunctions.

Intrinsic hindrances appear to blur a child's focus or concentration (e.g., ADHD, marijuana), or to prevent accurate interpretation of visual-spatial cues (e.g., non-verbal learning disability), or to provoke anxiety (e.g., OCD), or to disrupt thinking (e.g., schizophrenia), or to distort mood (e.g., bipolar disorder), and so disorganize a child's cognition. Psychiatric illness (e.g., manic excitement, psychosis, depressed mood, obsessions) undermines concentration, distorts ideas and reasons, distracts from academic and social tasks, and saps energy and motivation. Repetitive intoxications (and hangovers), interfere with focus and thinking, impair mood, and weaken motivation. Chronic marijuana intoxication, for instance, dissolves adolescent ambition and reduces the likelihood of sustained effort to learn or create.

Some of these neurological disturbances may delay or prevent—or produce atypical forms of—*readiness*. A child old enough for the next developmental hurdle may be ready in so eccentric a fashion that, to achieve that milestone the conventional teaching has to be revised to fit an idiosyncratic readiness. It is not that a dyslexic girl cannot be taught to read, for example, but exceptional techniques may be required for success, and the standard teaching approach may fail. Idiosyncratic readiness may require experience to be reshaped to make it apt. Special methods may remove obstacles or provide a detour.

Other equipment malfunctions appear not to be specific to a particular milestone. A general neuro-unreadiness can interfere broadly with a teenager's apprehension of experience and so render her unready even for skillful teaching or parenting. A generalized or repeated disruption in brain function can interfere with a child's apprehension and so block maturation. It proves impossible to prod a child toward empathy, for example, or to get her to plan for a coherent future, much less to write an abstract essay, if she is delirious with encephalitis, sedated from seizure medications, or chronically stoned. Genetic or congenital defects, mental illnesses, brain injuries, or toxic deliria all vitiate experience that otherwise, in a healthy and sober teenager, could usefully promote maturation.[12] By depressing a child's level of arousal or disabling her logic, or distracting her from concentrating, an intrinsic obstacle disables the equipment. By sapping all ambition or numbing perceptions or sinking moods or obtunding alertness, an intrinsic obstacle delays maturation.

There is a point in recognizing intrinsic obstacles. If not recognized, they become invisible walls that adults and children bang their heads against, exhausting themselves and losing patience with one another. Intrinsic obstacles should be removed, if possible, and circumvented if we are clever enough to figure out how to do so. Otherwise, persistent futile prodding and blaming wears everybody down. Teenagers who cannot concentrate, focus, stay awake, sustain motivation, or think abstractly cannot be bullied into growing up. They may feel a despairing frustration if adults push them to grow up but fail to recognize and ameliorate an intrinsic hindrance. Teenagers can only feel that they are being asked to do the impossible and so become demoralized. Such failures are corrosive to self-respect.

In some teenagers, unreadiness is an intractable concreteness. The absence of cross-contextual thinking (see chapter 7) is normal in preadolescent years, but on the cusp of abstract thought, preteen boys and girls begin to laugh at cornball knock-knock jokes and crude puns, which play upon amusing confusions between concrete and abstract logic.[13] By midadolescence, a persistent inability to generalize across contexts, to rise above specifics to general principle or abstract class, however, is an intrinsic obstacle of great importance. This, at least, is our clinical impression. For we have never seen a teenager become emotionally mature without achieving abstract thought. Interpersonal separateness, empathy, goals, plans, and ethical abstractions all involve thinking across contexts.

Rigid concreteness soon becomes anomalous. A teenager who cannot lift off from particulars into abstract concepts becomes increasingly eccentric. He gets stuck among tangibles: belongings, clothing, concrete actions involving physical things. He greets words like "honor" with rolled eyes ("whatever"). Stuck in muddy particulars, a concrete teenager cannot anticipate (or await) a fully imagined future, cannot discover conceptual common ground, cannot follow historical trends or think about ideologies or make comparisons. He cannot subordinate a concrete wish to superordinate principle. And so he cannot achieve adolescent maturity, because empathy, consideration, anticipation, planning, separate relationships, and social ethics all require a capacity to hold multiple concrete contexts in mind all at once and so discover a relationship among them.

Extrinsic Obstacles

An extrinsic obstacle interferes with the experience needed for maturation. Inasmuch as parents preside over that experience, extrinsic obstacles usually disrupt the parent-child relationship and interfere with parenting. Extrinsic obstacles impair parental concentration or attentiveness, accuracy of perceptions or steadiness of judgment. They disrupt or distort parents' sustained performance of two critical parental tasks: recognition and limit-setting. The result is a young person who does not get these experiences, which maturation requires.

A number of common obstacles can obstruct maturation. A listing of them (fig. 8b) does not imply that each one invariably causes delay. No two divorces are exactly alike, and not every adopted child has trouble with adolescent maturation. Not every child of over-worked, grieving, depressed, or divorcing parents, nor every son or daughter of traumatized or alcoholic parents, gets stuck in adolescence. However, among immature teenagers at Montana Academy there is a high incidence of these potential obstacles.[14] This listing implies that effective parenting can be disrupted in numerous ways, and that disrupted parenting can become an obstacle to a teenager's maturation.

Here's the chalkboard:

Figure 8B
EXTRINSIC OBSTACLES:
Potential Sources of Not-So-Apt Experience
> Death (of a Parent)
> Psychological Trauma (in a Parent)
> Depression, Anxiety, Psychosis (in a Parent)
> Bereavement (in a Parent)
> Somatic Illness (in a Parent)
> Marital Discord
> Separation & Divorce
> Adoption
> Substance Abuse (in a Parent)
> Immaturity (in a Parent)
> Character Disorder (in a Parent)
> Socio-economic Debacle (e.g., unemployment, war, homelessness, poverty, epidemic)
> Overwork, Over-commitment, Distraction (in a Parent)
> Ignorance (in a Parent)

Extrinsic obstacles disrupt maturation by interfering with parenting.

These listed conditions or events can disrupt relations between parents and children. They can interfere with parenting by dissolving family structure: *separation, divorce, bereavement.* They can undermine a child's or parent's confidence in the bond between them: *adoption, separation, divorce.* They can impair a parent's participation in a child's rearing: *psychiatric or somatic illness, overwork, immaturity, ignorance, poverty, addiction.* They can subvert adult authority: *divorce, illness, immaturity, ignorance, unemployment, addiction.* Each obstacle can interfere with a secure, intimate, warm, constructive relationship.

What Else Happens

In the context of any obstacle, the outcome depends upon what else happens. When a teenager starts smoking marijuana between classes or starts getting drunk on weekends, the prognosis will be vastly different depending upon what adults do about it. It matters greatly how parents handle an adoption or divorce. A parent's death or injury or illness, similarly, may be handled well, or badly. The prognosis differs accordingly. Other adults, acting *in loco parentis*, may take on essential parental tasks. In the classroom, a teacher notes a boy's inability to pay attention and helps to sort out the problem—and so removes a potential obstacle to his development. A counselor steps in to help stop a girl's chronic intoxication, and so removes an obstacle to her growing up. On the basketball court or baseball diamond, a coach steps in for a deceased father—to straighten out a boy who needs to fly right.[15] Lucky teenagers get what they need from adults who help out parents or fill in for them. In this sense, of course, it takes a village.

Whether the problem is intrinsic or extrinsic, *parenting* must be a part of the solution. When disrupted parenting is the extrinsic problem, the remedy will be to restore effective parenting. But even when the problem is an equipment problem, e.g., ADHD, the full remedy will involve parenting. Even after a boy starts on medication, or receives the tutoring or classroom structure he needs, his relative immaturity will still be a problem that will require deft parenting to overcome. An immature girl, placed on anti-depressant medication, still remains immature, and her prognosis depends upon effective parenting. This is why no pill yet invented can fully address the problem of immaturity. Once an intrinsic obstacle has been removed, it takes parenting to address the remaining childishness.

Recognition & Limit-setting

It is time to say more specifically what parenting *is*. It is time to say what children and teenagers need their parents to *do*. The two essential parental tasks are recognition and limit-setting—sustained over time. When an obstacle has been removed, these two parental influences will be needed to prod a delayed development onward.

First, children and teenagers need their parents to recognize them—in an accurate, honest, steady, hopeful way. The essential experience of *recognition* is to be understood, to see oneself reflected, as in a mirror, in another's eyes. When parents recognize a child accurately, in a friendly and honest way, they do what a child or teenager cannot do for herself—let her know who she is, where she stands, and that she is not alone.

Parents communicate their understanding during every stage of development and in every sensory mode—by holding a tired baby, by talking to a toddler, by winking at a five-year-old strutting in her mother's heels. It has an all-at-once visual quality. A child needs to feel seen to know she exists. A teenaged daughter needs parents to *be* there, to *watch* her, to *hear* her perform, to *touch* her with a reassuring hand. A son needs an audience, but beyond applause he needs parents to hear what he says, to respond to what they see. Parents need to make him feel, beyond words, beyond their capacity to explain themselves, that they get it about him, that they see his triumphs and his humiliations, that they understand how it is.

Children usually do not express this need explicitly any more than fish say they need water. Teenagers do not usually say, "I need recognition, Mom, so could you please *be* there?" But a child rarely fails to signal how much it matters that parents show up: to admire his finger-painting tacked up on a classroom wall, to hear her sing "The Volga Boat Song" with the choir, to see him dressed up as a goblin at Halloween, to hear her recite the *Torah* at her Bat Mitzvah, to hear him recite the Boy Scout Oath, to see her kick a goal, to watch him make a basket. Children need parents to see them do their homework, to witness the Wolf Badge ceremony at solemn gatherings of the Pack, to admire gold stars on spelling tests, to ooh and ahh at blue ribbons at Science Fairs. When a mother sees her son's report card and cries, "That's my boy!", her son has received his report card. Before she saw it and said so, all he had was a scrap of paper with a little ink.

It is almost impossible to overstate the power of recognition over a person's experience of himself. Children need to find their own faces in the family album—in first bikinis, swinging a bat, dressed up in the uniform of a Boy Scout, or as Belle of the Ball. A lack of recognition is painful. A sixty-year-old friend, a standout athlete in his adolescence, never recalls that triumph without saying sadly that his parents never came to watch him play. Both memories retain equal valence: his pride in playing for the state championship, and his grief, which forty years and the deaths of both his parents have not erased, that they had not come to watch him do it.

To say that children and teenagers need recognition is to say they need a deep, abiding, trusted, warm relationship. For recognition produces a parent-child relationship. It expresses that relationship, sustains it, makes it matter. To say what it means not be to recognized is to say what it means not to have a warm relationship in this world. It is to be alone. A lack of recognition leaves a child or teenager feeling unimportant, not of much use, baffled about what to do, confused about who he is, unsure of himself, invisible—*lost*.

Children and teenagers also need limits. *Limit-setting* is the second of the two parental tasks that are essential to maturation.[16] Recognition is critical, but it does not alone suffice to create a civilized personality. To goad a child to grow up requires the discomfort of constraints. Without set limits, "unconditional love" merely encourages unwarranted self-regard. Without set limits, children fail to grow up. They remain immature.

Why do limits promote maturation? Or, put the other way around, why does a lack of limit-setting produce obnoxious childishness in teenagers? To answer, we must begin with what limits are and what they do.

We are all born *self*-ish. This narcissism is normal. Limits are constraints that by their nature frustrate this entirely normal narcissism. Limits push selfishness to change. During maturation, limits force toddlers, schoolgirls, and teenagers to squirm about their selfish approach to problems and to others in their lives. Limits are not just a thwarting of a teenager's right to a carefree time. Parents must set limits in order to challenge that selfishness we all begin with, so as to help children to grow up.

To understand this essential role for limits, we need only consider what it is that deft limits thwart. Virtually every element of the flawed approach we have identified with adolescent immaturity is an aspect of childish narcissism: egotism, magical expectations about the future, lack of consideration, puppet relationships, and selfish ethics. Every element of that flawed approach cries out: *Me! Me! Me!* Every aspect of that unsound approach shouts: *Me first! Only me! I don't care about you!* Every element asserts shamelessly: *I'm entitled! I want it all now! I shouldn't have to wait! I shouldn't have to work! No, no—I expect you to work to provide everything I want—to wait on me!* Immature teenagers think rewards ought to come without effort. For immature teenagers, the rules do not apply.

Limits say: No. Sustained adult limits put pressure on childishness and push normal teenagers past the limited repertoire of childhood. Limits insist: *No, you're not always first,* and *No, it's not only about you.* They announce: *No, it's not all right not to care about others.* They say: *No, you are not entitled—you must work to earn it if you want it.* They call for a delay of gratification, for they say: *No, wait your turn.* They say: *No, not until it's time. No, not until I am ready, too.* And *No, not until you have done what you must do.* Limits refuse to rescue. They draw a line (within the bounds of what parents know a child can tolerate), and they say: *No, I won't do it (all) for you.* They prick the balloon of presumption by insisting: *No, others are not your lackeys.* They conjure a wider social order and make teenagers join it. For limits point to *social obligations, called duties, from which you are not excused and for which you may not expect to be paid.* Not least, limits challenge arrogant obliviousness to the constraints of civil society: *No, sorry, the rules do apply to you—**all** of them.*

In sum, set limits challenge the narcissism at the heart of the flawed approach that is adolescent immaturity. If adults thwart that childish narcissism with determination, and do so with loving understanding and recognition, children and teenagers tend to grow up. But if adults fail to set limits, teenagers do not grow up. The result is an entitled, presumptuous, selfish, arrogant teenager—who has been *spoiled.*

∽

These two essential tasks are the *yin* and *yang* of parenting. Accurate recognition must include a recognition that a limit must be set. Limits ought to be set within the context of recognition—and the solid parent-child relationship, which recognition fosters.

These parental virtues also need consistency, to be sustained over time. Children do not need parenting occasionally, as a matter of whim or adult convenience. To rear a child and adolescent well, to help a normal child to grow up fully, parents provide *recognition* and *limit-setting*, sustained over *time*.

The Essence of an Obstacle

All obstacles, then, turn out to be disruptions in the mutual recognition and limit-setting that sustains developmental progress.

Intrinsic obstacles, which disrupt neurology, undermine a child's capacity to use recognition or to grow under the influence of deft parental constraints. Inasmuch as it takes two to tango, recognition is not only a parental act, but requires a child to register that understanding. Limit-setting is not merely the infliction of punishment, but a complex encounter within a close relationship—in which a child or teenager must feel the anxious dysphoria that results from constraints. Congenital or gestational anomalies (e.g., fetal alcohol syndrome) disturb the development of the nervous system. Brain dysfunction adversely affects a child's responsiveness to parental influences—and may secondarily distort a parent's reactions to that disappointing child. Even mild disturbances, such as a non-verbal learning disability (NVLD), may alter a child's experience of his parents' recognition and constraints. This is true by definition of mental retardation, autism, and schizophrenia. By a similar logic other disruptions in neuropsychology, e.g., somatic illness, attachment disorders, defects in attention, post-traumatic anxiety disorders, mood diatheses, and chronic intoxications (e.g., marijuana), change a child's experience of adult recognition and prevent his making effective use of deft limits.

Extrinsic obstacles disrupt parenting. All my examples—adoption, death of a parent, parental trauma, illness or mental illness, parental addiction, divorce, overwork, adult narcissism, parental ignorance, or general socioeconomic catastrophe—disrupt a parent's capacity, more specifically, to sustain recognition and limit-setting. But the impact is potential, not inevitable. For example, some parents handle a divorce well, others badly. Attentiveness can reduce the negative impact. In this context, for example, a deft divorce would mean that each parent assiduously protects both parent-child relationships, and so sustains, for a child, both parental experiences of recognition.

Adoption is a special case, a potential obstacle. It has been our experience that in some families adoption undermines a teenager's faith in an unbreakable and exclusive parent-child bond. For teenagers, adoption introduces uncertainty about the legitimacy of a parent's authority or standing as a parent. Because adolescence raises stage-specific questions of identity (where a teenager came from, and where she belongs), adolescence challenges the parent-child relationship. And so adoption can disrupt a teenager's secure experience of recognition, and vice versa. Adoption can also make limit-setting difficult or impossible, since limit-setting relies upon a legitimate, strongly felt relationship.

In sum, obstacles disrupt—from within or from without—a child's or teenager's much-needed experience of adult recognition and limit-setting.[17] If unable to register apt experience, or if prevented from having needed parenting experiences because parents cannot or do not provide them, a stuck child or adolescent cannot move on to the next milestones. This being so, the first step in any remedy must be to remove the obstacle or find a way around it. But if developmental momentum is to be restored, removing an obstacle is only the first step—of a *two-step* remedy.

A Case: David (Part A)

David's debacle involved both parents, each differently, and also a brother. I present this particular family because, as in Helen's case, there are any number of illustrative obstacles. Also, David's troubles illustrates how the sources of a teenager's distress can remain obscure to him, not only because he himself, as a child, can have little idea about what he truly needs and is not getting, but also because, in this case, the source of the family's disarray is not present, not tangible. The culprit had already vanished prior to David's birth.

1.

By his second year at Tam High School, David's parents, Paul and Susan, could barely stand to be with him. Since puberty began, it seemed to them, David's defiant risk-taking had worried them more and more. They were shocked that, at age seventeen, he still had so many problems. He was bright, and in childhood had been precocious. As a school-boy he'd been an assiduous student, always got A's. He took saxophone lessons and seemed to have promise as a musician. But in the three years since middle school, David's grades had dropped from A's and B's to C's, D's, and occasional F's. None of his father's stern talks, stiff punishments, or reminders that he was "hurting his mother" resulted in any improvement in David's manners, in his cooperation at home, or academic performance. He quit the school band, refused to practice his sax, and his lessons stopped. Recently he had become less and less communicative; he seemed angrier and angrier, and his tantrums were intolerable. His father knew he was joining the wrong crowd. Paul discouraged David's friendships with scruffy skaters, who looked to Paul like grenades with their pins out, ready to blow, not at all unlike his son.

Paul and Susan recalled that things went off course when, in ninth grade, David tried out for the frosh crew and made the cut. His father, worried that he did not swim well enough and might drown if the shell capsized, refused to sign the permission slip the coach required before he would issue practice sweats. David became enraged. He stopped talking to his father at all beyond single syllables during excruciating, silent meals. He answered only direct questions with Yes or No. He took up smoking and left packs of Lucky Strikes for his father to find. When Paul confronted his son about this unsafe habit, David slammed his bedroom door. When Paul followed, he found himself nose to nose with his son, who was now as big and strong as he was—shouting and shoving. In the fracas David's lamp got knocked over, the bulb shattered on David's desk, a chair overturned.

Paul left his son a typed note, grounding him, requiring him to be home for dinner, and making sundown his weekend curfew "until further notice." As fall semester proceeded and his formal permission to row remained unsigned, no longer even discussed, David became even more provocative. He changed friends, leaving behind his prep jock pals to join "punks." Unable to work out with the oarsmen after school, he bought a skateboard without his father's permission, from college funds he'd banked from his summer job. Rather than come home, he practiced long hours of skating (and secretly smoked pot) with his new acquaintances. They met *behind the supermarket on Miller Avenue to skate up and down a cargo ramp. Paul summed up the falling grades, dubious company, and "obvious risks" and forbade David to skateboard—and confiscated David's board.*

David stopped showing up at dinner time. Paul drove downtown angrily, but very carefully, and found his son skating on a borrowed board. Because of this defiance, Paul cut David's allowance. He refused him the use of the car. And so David took to his bicycle and made himself scarce anyway. After a hostile dinner he fled to his bedroom and slammed the door. Despite apparent academic effort, David's year-end report card had: 2 B-minuses, 3 C's, a D, and an F.

In the fall, the start of David's tenth-grade year, relations became more tense on weekends when the crew left town to race in distant regattas. Because he seemed "mad all the time," David's girlfriend dumped him. As if to demonstrate what she had complained about, David picked a fistfight with a bigger senior she had begun to date, and the older boy broke out David's front teeth. To add insult to injury, from David's point of view, the principal talked to witnesses, learned that David had provoked the fight, and suspended him from the high school.

David found his mother weeping. When told why, he agreed, for her sake, to talk to her therapist. The psychiatrist diagnosed bipolar disorder and prescribed a mood stabilizer and antidepressants, which only annoyed David. He emptied the bottle into a toilet. "There's something wrong with you!" he shouted. "It's you two, not me! Why don't you and Dad take them!"

*Flustered, his mother told him, "David, we **do**."*

If he'd been asked, Paul probably would have agreed he himself needed a mood stabilizer. After he refused David permission to go skydiving with some acquaintances, David threw his plate of food on the floor. On the way to his bedroom, he punched a hole in the sheet rock. In a fury, his father called 911. David was so hostile when the officers arrived that they lost patience too, and when he swung at one of them, they wrestled him to the floor in front of his shrieking mother and handcuffed his wrists behind his back and hustled him into the back of their cruiser.

Clearly, from the point of view of a psychiatrist, David's symptoms added up to mood instability with a predominantly depressive tone—and so the formal diagnoses and prescriptions. But when we hear about the stormy course of events at home, it is not clear which is the chicken and which the egg. Are those struggles (with his father) the result of bipolar disorder? This diagnosis sounds like a biological diathesis, as if he had a primary neurotransmitter problem.

At this point, David demonstrates a global breakdown. David certainly was failing at school, at home, among peers, and all by himself. Noting this, we ought to look for the elements of a flawed approach. Personally, David certainly seems to be selfish with his girlfriend, self-centered, lacking in empathy for his parents, and oblivious to the future consequences of his present actions. At this point David was angry, impulsive, and defiant of his father's authority. His tantrums left his parents, cops, and teachers thinking he was insufferable. He lacked explicit goals beyond a wish to row or to skate, now. He had no other plans, and lacked a rationale for self-discipline. He was willing to be sneaky and to lie. In sum, his approach was flawed. For a young man in midadolescence, nearly ready to apply for college (if he wanted to go), David was grossly immature.

But how to explain it? Why did David remain childish? What obstacle blocked his path to more mature development? And what is he so angry about?

2.

David was conceived in the month before his parents abruptly moved off the mountain into the pine-and-redwood-shadowed lanes of Mill Valley. There was, from the start, something amiss in David's relationship with his father, who, red-faced with anger, sometimes called him by a name different from "David." Paul and Susan had discovered, on a narrow street, a redwood bungalow well set off from street traffic, on an ample lot. There, David built sandcastles under a giant spruce, and he pumped himself as high as possible on a safety-engineered swing set, secure behind a chain-link fence and padlocked gate.

In the days and weeks after his birth, Susan was grieving. She couldn't bear to nurse him. David's hungry mouth was too immediate, too direct, too raw a reminder. In those years she slept late almost every day—her windows shuttered as if even the dawn had been spoiled for her. In those years, she emerged about lunchtime from her dim boudoir to produce the unforgettable leitmotif of David's childhood: the arpeggio. Hour after hour Susan's fingers fluttered up the Steinway keyboard and back down again—up and back down, up and back down, up and down—in oscillations of pitch and crescendo that she seemed to produce on automatic pilot.

When David was old enough to ask, he learned that his mother practiced every day for a concert "in memoriam"—her professional debut. It took him awhile to notice there was anything amiss about this ambition. For David was young when he first learned of it, and probably did not even know what a debut was. Moreover, time only extended ahead and behind him for a short span. The future kept vanishing in mist, and so it was six or seven years before it occurred to him his mother's career floated in suspended animation. The date of her concert, always vague, never arrived.

Paul pitched in, took her place in David's rearing. David's first memories, then, were his father rocking his cradle more than he wanted it rocked, his father's bony chest as David bumped against it during walks at Muir Beach, or sucking his bottle while engulfed in his father's arms, unable to escape his father's tortured eyes. As a toddler, David could not elude paternal supervision, either. The other leitmotif of his childhood would be his father's stern imperative: "Watch out!"

Paul changed jobs. He left the firm after he'd abruptly lost enthusiasm for suing doctors over scars or drivers who had omitted to signal. He no longer wanted to point a finger about paltry mistakes for which a wretched defendant would pay for the rest of his life. Overnight, Paul changed direction. He took refresher courses at Hastings and switched to tax law—the consequences of which seemed relatively bloodless. He made an ample living helping Marin County matrons avoid tax liability. Every spring he did his family's own tax returns—as a form of penance. This worked out well when, after David's birth, Susan came down with chronic fatigue syndrome and fibromyalgia. Her doctors prescribed antidepressants to get her to sleep. So Paul moved back across the Golden Gate from the city to join a local firm with a few congenial lawyers and an informal style of practice that permitted him often to work at home.

David's toilet training was a struggle with Paul, who saw no reason his son shouldn't promptly get that unpredictable event under sphincter control. *"We don't want accidents, do we?"* he reminded his son. But spontaneous "accidents" are fine with two-year-olds, and were fine with David. This attitude would come between them. When David was two, Paul insisted he stay on his potty—with a seatbelt—for as long as it took—hours, if necessary. While David sat, withholding what his father wanted, his father drafted a will, or a lien, or a codicil, until David produced what his father demanded.

His early years were solitary. David was, in effect, an only child. There were few distractions. His parents did not own a television. Paul worked at home, supervising playroom and yard, but did not himself have time to play. Yet he resisted sending David to pre-school, given the risks of contagion. Until he was five, David had to content himself with safe toys and yard play closely watched by his father. Paul sat at his laptop in the corner of David's bedroom or watched from a picnic table within the perimeter of the fenced yard. From these sentry posts, he called to his son, "Watch out!"

Paul's caution seemed to have a paradoxical effect upon David, however, who startled his father, in his play, by enacting elaborate violent dramas—crashing toy trains, banging teddy bears together in noisy fights, monsters and ogres hiding in closets or lurking under his bed waiting to grab and eat him. Around Susan's cloistered routine, also, David and his father grew hot with one another in the friction of their competing wills. For David wanted his mommy, and he did not understand why she wasn't available. Paul tried to be thoughtful of his wife, feeling perhaps that he owed her this protection; that David's "bother" was his problem, by right, which prevented his uncomprehending son from entering that dim sanctuary where, after a rough night, Susan finally was asleep. When his mother emerged and, looking like a pale somnambulist, took up her position on the stool before the piano, David tried incessantly to dart past his father's restraining hand to interrupt her practice with his loving, climbing, insistent, squirming presence. Some days Paul had to go in to the office, of course. And when he returned, if he learned that David had been naughty, disrupting his mother's rehearsal for her elegiac concert, he spanked David's bare bottom.

When David was six, his father took the morning off to enroll him in kindergarten. Mothers brought most children to enroll, but David's mother no longer drove a car. When, after formalities, Paul *dallied on the playground to shout warnings to his son about getting hit with the ball or falling off the swings or the slide, the astonished teacher had to ask him to leave so that David could "settle in." She was surprised when he insisted upon watching the class at recess, but even more startled when he interfered with the children's play. Clearly it did not dawn upon her, at first, that Paul had not come merely to provide David a ride or to sign enrollment papers. He had come to reassure himself that the classroom and playground were safe enough for him to risk leaving David on his own.*

He was too young to notice the anomaly of his father's grim male face among all those smiling women. But in grade school David became a show off, as soon as his father left the premises. He outbid other students in derring-do: hanging by his feet from the chain rings, dangling by his knees from the bar atop the yard fence. It would have been impossible to describe the feeling—an exhilaration, a lightness, as if he could float or fly—that he experienced the moment he heard the slam of the car door and saw his father's Volvo vanish around the corner. Paul left instructions with the teacher to call if David were hurt "in any way" or showed signs of illness. They did call him the day, at age seven, when David climbed onto the roof of the custodian's shed and jumped into a pile of pea gravel, knocking the wind out of himself.

The spanking he got that evening, after his daredevil stunt, might have discouraged another boy, but not David. However, it made his father even more cautious. Probably for this reason, Paul refused to sign a release form for Little League. He came along on school outings. By seventh grade his father's presence at school caused David excruciating embarrassment—even more humiliation than other boys normally experienced. In eighth grade, while crossing the Golden Gate Bridge on a school trip to the De Young Museum, David hung his entire torso out an open window so as to wave at passing cars until, feeling a painful constriction in his chest, he recognized the driver of one of those cars to be his father, who had followed the bus and now raced up the outside lane to flag down the driver.

David doubted he would ever forget his humiliation when his red-faced father boarded the bus like a hijacker to drag him off. At thirteen, he realized he hated his father. His subsequent report cards let him count the ways. Given his experience, David knew better than to ask to try out for football, so he chose crew instead. He swam well. He thought there could be no objection to rowing in a boat with other students—the coach's launch alongside. Just in case, however, he stalled, making excuses, so as to secure a place on the boat before his coach, looking toward the first regatta, called home.

After speaking to David's father, the coach was kind, but cool. There was nothing he could do. "I'm sorry, Dave," he said, "but your Dad said no, and without a parent's permission, I can't give you a racing shirt." He seemed reluctant when he asked, "Any chance that your mother would sign, even if your father won't?"

*David doubted it, but he tried again. To his chagrin, his father was still adamant. His father seemed indignant that David had even asked. Irritably, he reminded David how his mother "worries" about him, how it was their job to "protect her" from worry. Aroused, David argued that no boat had ever capsized in the estuary, raising his voice in exasperation. But even as he shouted, he knew that this was not about logic, that he was stuck in a tar baby of ancient history he didn't understand and had little to do with. He could not have explained this. But what enraged him, beyond the simple no, was his father's implicit demand that he not only be thwarted but also **like** it—that he pretend he, too, could see imaginary dangers his parents hallucinated. All he could do was yell, "This is such bullshit!"*

Unable to bear his father's presence a second longer—and, in fact, sensing subliminally, in his molten rage, that he might hit him—David jumped up, overturning a lamp, and shoved his father aside. He rushed toward his mother's bedroom, wanting to make his appeal directly, without his father arguing the other way in that weary, pedantic fashion David could hardly stand. If he could just get rid of his father, he thought, if he could lock him out of his mother's bedroom while he made his case, perhaps this time, different from all the others, she would be loving. In his hurry, rushing past his mother's polished Steinway, he tipped over a large vase that stood beside the ebony music stand. Caught between purposes, he turned just in time to see the vase bang down and crack open, dumping its wilted flowers and a quart of brackish water into the strings and velvet hammers of her concert grand.

Is the explanation for David's later debacle here—in his

upbringing? This account of it, told from David's own point of view, suggests that the heart of the matter may well be in his relationships with his mother and father. However, David clearly does not understand and could not explain what the problem is, except that he cannot get his mother's full attention or get rid of his father's smothering protection. Certainly Susan seemed disabled, unable to drag herself out of bed in the morning, compulsively playing scales to prepare for a concert that never came. She seemed to be hindered in her mothering, a woman who couldn't bear to nurse, who avoided David, leaving his upbringing to her husband. And Paul seems unable, for all the effort he devotes to it, to stay on his son's wavelength, sometimes even calling him by another boy's name. He seemed to be entirely preoccupied with safety, and he was joyless. If David's mother was an elusive ghost, his father was the voice of the inevitable No—to anything that might be fun. By midadolescence, David made his own judgments as to what was safe. He knew what other teenagers and other adults thought of these dangers, and he lost all respect for his father's negative, overbearing constraints.

From an early age, David sensed the presence of a ghost. By midadolescence he sensed the presence of an enchanted remote realm, where he was not welcome. Yet he was nonetheless haunted by this unseen personage. His mother's faraway glances into that nether world frightened him. When she looked that way, she was gone from him. He had no idea what she saw or felt so sad about, though he had heard an account from his father—words that meant little, when he was so young. For it was hard to take seriously a person he had never set eyes upon. He hated his father's lectures and strictures. It seemed unfair to be bounded by events he had no responsibility for, to be expected to respect reasons that started in that spectral world he had never visited.

For us, if not for David, this case demonstrates the importance of history. To make sense of David's behavior, it is not enough to assemble a laundry list of his symptoms or misbehaviors. It is not even enough, necessarily, to know only what David has experienced or can surmise. To make sense of a teenager's experience, we need the sequence, so that we can infer the emotional significance of events. Since David's trouble seems to have so much to do with his parents, we sense that we also need to learn about them. We need their history too. An account of the past would be revealing. Among other things, one would need to know what happened before David's birth.

3.

Paul met Susan at a piano recital on the cliffs above the Golden Gate Bridge. He had recently become the youngest partner in a plaintiff's law practice in the city. After years of intense study and repetitious practice at UC Berkeley, Susan was on the cusp of a public career as a concert pianist.

On that afternoon at the Palace of the Legion of Honor, she had played Bach and Chopin—a graduation performance. Paul walked over from the grounds of the VA Hospital, where he had been taking a deposition for a lawsuit. He watched her—seated with eyes closed, lost in another world, fingers running up and down the keyboard as if of their own accord—and he fell hard. In her indifference to cause and effect, in her dreamy otherworldliness, he felt the differences in their temperaments—"like oil and water." There was about the two of them, he said, an immiscibility that made it miraculous they mixed so well, and so thoroughly, once they combined ingredients. It was sheer luck, they said to one another, against the odds, to find such happiness.

They married—right after her graduation—and purchased a crafted miniature bungalow perched on the eastern slope of Mount Tamalpais, overlooking Richardson Bay. As dawn poured sunlight through their picture window, perched high above the fog, they sipped lattes and held hands, looking down upon Angel Island and Berkeley, across the water. Every day, waiting until the last possible moment, Paul jumped into an SUV and hurtled down the mountain. Susan watched him go. Then she perched on her stool before the keyboard, warmed up with scales, and threw herself into Rachmaninoff and Chopin. From there she could glance down upon the towers of the Golden Gate as Paul would be crossing into the City. She could see the glass sky-scraper on Montgomery Street, where Paul prepared his cases.

A year after their wedding Susan gave birth to Isaac, a cheerful beautiful boy, whose avid suckling, as she happily nursed him, provoked her to joke with Paul that their son had the reflexes of a lawyer. Seeing his long fingers, Paul wondered when piano lessons should begin, and pictured their son on the stage at Carnegie Hall.

Isaac grew like a weed. He toddled around their diminutive unfenced yard after a beagle named Esau. While Isaac was entering the magic years, Susan became pregnant once again. Floating upon this happy news, Paul and Susan looked out over the Bay's galaxy of evening lights, mirrored in the water, and concluded that—unlike all those sorry people who could not live in northern California—their lives had been charmed.

One less auspicious evening, however, Paul came home to find the puppy gone and his wife and son disconsolate. With Isaac wailing, and later sleeping, in his carseat, Paul and Susan drove up and down the mountain for hours. Paul adored his son, and talked out loud to him, as he dozed, about the wonderful adventures that rascal puppy must be having. This made Susan laugh, despite her worry. They had high hopes, but after scouring the entire mountainside, they brought Isaac home, wearily, without the puppy.

In the morning, Susan felt nauseous. Paul overslept, and rushed to make coffee and gulp down his yogurt, reassuring Isaac, who was crawling under the table, about the adventure the puppy was having, and scanning the Wall Street Journal. *He kissed Isaac, and when he went in to kiss Susan in bed and to scribble down her shopping list, he left the sliding door open to the deck. Then he ran into his den to pick up his briefcase, rushed back to remind Susan he would be home late, then made a quick call to the office about his appointment to take a deposition in a malpractice suit in Corte Madera. Then he rushed out.*

Late for his deposition, Paul jumped into his Landcruiser and backed into the road. He paused to readjust his mirror and seatbelt. He got ready to launch himself down the mountain into another day, but something made him pause to glance back down his driveway. He'd felt something—a small something. But he was so distracted with all the next steps in his plan for the day that for a moment he simply stared, unable to recognize, at first, what he'd backed over—the powder blue, fuzzy small heap—facedown, his son, Isaac.

This is family trauma. The death of a child, not so uncommon a catastrophe in our paved world, is among the worst psychological blows men and women endure. Often enough, marriages cannot survive the strain of such a loss, of such guilt and recrimination. Heard in detail, this sad story demonstrates how profoundly trauma echoes down the generations.

Trauma comes in all shapes and sizes.[18] It is commonplace. It may not be the most frequent obstacle to maturation, but trauma makes both lists: as an intrinsic obstacle, when an overwhelming experience disorganizes the psychology of a child; and as an extrinsic obstacle, as in this case, when trauma disrupts parenting. Trauma is so commonplace that our emotional response to the news of it gets dulled by repetition and displacement. We forget how trauma feels, and we do not wish to recall. In magazines and papers we consider accounts of other people's traumas—famine, epidemic, natural catastrophe, genocide, crime, accident, and war—to be "news." Whether personal or collective, trauma surrounds us.

Isaac's death was personal, not a collective trauma. When an overwhelming horror is shared, when it is a collective experience, as was the Holocaust or the Rwanda genocide, then subsequent history probably ought to be written from a psychiatric point of view. For when trauma is shared, the sequelae also are collective. The psychological effects of trauma endure for decades. Studies of survivors of extermination camps reveal that most continue to be symptomatic (nightmares, anxiety attacks, intrusive memories, for instance) even after forty years.[19] Human beings dream repetitively of their traumas and, for a lifetime, can be reminded of a trauma by chance associations. Moreover, human beings tend to reenact their traumatic experiences or discover the apparent reiteration of such experiences in daily life. Freud called this repetitive reexperiencing of trauma "the repetition compulsion," and guessed, insofar as the stress response to trauma can be said to be voluntary, that such reenactments are attempts at mastery.

We infer that David's parents suffered, each in a different way, from chronic post-traumatic memories. Susan took to her bed, but could not sleep, enduring restless nights of insomnia, nightmares, or repetitive dreams in which Isaac came back to her, miraculously alive. These happy visions tortured her in the morning when she awoke, again and again, to the unbearable facts. Paul, for penance or reparation, took over the parenting of David without protest. He seems to have devoted his life to the prevention of another accident. In this sense, as in so many others, David was haunted by his brother's ghost.

4.

Susan followed Isaac's diminutive casket down the path between rows of memorial gravestones. After the brief service beside the diminutive pit, her legs gave out. She sank to the grass, and couldn't stand up to walk away. For weeks afterward, her legs would not carry her, and she could barely stagger from bed to piano bench. These were her only destinations, aside from her trips to the bathroom, where she glimpsed her haggard features in the mirror.

For months, when not counting sheep or praying for oblivion, she counted to three, four, six, or eight, as by the hour she sought the only consolation she knew in the music of Bach. She tried to avoid reminders. At every turn, however, some sound or chance memory or word provoked images of Isaac's face, the joyful sound of his giggle, the soft texture of his PJs with leather feet. She could not entirely escape into sleep, either, for Isaac visited her in dreams—alive, laughing at her "mistake" about his death. In her dreams, she experienced a startled and souring relief to learn she had been "so stupid," each dream suckering her, again and again, into believing her son alive again. Each time, when she awakened, Isaac died again. Every morning she had to look again into Paul's aggrieved face, its features run together like a dropped and broken egg, much the way he had come back to her bedroom unexpectedly, croaking in anguish "Susan!—oh my God!" She could forget this only for brief blank periods of numbed amnesia. These came to her mercifully from time to time. She forgot, and so she felt nothing—and then Paul's crestfallen face re-appeared in her bedroom. His groveling brought it all back.

Her second labor reminded her so vividly of her first son's birth that, when David arrived, she took no pleasure in his cry. In the following days Paul could not do enough to please her, to protect her, to ingratiate himself. Soon he annoyed her with guilty hovering, his indignant complaints to the busy nurses, his fussing over her diet, his endless smoothing of her blankets. And yet, she hated hated herself for resenting his presence. For of course she knew that he was so sick with horror that he willingly would have thrown himself off the roof if she had merely hinted that his doing so might distract her, even momentarily, from her pain. And so she tried to hide her revulsion. The fibs she told to reassure him were the first lies in their marriage.

When his re-expanded family left Marin General, Paul entirely took over the baby's care. He realized, without her having to say so, that she already had become weary of David, that she recoiled from nursing him, that she was afraid to cuddle him or coo to him—or in any way to become too fond. Paul understood this. For he, too, feared to love David. Yet he was caught. He had to care for this sad boy. For he knew that she had a right to be reluctant, but he did not. He knew he must love this boy, embrace his care and so expiate his lapse with unstinting sacrifice. He knew that this child had to live, for he knew that neither one of them would survive another loss.

So began for Paul an anxious labor of Sisyphus. He lived in constant anticipation of catastrophe, saw dangers everywhere. In the hospital he watched over David, alert to the possibility of a switched ID band, a nursing error, a nursery epidemic. As David rolled over, crawled, stood, and then climbed, Paul became ever more anxious, watching for falls, fatal contagions, uncovered sockets, frayed wires, overfilled baths, allergic anaphylaxis, mis-swallowed pabulum, pans of sizzling grease, an overturned tricycle, a car's malfunction, a rain-slick road. As David grew, Paul's red alerts simply shifted venue. He detected new dangers appropriate to each new stage of David's mobility: unlatched gates, bicycles that might wobble into traffic, half-swallowed bones, building sites, blows from baseballs or bats.

To David the fifteen years of his whole life seemed forever, but to Susan it was not long enough to abate her grief. By the time David reached early adolescence, she was playing Beethoven, Chopin, and Rachmaninoff again—the musical manifestation of her slow recuperation from the endless repetitions of Bath's variations upon a single theme. But she was not free of a constant ache, for a fibromyalgia syndrome had merely displaced her conscious pain, moving from mind to matter, from memories to her flesh and bone. Each anniversary was a terrible day—although less terrible, now, in the second decade. Among other torments, however, the day inevitably forced Susan to try to make herself not think that Paul had been to blame—a mute thought each of them cared enough to spare the other. But there were other days, almost as bad, when Susan saw another child learning a new skill. The spectacle of David's milestones—crawling, walking, talking, running, singing, riding a trike—forced her, involuntarily, to recalculate Isaac's age, to picture how far along he would now have come, to visualize his walking across a street, catching a ball or flirting with a co-ed. With each passing year it was harder to picture his face, and so she had to strain to imagine how he might have looked, as he became a young man. She suffered in silence about every milestone she would never see him pass.

For Paul, too, there was rarely a day, among all the days in all those years, when he did not catch a glimpse of that unclosed sliding door, and reach out (in his imagination) to slide it closed. There was never a turned key in an ignition or a shift into reverse or a reflexive glance over his shoulder when he did not have to endure a flashback to that feeling under his wheels.

Susan slept fitfully after she discovered in David's dirty shirt pocket a crumpled pack of Lucky Strikes. Paul slept very little after he found a discarded e-mail that revealed David's borrowed cash and a forged waiver that had permitted him to take off in a prop plane that Paul could imagine droning in rising spirals high over the golf course. In the panorama of his nightmare he watched the tiny blue figure pause in the wind-blown hatch and fling himself out into the empty air. Paul came abruptly awake—his pajamas sticking to his back, unable to catch a full breath—too late to stop seeing what he saw. He would not need to be dreaming to know the chute would not open, or to watch that boy hurtling through fifteen-thousand feet of freefall, or to recognize that powder-blue, fuzzy small heap on the fairway—face-down, his son, David.

Part 4
A Remedy

9   A Two-Step Treatment

$\mathbf{I}$F ADOLESCENCE WERE an overland race with stiff competition for all prizes, the maturity of every gearbox would be tested on every hill, curve, and straight-away. An adolescent transmission needs all available gears. Moreover, the young driver has to downshift coming into tight turns and shift up to passing gear on the straightaways. If a teenager were to fall behind the normal pack, catching up would be a major challenge. Although a troubled teenager has to stop to struggle to get it together, the race goes on, and the pack disappears around the next curve and vanishes beyond the hill.

On this long course Montana Academy is a pit stop, set well off the main track.[1] There, a trained staff helps teenagers and parents call a time-out and attempt repairs. There, an effort is made to install missing gears that the other contestants already have available. Then together, all the adults help a teenager get back onto the track and go on. The race is a long one; there is a long way to to to catch up, but still time.

Overview

To speak of a cure in psychiatry always sounds dubious, highly unlikely. In two decades of practice prior to opening Montana Academy—at the university, on hospital in-patient units, in my outpatient office—I have rarely had occasion to use that word. A cure in psychiatry is so improbable that a seemly humility generally prevents us from speaking of it. Even surgical and medical colleagues, who sometimes do cure a disease or prevent one, spend much of their professional lives attending to clinical problems they cannot solve. Certainly at Montana Academy we do not promise a cure—nothing like it. Yet inasmuch as immaturity is the cause of psychiatric symptoms and morbidity in teenagers, to grow up *is* a cure—or a radical prevention. When it happens, the result of maturation is the riddance of a cause, or a potential cause, not merely symptom relief. When it happens, what growing up prevents is a lifetime of character pathology.

So what should be the treatment for immaturity in adolescence? In this final section I present a two-step approach, which is not a fully elaborated technique so much as a clinical way of thinking about diagnosis and treatment. I will sketch the program we have developed at the ranch, and I will suggest how its elements make theoretical sense as a programmatic approach to adolescent immaturity.

In doing so, I will outline two key tasks that parents normally accomplish with their children, from infancy through adolescence and beyond, so as to provide them with apt experiences needed to sustain a timely developmental momentum. Specifically, I will explain how parents normally prod maturation onward by means of accurate, affectionate recognition, combined with deft, firm *limit-setting*—these paired tasks to be accomplished in tandem, attuned to a child's stage of development, and sustained over time. These two tasks are routinely important in normal children. They are, in a way, what effective parenting is. These parental tasks become the more critical, the key to a remedy, however, when a child has fallen behind and struggles with immaturity. [2] This is why recognition and limit-setting are built into the Montana Academy program. Our staff consciously try to recognize accurately and to set proper limits in everything we do together, just as competent parents do. Our ranch program has been shaped to these tasks, for the central goal, all but invariably, is to prod immature, troubled teenagers to grow up, and so to catch up with their age-mates.

To illustrate this approach, I will now sketch the treatment in the two cases (David and Helen) whose composite histories I presented in chapters 7 and 8, respectively. The reader, having come so far, may well now also ask, however, whether such composite outcomes are plausible, whether success, in these cases, has been exaggerated. To bring these accounts closer to actual clinical outcomes, therefore, I have asked a few parents of successful students to describe the transformations that occurred in their adolescent children. These parents provided these accounts knowing that they might well be published here. Their descriptions (in "Letters," chapter 10) are their own stories, told as they chose to tell them in their own diction.[3]

These clinical accounts and this anecdotal evidence is not a systematic multi-center, double-blind, placebo-controlled crossover study, but it is evidence. No such study can ever be done ethically, in our judgment. We could not randomize prospective students—to treated and untreated cohorts—or select, as a control group, a random cohort of students for whom we provide no treatment or sham treatment (placebo). Certainly other studies can be done. Some have already begun—and, where there is sufficient data, will be noted briefly in chapter 10. Others have not yet provided a critical mass of useful data.[4] Nor have we yet compared our results systematically to outcome results from other programs.[5]

Useful as such data might be, however, that comparison would be irrelevant to this argument. For I make no claim that residential therapeutic treatment is the only proper level of care, nor that Montana Academy has a better approach, much less the only approach to address these problems usefully.[6] I am not trying to demonstrate the relative efficacy of a particular method or the relative efficacy of Montana Academy compared to other programs. Montana Academy simply happens to be the location and the occasion for these observations.

I am trying to demonstrate something more fundamental. I am suggesting that for many troubled teenagers, the central source of a global dysfunction, the reason for so many failures at the tasks of adolescence, and the cause of so many symptoms, mistakes, and misbehaviors, is a relative *immaturity*. I am hoping to demonstrate that immaturity is a better, more correct, and more useful way to conceptualize many of the problems of troubled teenagers. In these cases, at the least, an effective, definitive treatment cannot be achieved by clustering symptoms as disorders and pursuing symptom relief with pills. Many students have already demonstrated that pharmacology alone often does not provide a remedy. Experience has taught us that to address immaturity requires going beyond symptom relief, to unstick an arrested maturation that is largely responsible for a teenager's global academic, familial, and interpersonal dysfunction. Experience persuades us that to make troubled teenagers grow up transforms their approaches to the challenges and opportunities in their lives.

In theory, to make these points I need only one telling case. To make these points should not require controlled studies or interprogram comparisons. For again, I am not trying to prove that one program works better—or even that it works at all. Instead, I want to demonstrate that immaturity is the central issue, and for this I need only one clear case in which a polysymptomatic, multiproblem, globally-flailing teenager changes her flawed approach, i.e., grows up, and in whom this transformation leads to a dramatic improvement in academic, domestic, and interpersonal functioning, reduces symptoms, and eliminates repetitive misbehaviors. To be persuasive, this transformation need not produce a saint or a graduate of MIT.[7] The outcome needs only to be a normal teenager, whose development now runs in parallel with other normal teenagers.

It would be icing on this rhetorical cake if, in this one clear case, that exemplary student arrived at the ranch in global disarray—after failing to improve in conventional outpatient therapy and assiduous trials of psychopharmacology—and, after catching up in maturation, began to thrive in all the venues of adolescent and early adult life. It would ice this argument if, as she matured, most of her symptoms abated and most of her medications could be stopped. This, you will not be startled to learn, will be precisely the story parents tell in their letters in chapter 10.

Although a single case logically could make the point, in these pages I have provided more than one. For we began by noting that immaturity looks very different from one teenager to the next. This being so, it may be more persuasive to provide a number of examples, out of all that diversity, rather than only one. After all, the common denominator is not to be found in the highly variable surface features in these teenagers, but rather in the deep structure of a "flawed approach"—which is immaturity.

Two-Part Diagnosis

Diagnosis is key. But a developmental diagnosis is not merely a question of fitting a teenager's specific symptoms into a prepackaged "disorder" cluster. A diagnosis of immaturity has two parts. To make that diagnosis we have to be sure, first, of the presence of the hallmarks (a) of a relative immaturity: the global break-down (chapter 1) and the "flawed approach" (chapter 2) that mark a relative immaturity in adolescence. Second, we must identify (b) an obstacle that hinders maturation.

To illustrate this diagnostic logic, here are tentative two-part diagnostic formulations for Helen and David:[8]

	Helen	**David**
(a) The "Flawed Approach" of Relative Immaturity	Self-preoccupation	Self-preoccupation
	Lack of Empathy	Lack of Empathy
	Magical Future (No Goals, Plans)	Magical Future (No Goals, Plans)
	Puppet Relationships	Puppet Relationships
	Sneaky, Concrete Ethics	Sneaky, Concrete Ethics
(b) Possible Obstacle(s) to Maturation (mo, fa)	Chronic Intoxication	Psychol Trauma (mo, fa)
	Traumatic Loss	(Pathol) Bereavement
	Somatic Illness (mo)	Depression (mo)
	Depression (mo)	Ignorance (mo, fa)
	Work/Personal Distraction (fa)	
	Separation/Divorce (all)	
	Ignorance (mo, fa)	

For this illustration, I have been overly inclusive rather than parsimonious. I mention a variety of possibilities from the potential obstacles (listed in chapter 8), so as to consider them all. In planning a treatment, we would not necessarily give equal weight to all of these potential obstacles. The point is that a relative immaturity, in either case, is no mystery. There is no shortage of potential sources of delay.

In brief, we might begin with the clinical hypothesis that Helen's preoccupation—first with her mother's illness, then with her parents' strained and broken marriage, and finally with the loss of her father—were hindrances to her growing up. Helen's marijuana use also may or may not prove to have been important. Certainly her parents' parenting already had been so attenuated—by her mother's illness and sedation, her father's distractions, absences, and self-preoccupation—that her drug use may not have been of much incremental consequence. And yet, when thinking how to put this family back together, to restore parental relationships and influence upon this lost girl, her substance abuse could well become a more central issue.

The clinical history suggests that, in his case, David experienced a prolonged lack of accurate recognition from his depressed, innervated, withdrawn mother. It appears that his father got locked into an enraging pattern of mis-recognition, that he spent a good deal of David's life trying to prevent an accident that already had happened long before David was born. It appears that his mother's protracted post-traumatic depression and his father's endless attempts to undo or expiate his horrifying negligence had everything to do with David's difficulties in growing up. His relationship with each parent had broken down so completely that they could no longer usefully set limits for him, either. By the final crisis they could not keep order in their own home, or make the parental *No* stick, without help from the police.

One diagnosis did not make my list of obstacles in David's case. If I thought he had suffered from a serious mental illness, I would have listed this obvious hindrance to his growing up. Certainly, bipolar disorder can hinder maturation. And a psychiatrist who saw him thought this was his problem, made the diagnosis, and tried to medicate his mood swings, as if a biological diathesis were the best explanation for David's behavior and the proper target for therapeutic intervention. However, as the full history makes clear, this diagnosis is not really necessary to explain David's unhappiness or his family's disarray. Moreover, there is little evidence, aside from David's symptoms (e.g., irritability, angry defiance), on which to base a genetic/biological diagnosis. And that diagnosis does not fit well with the sequences in David's history, which is to say, David's irritability, anger, deflated mood, and irascibility have obvious and proximate sources, and do not appear to surface mysteriously and anomalously from a murky biology.

Here it may be worth digressing to think out loud about David's diagnosis. Certainly I am not allergic to psychiatric diagnosis or to an indicated pharmacology. But I also think that to a doctor who has only a hammer, all the world looks like a nail. Because outpatient psychiatrists usually have little available containment to offer, aside from medication, and insofar as managed care has eliminated hospital admission except under conditions of dire imminent emergency (and sometimes, in my experience, even then), it is not surprising that symptom diagnosis and a reliance upon medication are common clinical reflexes. But parsimony ought to prevent our rushing to a diagnosis like bipolar disorder in a young man, since this diagnosis has a dire prognostic significance and encourages a strictly pharmacological approach. Therefore, in the absence of an unambiguous family history of serious mood pathology, and lacking evidence of an unambiguous manic episode, I am reluctant to make or readily to accept this portentous diagnosis. For the same reason I would hesitate to medicate David's symptoms—or to imagine, if I did treat some of his symptoms with pills, that I had finished the job.

A Two-Step Remedy

The logic of relative immaturity implies that treatment should have two aims: (a) to remove the obstacle(s); and (b) to provide a parental shove to restore lost momentum. More precisely, the first step should remove or mitigate the obstacle(s) insofar as this can be done. And, more precisely, the second step should prod a dallying child to catch up in maturation insofar as that is still possible. Certainly there are "equipment" problems that cannot readily be undone—e.g., brain injury. Surely there are also disruptions in parenting that cannot readily be rectified, either— e.g., a father's death. On the other hand, many intrinsic hindrances can be mitigated. ADHD can be treated with stimulants, depression with anti-depressants, chronic intoxication with sobriety. There are extrinsic hindrances that can be removed, such as a parent's distracted preoccupation with a demanding career, or a parent's ignorance. An alcoholic parent can achieve sobriety. Parents can collaborate gracefully in a divorce or seek treatment for a post-traumatic stress response or somatic illness, the deft management of which can make an afflicted adult more available for parenting.

(a) Remove the Obstacle(s)

This first step, which may take any of a wide variety of forms, is precisely what competent conventional psychiatry and psychology try to accomplish. True illnesses in parents or children can be treated (medication, psychotherapy). Academic disabilities can be treated (e.g., ADHD), and school performance supported with skilled teaching, classroom structure, and clever curricula. Somatic illnesses in adults or teenagers can be treated well or badly, and children can be helped to adjust to what cannot be cured. Substance abuse, whether in a parent or a teenager, can be confronted and sobriety encouraged. Loss, trauma, divorce, adoption, and other potential disturbances in the parent-child relationship can be well-managed or treated (psychotherapy). Parental communication and collaboration can be repaired or improved, ignorance turned to skill, distraction turned to focused recognition and deft limit-setting. And some problems, deficits, idiosyncrasies and post-traumatic sequelae can be faced, accepted, or worked around.

At Montana Academy, where beds are limited, we pick parents as carefully as we select students. A parent's willingness to face up to inadvertent, mistaken, or unavoidable hindrances, to recognize his contribution to a son's or daughter's disarray, makes all the difference in a teenager's prognosis. When there have been disruptions in parenting, there is no substitute for a mother or father's willingness to accept help (advice, direction, therapy) and to pitch in to remove the hindrance. Over the years we have learned the hard way that, absent that parental willingness, we will not succeed, and may as well not start. Thus, for example, we will not enroll a teenager whose divorced parents are still fighting over custody or money, who are determined to punish an ex by means of battles about the children. We require both parents to collaborate with daughters or sons, with us and one another—even if only to act in the best interest of the child. Parents must pitch in. We will not enroll a teenager whose parents wish to drop him off like a lawnmower to be repaired. We require parents to participate actively, willingly, and to face up to their own contributions to the problem and their own responsibility for the solution.

For parenting is the second step. These expectations have nothing to do with figuring out who is to blame. We require parents to commit to parenting only because, after obstacles have been removed, whether intrinsic or extrinsic, the second step invariably has to be a vigorous, clever, assiduous, determined, loving, and sustained effort at *parenting*.

This is true because parenting is what makes children grow up. Parenting is what makes teenagers catch up by growing up, and "parenting" is essential, even when biological parents are not available. When others—adopted parents, teachers, grandparents, older siblings, coaches, and therapists—step in to help, they act *in loco parentis*. Parenting is absolutely necessary. For when an obstacle has been removed or minimized, the result yet is merely a *ready* child—or, if not fully ready, a child as ready as we know how to make him. To make the next milestone, a ready child still needs the *apt experience* parents provide—if he is to grow up and therefore catch up. The push past the old point of obstruction is a parental push. Prodding a ready child to grow up is what parents (as parents) do.

(b) Parental Push

That parental push, as I have suggested elsewhere, comes from a combination of *recognition* and *limit-setting*, which must be sustained over *time*.[9] This combination guides and pushes onward a normal child's maturation. It also pushes onward an immature teenager, who needs to grow up and catch up. But when a teenager is relatively immature, this salutary task becomes more difficult. When development has been obstructed and delayed, the parental effort involves heavy lifting. It is my impression that this remedial effort is much more difficult and less sure of success than the prodding that produces development that takes place on schedule. It is also more difficult since a teenager in trouble becomes less tractable, himself, not more so. He becomes demoralized, distrustful, unhappy, angry, and harder to get along with. Remediation may mean that parents have to put aside work and pleasure to pay renewed attention to an unhappy, often unpleasant, teenager.

Much that parents need to do is painful, the remedial tasks unwelcome. For remediation requires parents to face their own past mistakes. It means accepting criticism, getting past comfortable denial, putting aside glib excuses, letting go of defensive self-justifications. It can mean shame, even guilt. Moreover, it may mean cooperating with an ex with whom one is furious. It may mean learning to parent differently— and what old dog wants to learn new tricks? It usually means change— and who wants to change? It can mean facing facts, admitting mistakes, enduring empathy for a young person's pain, and so feeling that pain. It may mean thinking about someone besides oneself—which is to say, it may mean growing up. Who wants to have to do all that?

Moreover, this second step—parenting—is the more difficult for some parents, because it cannot be delegated to employees or professionals. For recognition is the context for limit-setting, but it is still limit-setting that goads a child to catch up. The authority for meaningful limit-setting can only come from parents. A typical outpatient therapist cannot accept this delegation of authority—nor do conventional therapists want it. Even if parents wanted to delegate their authority, an outpatient therapist usually cannot (and certainly does not) set limits for teenagers. Limit-setting is not, even in theory, a technique therapists imagine themselves putting to use. Recognition, on the other hand, is close to the hearts of therapists. But setting limits does not readily fit with Freud's therapeutic rules of abstinence and anonymity, aimed at adult patients. Most competent therapists are taught not to intrude into their (adult) patients' life decisions, not to reveal their own feelings or values, not to presume. Most therapists have accepted these proscriptions, and have extended them from work with adults to psychotherapy with teenagers. At the most mundane and practical level, therapists learn the hard way that a teenager who is sent unwillingly for psychotherapy and receives from his therapist any blunt criticism, or attempts to impose discipline, may well never come back. It is all about recognition and not much about limit-setting. For these reasons, too, outpatient therapists cannot get parents off the hook for setting limits.

Moreover, our culture is not very helpful, not very supportive about parental attempts to set limits. I have argued, here and elsewhere, that firm limits prod teenagers to give up childish narcissism. But when was the last time, beyond his family, that a sixteen-year-old boy from any contemporary upscale American suburb has been told No about much of anything? Is there much he cannot have right now?–keys to a car, tutoring, guitar lessons, money, sex, booze, marijuana? What else do the ads on television and radio and the internet tell him, but that he deserves to have anything he wants? Even if parents provide reasonable constraints—set curfews, insist upon schoolwork before partying, proscribe certain kinds of adolescent sexual or drug-related behavior, keep track of where she is, and with whom—what chance do such parents have, if a son or daughter wants to resist? Most sons and daughters leave home in the morning and come back at night, and while they are away, their parents may well have little idea where they are, what they are doing, and with whom.

Certainly, this is true of the troubled teenagers I am describing. How do I know? Because once troubled teenagers arrive at wilderness programs and therapeutic schools, they gradually come clean and, as part of a therapeutic ritual, write "letters of accountability" to their parents. In these missives young people catalogue, with all the frankness they can muster, what sneaky, under-the-radar behavior they have not heretofore told their parents about. This ritual usually ends with teenagers feeling better and parents feeling worse. After reading accounts of sexual license and vulnerability, drug use, molestation, and rape, about lies and sneaky manipulation, parents usually express shock that they were so gulled, that a son's drug use was so very much more extensive and so much more dangerous than they had imagined; that a daughter had been so unsupervised and vulnerable, that she was so wretchedly exploited (often while intoxicated), bullied, molested or raped. The parental leitmotif after digesting a son's or a daughter's letter of accountability all too often is, *We had no idea!* Only later does it also occur to them, usually with indignation, if not rage (along with shame and guilt), that no other adult, not even other parents, "ever bothered to tell us that this was going on."

This is not the occasion for a detailed discussion of the essential push that can prod a troubled teenager to grow up, and to catch up. Elsewhere I have described these essential parental tasks: *recognition* and *limit-setting*.[10]

Here, instead, I will dramatize what a remedy looks like, particularly when it leads to restored developmental momentum. To this end, I describe Helen's treatment at the ranch, followed by David's.

A Case: Helen (Part B)

We left Helen (chapter 7) passed out after ingesting fistfuls of her mother's medications. Her father, Ted, never did come home to discover her, waiting for him in the front bay window. Luckily her mother, Linda, got up to visit the bathroom and did find her—comatose in a puddle of vomit. By this serendipity, Helen did not die.

Her act, or her gesture, had many meanings. We can infer the message it was meant to convey from some of her symbolic choices—her mother's pills; her father's baseball cap; an alcove overlooking the driveway, where she always awaited him, as her final resting place. These choices were not lost on her parents. In retrospect they recognized other meaningful clues: her falling grades, her arrests for drug possession and shoplifting.

This solitary suicide attempt brings up a leitmotif commonly heard among troubled teenagers—the Mayday cries for help broadcast on adult frequencies that kids know no adult has been monitoring, the emergency flare fired into an empty sky from a sinking ship. They seem, in retrospect, to have been "cries for help"; but they are indirect, not so obvious, and likely to be missed. Yet they also clearly are intended for an absent or oblivious adult. Over the years, listening to unhappy histories, I sit up and listen when parents tell me how "shocked" or "surprised" they were to discover a son or daughter afloat on a makeshift raft, surrounded by sharks. After a suicide there is usually a lot of talk around dinner tables all over town about "hints" that (s)he was in trouble.

What is common among these gestures is that they are hints, not shouts; that they are covert, not explicit; that they are directed to those who are not paying sufficient attention, but are likely to be heard only by those who are listening carefully. In this way they seem to be asking for help, but they do so in such a way that they are more likely to dramatize a lack of help, a lack of attentiveness—a lack of recognition. They seem symbolic messages, which can be interpreted to mean, *I am in trouble, and you are not getting it!*

Whenever I hear about such provocative, half-obscured misbehaviors (shoplifting, self-laceration, covert vomiting, extreme weight loss, thefts of a parent's cash, a credit card belonging to the mother of a friend, or sneaking out at night) involving a lost and unhappy teenager, it occurs to me that they are distress signals.[11] The message is: *I'm in trouble—is there an adult on duty?* In Helen's case, the message was even more grim: *I am dying—and you are not here.* Or perhaps: *You are oblivious—and it is killing me!*

1.

Her parents' broken marriage reconstituted itself, such as it was, outside the ICU where Helen was comatose, then stuporous, in the hours after her stomach was pumped and her fluids and electrolytes restored. She had absorbed a lot of medicine, and it took hours for her consciousness to clear. In that time, her parents began a conversation that would last for several days.

Both parents were alarmed. They were furious with one another, and mutually contemptuous, when it came to other matters, of course. But prior to Helen's discharge from the hospital they already had agreed to insist that she see a prominent psychiatrist, who diagnosed major depression and prescribed Effexor. When the doctor met Ted and Linda, he was somber about the risks. "She nearly did it," he told them. "And she gave little warning, and she left no note." These facts particularly bothered him. "She wasn't trying to manipulate," he said. "She was done."

The doctor was dubious about a plan for her to come home to be with her mother. For he saw that Linda was unable to supervise her much of the time. Nor could Ted continue to work and pay the bills if he had to stay home to make sure Helen was safe. The doctor did not wish to sign off, and take responsibility for, a casual discharge plan. He did not think their plan was good enough. "She needs structure, people around her." He urged them to consult an educational consultant he recommended. They did, and, after a careful evaluation, the consultant urged them to enroll Helen in a therapeutic boarding school.

Linda resisted this plan. So did Ted. Montana was a long way from Connecticut. But the consultant said their daughter needed a psychiatrist on staff and good psychotherapy, if she were going to make it. Her parents could not argue with the fact that Helen had attempted suicide with her mother's medication, which she had gobbled down from her father's baseball cap, and that she did so with a cell phone in her pocket (with which she could have called Ted), and that she was down the hall twenty-five yards from where Linda had been asleep, giving no warning, leaving no note. And so they were angry not to have any closer alternative to this plan, and upset that they were arguing about Helen again, but in the end they flew together to Utah and Montana to visit a recommended wilderness program and a therapeutic boarding school—and to make decisions together.

They also flew together because the admissions director at Montana Academy warned that there would be no chance for a place unless they came together—and were both very much behind the plan. At the ranch they were told politely, but in no uncertain terms, that treatment would take time; that the terms had to include their both showing up regularly, and their own therapy. All this seemed a bit much. Yet the students at the ranch seemed strangely happy and engaged. Over lunch some of them talked with Ted and Linda in a friendly, but also very forthright way. So they promised the admissions director in writing that they would persist in the program start to finish; that they would agree not to give up or get talked out of the therapeutic process by their articulate and wily daughter; and that they would consider themselves to be part of the problem and essential contributors to the solution.

Ted and Linda paused to consider. They were shocked that it had come to this, that the solution seemed to demand so much of them. They also had been badly frightened by Helen's near-miss, right under their noses. They wept a little, then nodded to one another and reached for their pens.

This commitment, we had to learn the hard way, is one secret about a healthy ranch culture in which teenagers can grow up—that *all* parents sign on and stick it through difficult times to come; that all parents participate actively; that all parents support each other's family efforts. For if one parent fails to show up, all the students know. If parents fail to support the rules of the school, all the students know it. If one student's parents "pull" him when he looks a little better, or talks glibly about a magical cure and a bright future, then every student at the ranch will be upset, will wonder whether they can talk their own parents into quitting, whether they really have to do the hard thing it is to grow up.

In other words, these are not policies aimed at individual cases or any particular student or parent, but are aimed instead at the ranch culture. In an out-of-the-way corner of the nation, the parents at Montana Academy do what all of us, in the broader culture, should do. They join together in a common determination, in mutual support for each other's children. This is, in effect, a political act—a joint communiqué to all the teenagers living on the ranch—whose unmistakable meaning is this: we adults are all going to show up, to help you, to pitch in, to do our part, and will pool our adult authority to hold the container firm for your growing up. We select parents who appear ready for this political collaboration, as parents.

Understandably, parents think that this is a lot to ask. Not all of them really want to have to show up, to have to make themselves vulnerable, to have to admit to mistakes, to face their angry or sad children. Yet there is no hope to help teenaged sons and daughters if their parents absent themselves. Helen's parents already had tried that approach to rearing her—it led to an ICU. They saw no point in trying that approach again.

2.

On the day of enrollment both parents came, as they were asked to do. The therapist predicted that Helen would try to "divide us—that is, the school and her parents—by making you feel guilty, or telling you she's fine, or that we're feeding her worms." Her parents agreed to stick close together with Helen's therapist, and not get split apart.

Helen quickly settled in and immediately set to work to split the school from her parents. She tried to split her mother from her father. She told her therapist that the teacher thought she was "stupid." She split one new acquaintance from another, too, and the other students on her team confronted her about it—again and again. She seemed gifted at saying one thing to A and another thing, slightly different, to B, the sum suggesting that A and B were mutually filled with contempt for one another. Helen's therapist, who came in for some of this treatment early on, spent hours on the phone with Helen's parents, mapping out the problem and its solution, clarifying that, at the ranch, the kids were really not fed worms or exploited to save money on the janitorial help.

The therapist spent hours getting to know Ted and Linda separately, and when she had them on the phone together, she helped them to confront their daughter about her "splitting." They told her, in no uncertain terms, that they were together about this (whatever else they were not together about), that they expected her to settle down and get to work; that they would not agree to take her home to either one of their households before she had finished the program; and that, if she kept trying to play them off against each other, they would only call together. With advice from Caroline, their therapist, they told Helen that each of them was seeing a therapist also. They promised that they would both come to the ranch to participate. They said that they were going to have it out with her, as needed. And they expected that she had some blunt things to say to them, too.

These first steps might sound easy. But in fact they are the test of the adult alliance. If, at this point, any of the adults welch on this parental alliance, the entire effort fails. A teenager's resistance manifests itself in a refusal to get to work (e.g., at school), a refusal to make friends with staff or peers, a refusal to follow orders, and in repeated, deft attempts to divide her parents from the staff, or make side deals.

If parents fail to stand behind the program and process, if they make side deals (e.g., "Be good for two months, and then we'll see"), or if they miss phone calls and again absent themselves from a son or daughter's life, then the process stops before it starts—and goes no further. No growing up will happen without this first set limit. No growing up will happen unless parents pass this first test, which their children inevitably put them through. Or, put the other way, when parents become clear, firm, and aboveboard about setting a limit, when they stand up to their children's wheedling or threats, then their sons and daughters settle in and get to work—and look (and feel) relieved. "Finally," they appear to be thinking, "grown-ups are on the job."

3.

Helen promptly settled in. She began to work at school for the first time in months. In written work she was clever, and she was a perfectionist about her homework, keeping track of details. Her notes were exemplary. Yet we noticed that in class and over the lunch table, and in the dorm, she was awkward with peers. Adults saw her as thoughtful, and capable of consideration. But she was incapable of a similar consideration for her classmates. Instead she was selfish, demanding, hogging staff time and attention. We noticed that she looked like a spoiled, only child—which, of course, she had been.

This entitled narcissism became more pronounced. In the early months of Helen's stay, she had to settle into a schedule in which all aspects of her life were under scrutiny, under control, and in which all rules applied to her. She was expected to get oriented, to know all the teenagers and adults in her life; to master the rules and the schedule and the dress code; and to settle into a highly structured daily life. Here she initially had trouble. She failed to obey the dress code, to put scattered belongings back into her backpack during lectures, and she tried to skip sports, which are obligatory. In these encounters with team leaders, teachers, and coaches, she acted as if she had not noticed that they were there to be taken into account, or as if they were too stupid or incompetent to be taken seriously. This produced a series of unpleasant confrontations, which her therapist helped her negotiate—and a return, at one point, to start over, quite literally, at the beginning of the program. In effect, she was told that "learning to accept the rules is A—and you will not go on to B or C, let alone D, until you get this straight."

Helen resisted. She went on strike—refusing to do her chores. She "just wanted to do school, and not all this program stuff." For a few weeks she spent all her "free" time moving gravel or sawing firewood alone, and she got seriously bored. "C'mon," her therapist suggested. "Let's get beyond this. It's not all that awful for there to be adults who have authority around here."

She continued to split, to try to divide and conquer, and she managed reasonably well. Her phone calls with her parents were perfunctory, and she punished them "for sending me to this ghetto place" with contempt or sarcasm. When this happened, her therapist ended her phone call on the spot. On campus, Helen refused to trust the adults responsible to help her. She was critical of their every fault, presumptuous about her right to sit in judgment, and not grateful for their courtesies. However, the adults on campus were quick to take on her presumptuousness—and not to put up with much of it. Then other students on her team began to object to her rudeness, in particular when she spoke in a presumptuous way with their beloved therapist or team-leader. Helen's obvious belief that she was "above everyone else" got a lot of criticism from her teammates, who told her they did not much like her self-importance. On the other hand, the adults (teachers, team leaders) admired her quick wit and intelligence, and told her so. Her presumptuousness invited a lot of direct criticism from teammates, but they also made it clear that they were trying to like her.

It is commonplace for new students to reenact the enduring dynamics of their home lives at the ranch. They reenact these, casting staff and students as *dramatis personae*, who play all the parts in key relationships and family motifs from recent history. This is a good thing, a "transference" of the drama of the old context into similar dramas in a new context. In this respect, for example, Helen behaved, in the midst of a dorm full of other girls and a team busy with her teammates, as if she were an only child. She wanted all "parental" attention, and she wanted it now. She behaved as if adults had no legitimate authority—as if the rules did not apply to her, as if she could make decisions affecting the team without permission. She acted as if her therapist and team-leaders were ineffectual parents—not to be taken seriously.

The proper response? Firm limit-setting, unpleasant consequences, a putting on hold of all the new privileges and options and fun she wanted to join in. The messages: "First A, B, and C, and then we will be glad to talk about D"; and "No, you're not the only young lady who lives here (or needs a teacher's time)"; and, "Not yet, because you have not yet earned that privilege." These messages, implicit in the program constraints and in the No that the staff was quite willing to say, confronted Helen's residual childish narcissism. They pulled for consideration, empathy, goals and plans, separate relationships, and a social ethic.

4.

In the course of her individual therapy, it came time to review her relationships with her parents, her own history, and it came time to face up to her own arrogant contribution to her many difficulties. This was a painful process. At times she treated her therapist with angry, caustic contemptuousness, and she provoked in staff adults both consideration and indignation. When Helen got slapped down, there were tears, apologies, times of shame. Helen had to be asked, at critical junctures: "Who the hell do you think you are?"—the quintessential question for a spoiled teenager in the face of open rudeness and presumptuous grandiosity.

This sounds easier than it is. It is difficult to get it right in confronting presumptuous, arrogant narcissism. It is not effective simply to punish arrogance. We do that, of course. We do not think it is any help to put up with too much of it, or to make nice about it. For this only makes it seem OK. Yet adults (and other students) must grit their teeth long enough to develop a caring relationship with a swaggering teenager before confronting presumptuousness, entitlement, and obliviousness to rules. When I get it right with an arrogant student, I already have an important, warm relationship before I cut him down to size. And when I do, the result is a squirming dysphoria. There is shame as well as anger, anxiety as well as self-importance. From this unhappy mix of feelings comes new maturity—a reflexive taking of others into consideration. The point is, however, that this useful shame and anxiety would not occur unless a student knows me well enough, likes me, and hopes that I like and respect her, too. Only then does my expressed displeasure leave her squirming. Without a relationship, she only needs to feel a dismissive anger (at me), nothing more. Attempts at limit-setting without a relationship, based upon affectionate recognition, have no useful effect upon maturation.

5.

Meanwhile, Linda and Ted met with their own therapists. They sorted out their own histories—and found echoes of those histories in their parenting and in their marriage. In meetings with Caroline at the ranch, they sorted out the pros and cons of the divorce, wondered how it all might have been otherwise, and sometimes they both came out of those conversations with their cheeks wet with tears. In the end they decided that what had happened could not be undone. Linda was bitter and felt abandoned. Ted was guilty and ashamed, but angry, overworked, and overburdened, and, in the end, unwilling to go back. He had already started another relationship, which he wanted to pursue. They struggled with this suspense, and to come to terms with their decision, and they did much of this without pulling Helen into the middle of it.

By her sixth month, she was ready to face them. She and her therapist shifted gears, and began family therapy in earnest. Together, when they were ready, Ted and Linda told Helen that they were going to live apart, but would do their best to be, together, her parents. They would try to keep to the same rules for her, to stay friendly and collaborative in parenting Helen. They agreed on the wording and meaning of the message that they would give her, and cried a little, together, and then faced their daughter together, too. Helen wept. And for weeks, even after Ted and Linda left Montana to return home, Helen was hard to console.

In weekly conversations, her parents worked with her separately, each one individually, at first. For she would have to make a separate relationship with each parent—and find a place in each of their homes. It became Helen's task to renegotiate her relationship with each of them, separately, to have it out about the past and to imagine two new distinctive relationships for the future. Her parents came separately for visits every eight weeks. She met with them in painful, tearful therapy hours, sorting out her past struggles at home with Linda, and finally shouting, in her rage and grief, at her father for walking out on her mother—and on her "family."

This was the heart of Helen's psychological work at the ranch—a separation of herself from the adult strife and partings of her parents' divorce, an extraction of herself from her parents' marriage and separation, a gradual acceptance that there no longer was a marriage for her to rescue. She came to accept that, in any case, it never had really been possible to rescue a marriage her parents did not themselves sustain. So she came to accept that they had to do what they had to do—and it was not her business to keep them together. And so she had to walk away from that Once-upon-a-Time family she idealized.

In this they had to work together. For her parents, too, there was a deal to cut. They had to divide the family assets. They had to negotiate a *modus vivendi* with a shared daughter. They had to try to part ways, to let bygones be bygones. For Helen, there was rage, first, and then grief. Working through it took time. It would take her more time, long into the future. But she began to realize that, when she had grieved, there would come a time when it would be time to turn away, to go on.

6.

By this time, Helen's relationship with her team-leader was deeply meaningful. Margaret was old enough to be her mother. They had heart-to-heart talks before bedtime. The relationship with her much younger therapist was close and trusting, like having an older sister. Helen rode horses with her therapist. When Helen joined the horse program, she shared this common avocation with her therapist. Helen also began to care for the ducks that waddled around the pond, quacking in the middle of the campus. She took over this chore, defending it against all comers, and had to be made to share the ducks with other students, who also fell for them. Yet she had her own very personal time with the mallard male. They could be seen together in the morning, when I came in—Helen seated, giggling at him, on a stump at the edge of the pond. The mallard quacked in circles around her, coming close to poke his beak into her fistful of grain.

By the end of these months of family work, Helen was doing well in all areas of her life at the ranch. She was an A student in school, participating well. She had close relationships with all of her teachers, but particularly Lya, the Spanish teacher, with whom she ate lunch in the Spanish classroom one day every week. Helen and her parents began to flesh out mutual expectations for visits and to establish a plan for two bedrooms in two households. All three were on pretty good terms. Helen was sad about her parents' unhappiness, their separation. She was disappointed in them in painful ways. But she also had begun to think that her own life was going to become a separate matter. She began to anticipate college, and to picture herself going there on her own. She accepted that her parents were adults, after all, and had to be allowed to live their lives as they wished. There was still a grief in this, which affected her for months. But it became a grief she could talk with them about, and write poems about in creative writing class.

The hardest task for Helen, in the end, had been her reluctant struggle to make intimate friends with other students her age. She began a little stand-offish. She had never had close teenaged friends. She had been so preoccupied with her parents that she never had time to master the skills of the coquette and gossip, to test boundaries of trust and loyalty, to allow herself to confide. Among her roommates and teammates and, in time, among considerate boys on campus, she made friends. She attempted to act out sexually, early on, to skip emotional intimacy and to jump into sexual acts, which were a lot easier to pull off than intimacy.

At first she had great trouble getting close. For she could be difficult, sharp-tongued, contemptuous of childishness and boyishness, sarcastic, as if she expected all friends to be adults like her father. She betrayed a few confidences with girlfriends—just as she had betrayed her mother— and got called on it by bitter almost-friends. This was painful. Yet in time she got better at it. Soon she could be trusted with a confidence, trusted to keep her hands out of boys' trousers, trusted to hear a boy confide his affection to her—and trusted to listen to his troubles with his mother. In time she could be empathic with new students coming in, no longer threatened by their wish for time with the adults. She was amused by them, by their anger and resentment about their own parents—so much the way she had once felt about her own. She was considerate with her team-leader when she had to take time off to care for a new granddaughter.

Consideration, empathy, and an ethic that includes loyalty and trustworthiness get worked out in discussions that center on the lives teenagers live with one another at the ranch—in dorm bedrooms, at the team table in the dining room, in academic classrooms, and in daily group meetings—at which any criticism or admiration a girl feels for anyone else on campus is fair game. At the beginning new students have to learn the rules, face and accept the reasons for their enrollment at the ranch, and say what they mean directly, albeit tactfully. More advanced students become preoccupied with goals and plans, debates over principle or over ethical indignation or admiration.

As in a family, there are at the table and in the dorm a variety of students—some of whom have just arrived, licking their wounds; some who are in the midst of battles with parents; and some who are getting ready to bid the team and school farewell. As in a family, there are also adults, who have opinions and guard the boundaries. As in family discussions, the young learn from and identify with older students and with adults.

7.

In the last months of her stay a the ranch, Helen clearly had energy to spare—and, as she was less burdened by her parents' troubles, she became involved in other teenaged activities. She joined weekly group discussions about substance abuse. She joined AA trips to town, well-aware she had been headed for serious trouble prior to her enrollment. She wrote essays, poems, and short stories in creative writing and Brit lit, and she published poems on the school Web site as well as essays in the weekly school newspaper, Back at the Ranch. She became a favorite among her teachers, who admired her intelligent, sarcastic wit and thoughtful essays. She joined the cross-country team, got close with the coach, a young therapist who ran with his team. She got into shape and became a slim, lovely young woman.

Perhaps it was no surprise, despite her reluctance to come to the ranch, that she was going to have trouble leaving. She made a series of trial visits to her father's apartment in New York. She went home a couple of times to redo her bedroom in her mother's home in Connecticut. She and her father made a week's visit to a number of colleges she wanted to apply to, and she prepared for the SATs and took them one Saturday morning at the community college in Kalispell.

All this went as planned, but she came back from each visit feeling riled up. It took her hours in therapy to sort out what she was so mad or sad about. Fixing up her new bedrooms, choosing photographs to pin on her bulletin boards, shopping for posters to put up on her walls, simply emphasized that now she had two bedrooms, not one and two households, not one family. She felt divided. And as she adjusted at each place with one or other parent, she felt the absence of the one who was not there, and she felt as if a hole had been cut into her. Her grief returned. She was surprised how painful those trips were—and worried again that she would not be able to get on with her life, that she would remain stuck in the tar-pit of her parents' unhappiness. But she managed, gradually, in ways concrete and abstract, to deepen her relationship with each parent. This much she could do. What she could not do, what made her suffer about her failure, was put her Humpty Dumpty family back together again.

Often students get to the end of the program and prepare to recross the cattle guard, to reenter what they often call the *real world* of American mass culture, and feel a surge of the old unhappiness, a resurgence of urges to misbehave—the upset, the conflict, the issues that once brought them to the ranch. This is normal at the end, when it is time to say good-bye. In this sense, parting raises all the old issues. It provokes an irrational fear that nothing has really changed.

8.

When she graduated before the assembled students, staff, and parents, Helen thanked her parents for coming with her to Lost Prairie. She spoke with feeling about her worry over them, about her worry that her mother would be lonely, her father guilty and overworked. She spoke of her dream to become a veterinarian, or maybe a naturalist, "someone who gets to hang out with ducks." She told her roommates how much she loved them, how much they had meant to her. She thanked her parents for "taking the trouble to take me here, where I could stop being sneaky."

She spoke about "home"—and what it meant to her now to have homes with each of her parents. Then, weeping openly at the microphone, she said to her friends, her team, her therapist, her team-leader, and her teachers—as well as to her parents—that she now had three homes. No doubt she would someday make herself comfortable in other places: at college, and in her own household when she had her own family, assuming she ever found the courage to marry. But who would have thought, she wondered, that a girl from Connecticut would feel so very much at home in Montana?

A Case: David (Part B)

When we left David in chapter 8, he was handcuffed in a police cruiser. He had been failing across the board—at school (although he was bright), at music (he quit the band), and at love (his girlfriend had left him). He had been expelled from high school for picking a fight, had lost two front teeth, had punched his living-room wall and had been expelled from home. He had come to a crisis—a global breakdown, surely. David's approach to his life was flawed in all the familiar ways. He demonstrates in spades, at age seventeen, the elements of what I have called a relative immaturity. Not only did he behave childishly, but he seems *only* to be able to behave childishly.

What obstacle(s) prevented David's growing up? In brief, it was his *parents'* parenting that got disrupted by his brother's tragic death. It was his parents' capacity to recognize him accurately, to see what *he* was, what *he* needed, what *he* cared about, what talents *he* had, what promise *he* might hold. His father appeared to be able to see in David only another accident waiting to happen, one that, once again, might be all his fault. Paul could only mis-recognize David (i.e., see him as if he were someone else). His mother, living in the dim penumbra of a protracted grief (or depression), hardly saw David, who was, from the start, the unbearabale reminder of her loss.

This parental reluctance to recognize him left him lost and angry. David tried to stand up to his father's false reframing of his existence—his determination to make David out to be a wantonly careless boy who kept criminally upsetting his mother. David had to resist his father's attempts to make him out to be what he was not, to hold him responsible for a fatal mistake he never made, to call him to account for a sin he did not commit, and to anticipate a doom David had no reason to believe his own.

1.

At the juvenile court hearing on San Pedro Road, the judge suspended David's sentence at their attorney's request, so that his family could follow the advice of an educational consultant to send David on a wilderness trek. This, she suggested to his parents, would start David out with an attitude adjustment. If he did well, she told them, he might be enrolled in a therapeutic boarding school on a ranch in Montana.

Hours later, a very large, onetime Dallas Cowboys lineman met David in his bedroom, helped him carry his boots to his rental SUV, and in a friendly way conducted David to a venerable wilderness program *in Oregon. At the base camp David was issued a backpack, basic camp equipage, and simple provisions. Still in a daze from the sudden change in his life's direction, David shouldered his pack and followed a team of young adults and five other teenagers into the Oregon outback.*

A sudden disappearance into the "wilderness" has become the entry to the world of "alternative" (nonmedical) and "emotional growth" treatment programs. Ten years ago, when I was a conventionally trained, board-certified psychiatrist, I had never heard about irascible teenagers whisked off by friendly "escorts" to "wilderness." I was as ignorant, a decade ago, as are most conventional psychologists and psychiatrists, some of whom, having offered very little to very troubled teenagers in outpatient offices, and having rolled over entirely to managed-care intrusions—so that inpatient hospital facilities have become unavailable—now express their noisy indignation when parents resort to "alternative" interventions.[12]

However, a decade of deep experience with some of the best of these programs has taught me that, in good hands, a few weeks in a "wilderness" program can produce a remarkable change in attitude among troubled teenagers. All but invariably our students at the ranch have started with a "wilderness" experience, and we often insist upon it prior to enrolling a stroppy teenager. When our students have emerged from these programs, they themselves swear by the experience. Many decide that they want, someday, to become wilderness therapists. And they are proud to have overcome a major physical and emotional challenge. They would say that "wilderness" changed them dramatically, and for the better. This is also what parents tell us.

In the last decade these programs have changed, too. Although the original concept was of a sudden exile from an invidious teen culture, a radical cleaning up from drug and alcohol use, a serious physical challenge that teenagers are helped to meet, and a radical rethinking of recent events—it was, in particular, the global breakdown that provoked their parents to call an educational consultant. These days, the therapists who join teenagers on those treks are well-trained, often with PhDs in psychology.

Why should this be so helpful? I have come to think that limit-setting may be the key intervention with most of the immature students who come to Montana Academy. There is nothing quite like a sudden exile from the city or suburb to the high Utah desert to communicate a very firm parental limit. For a big, strong, angry boy, who is no longer taking direction from a mother and father, there is nothing like waking up under the stars to a cup of cold rice and beans to understand the parental determination that this is going to change. We have come to think this kind of wilderness experience a very good way to prepare for enrollment at a residential therapeutic school like Montana Academy. Only those who have no experience with first-rate wilderness programs will think otherwise.

2.

David completed his exile six weeks later. His therapist spoke of him with pride, enthusiasm, and optimism. After an initial tantrum David had settled into the group of his peers, accepted the challenge of the strenuous days of hiking and rudimentary diet, the necessity to make his own fire from scratch, and to carry his own and some of the rest of the team's gear. He began to pass tests for promotion with panache and with distinction. When he came out, his parents were there to meet him. He proudly built the fire, cooked them their dinner, and bedded down with them under the stars. Intensive group discussion followed, and then his parents took him out to their car and headed north.

They at first had wondered if that was it—whether they should simply take David home. But experienced therapists and educational consultants advised Paul and Susan not to make that mistake. The short trek had been a good start. But the deeper change he needed so badly could not happen so quickly. Molly (their educational consultant) asked them how many times they ever wanted to call 911 again? They flew to Montana to visit, and when David demanded to be taken home, and bristled when they said No, they knew they were right to say No.

On a crisp fall day, they flew with David from San Francisco to Kalispell, rented an SUV, packed in all David's new gear, clothing, and school supplies, and drove for an hour—in silence, most of the way—down a winding country highway to the turnoff. Then, still quiet in the car, they climbed a piney ridge and started the steep descent into Lost Prairie.

By the time David arrived at Montana Academy, the school and program had settled into an established, coherent structure. There were sixty-nine students already in residence in log dorms with spacious lounges, and some of the senior boys on his team were assigned immediately to "mentor" him—to welcome him, to show him around, to teach him how to settle in, and to reassure him that they, too, had once felt new and unknown, and that he would be all right if he settled down and settled in. Dr. Parker, one of the older clinicians, met him when he got there with his parents, and that afternoon they spent a couple of hours getting acquainted in a friendly conversation that David did not find difficult.

3.

David quickly adapted to a new routine. He attended three academic courses each morning, in classrooms with fewer than twelve students. He met daily in groups with the nine other boys on his team, with whom he also ate all his meals in the lodge, did chores in the kitchen and dorm, played basketball during sports, and bunked at night. He and Dr. Parker called his parents at the end of his therapy. In school, at meals and in the lodge, he met the forty other boys and thirty girls, who quickly sized him up. Some girls already thought he was "cute."

In fact, adults and teenagers on the ranch quickly made sense of David. They watched how he did as a student, teammate, worker, and potential friend. They saw him as a son, as a boy trying to figure out what to do in psychotherapy and groups. In the classroom, he quickly got to know his teachers well. The Spanish teacher invited him back to have lunch with her in their classroom, and the creative-writing teacher asked him whether he might be interested in the school newspaper. They saw his early academic work, noticed his curiosity and intelligence, and told him they thought he had promise as a student. In groups, boys asked him blunt questions. In the kitchen and in the dorm during morning clean-up, his team watched how he did his chores, whether David pulled his weight, how well he cooperated.

In short, tens of people watched his arrival closely—as they would at any school. But on the ranch David also had to face those same adults and kids in groups, where he was expected to be frank about his thoughts and feelings, and where they would notice his attitude, his manners, his kindness or meanness, even whether he bathed with soap and washed his clothing. In short, David found himself in a fishbowl. There were few secrets from adults. The culture contained sufficient ethical sophistication for mature students to recognize that dirty secrets were not good for anyone. Someone always "told."

On that first day, David also ran into limits built into the ranch culture. There were things he used to do that he could no longer do because they were not allowed on the ranch. He could not use a cell phone or headphones, drive an automobile, or play a computer game. He could not smoke, and there were no drugs or alcohol on the ranch. Freedoms were not entitlements to be had just for showing up. There were privileges that, as a beginner, he could not have. There were attractive options he would earn only by responsible behavior sustained over time. He had not yet demonstrated at the ranch that he was responsible or energetic or constructive or trustworthy enough to be allowed, for example, to go into town, or to make phone calls to old friends.

The public culture, shared by all, was Spartan. There were no TVs on the ranch. Movies were regularly played for all the students at once, not on private laptops. No blasting music made conversation superfluous. There was little jewelry or makeup, no designer clothing, little vulgarity or careless diction, no threats, no slander, no fondling, no wandering off without staff permission. Adults were an intimate part of this new world, which they supervised. He had privacy, but staff also came into his bedroom to say goodnight and into the bathrooms to check his chores. In the dining hall, they ate their meals at his table, and his therapist presided over the team's frankest discussions.

Even before his first therapy session, David felt the eyes of others on him. The surrounding country was huge, the community small— seventy teenagers and seventy adults. David made friends with other boys, pretty girls, and some adults. His team admired his athletic spunk, his willingness to throw himself into a game, to go for it. Teachers liked his readiness to debate, but put limits on his willingness to argue about the rules or the expectations. Dr. Parker accepted his indignation about "not needing any of this," but found ways also to help David talk about his parents, his dead brother, his fury about his mother's locked door and his father's locked gates. Pretty soon, David felt that Dr. Parker "got it" about him. He knew that Parker liked him, even if for a time Parker had wearily to put up with David's noisy complaints about "the stupid rules."

Limits enraged him. He hated to be told that he was "not ready" for X or Y privilege, to discover that he could not do something he had yet to earn the right to do. The rules simply applied to David—all of them. This was a first premise of his treatment. Not only that, his unwillingness to accept that all the rules applied to him provoked one of the first confrontations he had with his team-leader, Seth. He did not like this argument, because he thought Seth was pretty great, and Seth clearly had no respect for his "childish" opposition to reasonable rules.

This came to an emotional crisis when his mother first came back to Montana to visit. When he was not allowed more than one night off-campus with her because he had not yet demonstrated that he could courteously manage it, he demonstrated the wisdom of Dr. Parker's precaution by throwing his first public tantrum—stomping out of group and slamming his knuckles into the Sheetrock. Then he picked up a textbook someone had left on a table and knocked a framed picture off the wall, shouting, "Dr. Parker, you bastard! You want to keep me away from my mother!" And so he lost the one night.

When his mother arrived on campus, David refused to agree to the limit Dr. Parker had set. Dr. Parker asked him in a kindly way to control himself, even though he was frustrated. But David fumed and swore under his breath. Dr. Parker, who had prepared his mother for her part, then told David somberly, while his mother nodded sadly, that if he was not yet up to a visit, if he could not control his temper and accept the rules willingly, then his mother would have to go back to town alone.

Susan confirmed this plan, admitting that "it would upset me not to see you any longer today," but agreeing that "first things have to come first." When he could not stop glaring and cussing under his breath, she stood up to cut the day's visit short, saying she would "come back as soon as you can control yourself and accept the rules."

David shouted, "You don't love me!" and lunged from the room, slamming the door. Dr. Parker sent Seth to intercept him, and he walked Susan out to her rental car. She tried not to let David see her emotional struggle, but once past the gate she wept all the way back over the ridge, certain that her heart would break.

The next morning she was back. At their group meeting, his team helped David settle down and prepare for anything she might say to him. He did not repeat his tantrum. Although limited to the ranch because of his tantrum the day before, David and his mother spent the day walking the fence line and talking together in the lodge.

Perhaps it already will be obvious what Dr. Parker and his staff are doing. This is a description of steady recognition and limit-setting. One obstacle to David getting what he needed had been his mother's fragility and aloofness, even her avoidance of him. Therefore, here it is Susan, not Paul, who has come to set a firm limit and stick to it in the face of David's defiance. In this tightly organized community, many limits are built into program structure—prohibitions, rules, constraints, schedules, and assignments. David squirms and resists, complains about them, protests he "does not need this," and accuses his mother of not loving him. But he manages to comply when limits are firmly set.

David feels them painfully. After a lifetime of missing his mother, what could be harder than for her to come to visit and then suddenly go away again? This is painful to read, and none of this is easy. Yet it is only limit-setting that can confront and diminish David's childish narcissism—his angry demands, his tantrums when frustrated, his threats and his pouting. Yet when he negotiates these constraints with dignity, he is recognized for it in an affectionate, loving way. It is no longer that David simply cannot get to spend time with his mother. Now he can, so long as he accepts constraints. He may be confined to the ranch; but because he recovered his poise, his mother comes to share this constrained day with him. That, after all, is the closeness he misses and longs for.

4.

Once past all attempts to talk his parents out of their decision to send him to the ranch, and once past two weeks of homesickness, David began making a success of ranch life. He did very well in Spanish and math, where his teachers did not hide their pleasure in his good work. They saw his promise and expected great things. He joined the school paper and wrote a profile about the Spanish teacher. He made three friends to hang out with during common breaks in the day. He ceased to argue about the rules, most of the time. Eight weeks after he arrived, he got promoted to Moon Clan.

This promotion meant that he had more choices, for example, of weekend activities. He fell off a mountain bike coming down a wooded hill too fast and broke his forearm. In January he became the most daring snowboarder on the mountain—and prompting Dr. Parker to hold him back from a weekend of Big Mountain activities until he could wonder, with David, what all that risk-taking was for.

When his parents came to visit at the Christmas break, Paul rented a condo at Big Mountain, and David earned three nights with them. He told his team he hoped to show off for them how well he had learned to 'board—and they cautioned him, inasmuch as his risk-taking had become a public issue after he broke his arm. By then he knew he was angry at his mother not because she was so unreasonable, but because he longed for her. On the phone, he asked her to ski with him—and she promised she would. He already knew he could hardly stand to be with his father, who seemed "always on me." His father, he told his team, was "no fun." He just kept "trying to tell me what to do, or what not to do, all the time." But David also had begun to see that this caution had something to do with his father's anxiety, his father's fear that something would happen to him, that he might lose David as he had lost Isaac. Knowing this, David tried on the phone to talk with his parents about his frustrations, and, for a time, he even thought they got his point.

But when Christmas break came, his mother turned out to be "too tired" and her back "hurt too much" to ski very much. She spent most of his three overnights closeted in her bedroom, coping with a headache that seemed to be provoked by the glare of the sun off the snow. His father canceled his own skiing so as to stay with his wife. So David got to go onto the slopes only when a few other students arrived with a few staff, who happened to be skiing on Big Mountain, too. Otherwise he would not have been able to board at all, and would have had to spend the weekend in the condo, leafing through magazines. In the end his parents came to Montana and went home again without ever watching David on his snowboard.

All the same, they were offended by his behavior. His father complained afterward about David's "bad manners," which had "not improved at all." At the restaurant, he said, David could "hardly be civil." Maybe it was better that now he muttered, rather than yell, but his father told him that his mother had heard him grumbling that her fatigue was "a crock," that all his life he had been "motherless." His father was furious that David "ruined a perfectly nice dinner" and "made your mother wretched!" He drove David back to the ranch in all but total silence. When David got out of the car, he only could manage, "Yeah, thanks."

Paul's long drive back to Big Mountain was grim. He wondered whether David was getting anything out of this expensive "treatment." Here seemed to be "the same old thing." He was bitter about other things that seemed not to change, either. He knew he would find Susan prostrate, turned away in the darkness. And he knew that all night, off and on, he would awaken to her whimpering. What bothered him most, however, was something he was not entirely sure about. All the way to the condo, he tried strenuously to recall the inflection in David's final remark. For it had dawned upon him after David trudged up the stairs to the lodge that, despite all he and Susan did for David, his son's thank you had sounded a little bit sarcastic.

It becomes apparent here that there will be no miraculous cure for all that prevents David's parents from intimacy with him, from closeness, from getting "it" about him, from seeing him clearly. Surely most parents are set in their ways, shaped by formative relationships and histories with their own parents, by traumas endured, by the critical or cautionary voices of their own parents, which echo in their ears. Parents often do better. They almost hold their tongues. They drag themselves home from a demanding career and try to make time. They try not to say what they are thinking. But parents are hard, if not impossible, to change in a fundamental way. This being so, it may have been inevitable that his parents' visit would prove to be a disappointment to David— merely a replay and a reminder of his prior frustrations about his mother's "fatigue," his father's angst and fault-finding. David, too, felt that this had been the same old thing.

Yet he was no longer the same. Fortunately for young people, it remains possible to renegotiate relationships with "father" and "mother" even after leaving home, even after parents are gone. It is possible to some extent to work out the residual knots in those relationships by working out new relationships with others who stand in for them. A good deal of this repetition, of these attempts to do it differently this time, takes place within such symbolic substitute relationships. In these new relationships, the echoes of the past can be reexperienced and recognized. Many of us feel the presence of those virtual parents, who haunt our nights and days.

Similarly, there inevitably are echoes from our own childhood experience in our relationships with our children.

When such unconscious echoes sound in psychotherapy they are called transference. When this happens, a therapist stands in for some past important figure, often a parent. And a skilled therapist hears these echoes. He recognizes the role played; he knows the history, and listens for it. What he then says or does "in the transference," he frames with a deliberate ambiguity. For the conversation is taking place, in this sense, in two time zones: one present, one past.

5.

In the spring, Dr. Parker's toddler son became ill. Again and again, he developed high fevers, but there was no diagnosis. So again and again Dr. Parker had to vanish from the ranch, usually without much warning, so as to attend to his son in the hospital.

David accepted the first missed therapy appointment without comment. But as spring break neared he grew anxious to get promoted to the next level of privileges in the program, so that he could have more days at Big Mountain on a ski pass with his parents. Perhaps this time he would manage to show them what he could do.

For this reason, he resented his therapist's many absences without meaning to. He got irked when he learned his promotion would require Dr. Parker's signature before it could even be discussed by his treatment team. He was put out because he had not been able to see Dr. Parker alone in his office for two weeks.

Then, arriving on a Monday for his regular meeting, David found only a scrawled note in a secretary's hand announcing that Dr. Parker would be gone "until further notice." Angrily, David scrawled on the note still taped to Parker's door:

To hell with your son—he's not that sick! What about me?

Parker returned three days later and found the note. He called David out of school. When David arrived, looking sullen, Dr. Parker said, "You forgot to sign your note." David conceded that it was his scrawl.

*"Well, OK, what about **you**?" Parker said.*

"Oh, nothing."

"Sounds like you needed something. You said, "'What about **me**?'"

"Not really," David muttered.

"Wait," Parker said. "Your parents are coming to visit. Is this to do with that?

"Not important," David mumbled.

"You were up for promotion," Parker recalled. "Did you get it?"

David shook his head. "I didn't have your signature." When he glanced up, feeling shy, Dr. Parker was looking at him with friendly concern.

"You're angry with me."

David stared at his shoes. "Not anymore."

"No. But let's hear about it."

David launched woodenly into an account of his parents' coming visit, his hope this time to snowboard with his mother. When he got to his complaint, he said softly, "You're never here when I need to see you."

"Yeah," Parker said. "Never?"

"I just needed a damn signature, which you could have done in a few seconds. But nobody would bother you. All you could think about was your other ... ."

After a pauses, Parker said, "My 'other'..."

David blushed. "I'm so sorry, I..."

"You're being polite, but you were furious. Yes?"

"Yeah."

"I was so preoccupied with my 'other' son that I forgot about what you needed—even so small a thing. It wasn't like you were asking much."

"Yeah."

They both stared into the forest. "The worst of it," Parker said, "was that this was not the first time in your life,..."

David began to cry.

"You know what I mean?" Parker looked at David kindly, nodding. "Of course you do," he muttered, "...all your life."

"I could have been dying," David sobbed. "I never could figure out what I had to do to get her to come out of there. My dad guarded the door like a junk yard dog. He never would tell her I wanted her. He always put his fingers to his lips, like this—shhhh! shhhh! Like she was asleep in the middle of the day. And he would never even tell her."

"And he wouldn't sign," Parker remembered, "so you could join the rowing club."

"No. Like I wanted to enlist in the Marines!"

"I know," Parker said. "It didn't seem like much to ask." He glanced at his calendar. "When do your parents arrive?"

"Friday."

Parker said, "OK," as if lost in thought.

"'OK' what?" David finally asked.

Parker smiled and looked at him directly. "Time to join the club."

"What club?"

"The club of men," Parker said. "Unfortunately you can't skip the initiation, which is the disappointment we suffer when we realize that our godlike parents are not what we wish they were—not as big, not as strong, not as wise, nor as consoling as we once thought they were, or could be, when we were little. You get to join the club when you suffer seeing that they just sweat and wear socks like everybody else, even when they do their best. You see that they were just doing the best they could. And the initiation is knowing that sometimes the best they could do was not good enough."

David nodded.

"We feel this disappointment, and we have to change our view of them—or go on blaming ourselves for their failings. They get smaller and smaller, down to just human size—not gods anymore, but just like ourselves. How we hate that! We do not like to see how mom or dad lets us down—and, worse, that they couldn't help it, because they never were gods. We thought they were. We can hardly stand it when they let us down, and we have to see that they never were.

David's tears wet his cheeks. "I used to get so sad."

"Yeah," Parker said. "I know."

David started for the door, rubbing and wiping at his eyes.

"Oh, David?" Parker called after him, making him pause at the door. "I'll take care of your promotion and your pass," he said. "Not your fault."

"Thanks," David said huskily, hiding his tears.

"David?" Parker called again.

"Yeah?"

"Sorry I let you down."

We will leave David there—and bid farewell to these composite students—Pauline, Helen, and David, who have served their purposes. Before closing this book, however, we need real parents to say in their own words—not by means of composite cases—what their actual experiences have been.

We need true outcomes.

10   Outcomes

WE HAVE COME FULL CIRCLE. Beginning with symptoms, signs, and misbehaviors that described a global breakdown in adolescence, we rehearsed a *flawed approach*, described so many times by visiting parents, which made sense of a troubled teenager's bad decisions and perseverative academic and interpersonal failures. Then we reviewed the stages of normal maturation so as to consider the possibility that a troubled teenager's unsound approach results from an disrupted maturation. Finally, we reviewed potential obstacles and how they might hinder maturation and so cause a developmental delay.

One Hypothesis—Immaturity

This carefully developed argument is a clinical theory—an *immaturity* hypothesis. Its explanation for adolescent global breakdown is radically different from conventional psychiatric (*DSM-IV*) diagnosis. For this reason its treatment implications also differ dramatically from the reflexive polypharmacy that is now commonplace in the standard contemporary treatment of a broad range of symptoms and misbehaviors in troubled teenagers. Like other meaningful scientific theories, this immaturity hypothesis can be tested, for it is a causal theory. Its predictions can be checked against empirical results, and so the hypothesis can be falsified (disproved).[1]

The immaturity hypothesis, we should note before going any further, seems compatible with modern neuroscience. For example, in these pages I have quoted from Daniel Siegel's synthesis of neuroscience and developmental psychology—and certainly Siegel thinks the two are compatible. In his book, the frontal lobes appear to be a key anatomical locus for many critical aspects of adolescent maturation—and for those aspects of an adolescent "flawed approach" that I have linked to adolescent *im*maturity. Or again, Elkhonon Goldberg, after a lifetime's study of the frontal lobe's "executive" functions, links the prefrontal cortex to the achievement of empathy; the capacity to form goals and to make and follow plans; the differentiation of self from other; and the capacity to think ethically—all in a cortical location where neuro development climaxes at about age nineteen. [2] Although Goldberg studied brain-injured adults rather than maturing teenagers, his anatomical correlations would apply in either population. Goldberg points out, in an aside, that injury to the frontal lobes leaves an adult helplessly behaving "like an adolescent."[3]

To any empirical test of the immaturity hypothesis, one set of key predictions involves the outcomes of treatment. That is, if a troubled teenager's blocked development can be unblocked, and developmental momentum restored, so that he catches up with age-mates in maturity, then the prediction would be that his approach to the tasks of adolescence would cease to be flawed. The prediction would be that he would cease to fail globally at all the tasks of adolescence, that most troubling symptoms would vanish, and that he would cease to need psychiatric medication aimed at those symptoms.

An Alternative Theory—Disorders

The contemporary alternative "null" theory is (what I will call) the *disorder* hypothesis. Since the publication of *DSM-III* in 1980, American clinicians have been taught to diagnose the multiple, protean signs, symptoms, and misbehaviors of troubled youth as pathological descriptive syndromes, called "disorders." For illustration, here are the descriptive diagnostic criteria for one commonly diagnosed adolescent disorder:

OPPOSITIONAL DEFIANT DISORDER (313.81)[4]

A. A pattern of negativistic, hostile, and defiant behavior lasting at least 6 months, during which four (or more) of the
following are present:
(1) often loses temper
(2) often argues with adults
(3) often actively defies or refuses to comply with adults'
requests or rules

(4) often deliberately annoys people

(5) often blames others for his or her mistakes or misbehavior

(6) is often touchy or easily annoyed by others

(7) is often angry and resentful

(8) is often spiteful or vindictive

Note: Consider a criterion met only if the behavior occurs more frequently than is typically observed in individuals of comparable age and developmental level.

B. The disturbance in behavior causes clinically significant impairment in social, academic, or occupational functioning.

C. The behaviors do not occur exclusively during the course of a Psychotic or Mood Disorder.

D. Criteria are not met for Conduct Disorder, and, if the individual is age 18 years or older, criteria are not met for Antisocial Personality Disorder.

These are typical criteria for a *DSM-IV* disorder: a laundry list of symptoms and signs from which a certain minimum number must be "present"; a requirement that "functioning" be disrupted; and, usually, disqualifiers that tidy up the inconvenient truth—that these symptoms and signs also are listed among criteria for other disorders. When specific signs and symptoms also can be observed among normal subjects, there is an added requirement that they "occur more frequently."

This particular (oppositional-defiant) disorder resembles a description of "global break-down," although clearly it is not the same. As demonstrated (in chapter 2), multiple *DSM-IV* disorders may be assigned to teenagers who are failing across the board at the tasks of adolescence. The point here is that the immaturity hypothesis is a causal explanation for global dysfunction, whereas the oppositional-defiant disorder is merely a geneal description of that global dysfunction, lacking an etiology. Moreover, the criteria for this particular *DSM-IV* diagnosis only (again) begs the question: what *is* a disorder? A congenital defect? An addiction? A response to trauma? A dementia? An intoxication? A genetic flaw? A maimed personality? A form of badness? The term *disorder* has been applied to any and all of these kinds of pathology.

A *DSM-IV* diagnosis usually tells little or nothing about cause. A disorder is *only* a descriptive syndrome. As a rival hypothesis, it offers little more than a universal occasion to prescribe medication to suppress symptoms. If in medicine we did likewise, we would accept "belly pain disorder" as a final diagnosis, find a cohort of "belly pain" patients who meet the descriptive criteria, and try them on various medications until one "helped." This nostrum would then be prescribed to "treat" the disorder. Yet, we would be no closer to answering the question: help with *what*? Treat *what*? In medicine, to "treat" belly pain without a causal diagnosis is considered to be medical negligence.

Clinical Patterns

The immaturity hypothesis, on the other hand, is a causal explanation. Its thesis is that immaturity *is* a flawed approach which produces a broadly-based dysfunction. It predicts that many problems of troubled teenagers will go away if a childish teenager can be helped *to grow up*.

We do not have definitive, double-blind studies to confirm or falsify this prediction, or to test the two hypotheses, side by side. But broadly speaking the immaturity formulation is confirmed by clinical experience. It explains the flawed approach we have described, locating its elements among normal developmental precursors to the mature adolescent repertoire. It is parsimonious compared to the grab bag of "disorders" that clinicians must resort to if they want to represent a globally dysfunctional adolescent. Immaturity suggests a unitary cause, a common pathway, for most of the pleomorphic signs, symptoms, misbehaviors, and problems of troubled adolescents.[5]

The more compelling test, however, will be the *outcome*. In a flailing teenager the immaturity hypothesis predicts that if and when he catches up, developmentally, then his symptoms, signs, misbehaviors, and psychosocial floundering will all improve. It predicts that if and when he achieves a full (mature) adolescent repertoire, his symptoms (or most of them) will abate. It predicts, therefore, that medications prescribed to relieve those symptoms will become superfluous and can be discontinued. The immaturity hypothesis suggests these results from a recovered maturation will not be subtle, but rather will be obvious, even striking.

On the other hand, if the immaturity hypothesis were *not* true, there should be no linkage between immaturity and the manifestations of global breakdown. If *not* true, then a restored developmental momentum would *not* remedy the signs and symptoms of conventional-psychiatry

DSM-IV disorders. If the disorder hypothesis with its prescriptive pharmacology were the better way to understand and treat a global breakdown in adolescence, then reduced symptoms and improved, even optimal, academic and social functioning should coincide with vigorous, sustained polypharmacy—and would *not* coincide with reduced or eliminated need for medication. But if the immaturity hypothesis is a better causal explanation and guide to treatment, then reduced symptoms and improved, even optimal, academic and interpersonal functioning ought to coincide with improved measures of maturity and with much reduced or an eliminated need for psychotropic medications. In short, to compare these two alternative explanations, we need to learn what happens when a troubled teenager grows up.

∽

At the ranch our treatment plans are intended to help teenagers recover developmental momentum (a) by removing obstacles to maturation or mitigating their effects, and (b) by prodding a "stuck" teenager to catch up with age-mates. A strong clinical alliance with parents is a first goal. A strong staff alliances with a troubled teenager is next. After that, the therapeutic tasks are to promote accurate, affectionate recognition and to provide firm, deft limit-setting—and sustain both over time.

By no means do we always succeed. But this is irrelevant to the test of these alternative hypotheses; our particular program's rate of success or failure is not germane. This is an important point. To test the immaturity hypothesis does *not* depend on the efficacy of our treatment method or how often we successfully prod an immature teenager to grow up. It is *not* a question of whether we always or only sometimes produce this desired result. It is instead a question of whether, *when we do* succeed, then: symptoms abate; academic enthusiasm and competence improve; parental relations can be renegotiated on new terms; separate friendships and grown-up romantic relationships emerge; and morale and self-respect dramatically change for the better. These criteria offer a test of the immaturity hypothesis.

Observations
Clinically we see a strong, one-to-one correlation between gains in

maturity and improvements in academic and interpersonal functioning. This is not a subtle clinical finding. When childish teenagers grow up, academic, familial, and interpersonal problems become tractable. As expected, these tectonic shifts occur along predictable fault lines:

FROM:		TO:
Gross self-preoccupation	⇒	Consideration for Others
Lack of empathy	⇒	True Empathy
Wishful thinking	⇒	Goals, Plans, and Self-Discipline
"Puppet" relationships	⇒	Separate Relationships, an Acceptance of No
Selfish Ethics	⇒	Abstract, Social Moral Ideas

To detect these shifts does not usually require seismic equipment. They are robust findings in parental surveys that ask parents to recognize changes in attitude and approach.[6] When troubled teenagers begin to grow up, parents readily detect the change. Clinicians do, too, and so do teachers. I find it most convincing when these shifts reveal themselves in everyday diction on mundane subjects, and a new mature perspective gets expressed spontaneously, as no big deal, when no privilege or new status is at stake, when no one is trying to sell anything. Here are a few examples:

- A heretofore self-preoccupied boy asks me in passing, "You OK, doc? You look kind of tired." And I register: *empathy*.
- A girl, heretofore an entitled brat, notices that I am busy at a time I promised to talk about something she wants. Instead of her characteristic worry about herself, she suggests, "Maybe you'd rather talk later." And I think: *consideration*.
- A heretofore heedless young hedonist comes to discuss his academic courses and tells me: "If I am going to start college next fall, I figure I need to take the SATs in May, so I better take algebra II next block, because Tim will be on vacation after that, and he won't be giving the course then." And I register: a *goal,* a *plan*.
- A girl reports in confidence that she has announced to a friend that if he does not confess that he huffed gasoline from a lawnmower tank, she will tell on him—"even if he gets really mad

at me for ratting him out." She realizes no true friend would let a friend damage his brain—and this is a selfless act, which may cost her something, an unselfish concern for another, and it is principled (about what a "friend" is), rather than concrete. So I register: an *abstract, social ethic.*

- On a Monday a boy makes a face that looks like he just sucked a lemon and says, "What a lousy weekend!" He complains that "the guys in the dorm were jerks," and launches into a description of his own behavior a few months before, which he no longer thinks acceptable. And I register: *change.*

This last complaint is typical—a boy who does not realize that he has changed, that he has matured. In general young people rarely recognize that they have changed or that they have grown up. Sometimes it upsets them (as above), and they feel less a part of the crowd, and a bit lonely. Not until an adult recognizes this shift in attitude, and marks it as a legitimate source of pride, will they see it in themselves. Often young people assume instead that others have changed, that others have begun to behave in a peculiar, offensive way. A teenager can be as oblivious to his own maturation as Mark Twain recalls that he was, himself:

> When I was a boy of 14, my father was so ignorant I could hardly stand to have the old man around. But when I got to be 21, I was astonished at how much the old man had learned in seven years.[7]

Because teenagers usually do not notice changes in themselves, parental recognition makes an important contribution. For an adult to acknowledge a boy's new maturity strongly sustains that new maturity. To help a girl make sense of puzzling new feelings, or to register that she is becoming a fine woman, turns out to be profoundly encouraging.

If maturation correlates with striking changes in academic and interpersonal functioning, we have observed that the contrary also is true. When a boy does *not* grow up, when over time his approach does not shift, then he also does *not* spontaneously progress to an improved academic and interpersonal functioning, no matter how much Prozac or Ritalin may be prescribed. It is possible to improve school and dining hall behavior with strenuous adult nagging; but without this internal shift to a more mature approach, this improved behavior regresses as soon as adult compulsion ceases. At the ranch our most painful failures, in this sense, confirm the immaturity hypothesis. They also confirm that, in the absence of recognition and limit-setting, childishness does not spontaneously resolve itself. Particularly this is so when an obstacle to developmental progress remains or deft parenting continues to be unavailable. When maturation does not occur and a childish teenager becomes adult, the result is a *character disorder*.

Digression—The "Criminal Mind"

This last point, which touches upon our penal system, warrants brief digression. Our jails and prisons appear to be crowded with persistent immaturity, with men and women already well into adult decades who still manifest a childish approach to interpersonal relationships and economic challenges. Some years ago, a criminologist named Samenow published a provocative theory of what he called the "criminal mind." In his book, he insisted that certain deviant characteristics of a criminal approach to life made criminal behavior inevitable—and that liberal do-gooders were foolish to think that this problem could be addressed by appeasement. The problem, he argued, was dyed in the wool, and he noted that in the histories of criminals this deviant approach was evident since early childhood. Entirely oblivious to child development, he pointed to the selfishness and the illogical thinking of these people from childhood onward, and claimed that adult criminals who committed crimes were not like the rest of us. [8]

Their deviant approach he described:
- **Floridly Narcissistic**, preoccupied with *me*—an abiding conviction that if I want it or I want to do it, and want it now, I should just do it or take it, even if exploiting or harming others;
- **Lacking in Empathy**, lacking (as prosecutors point out) in remorse, indifferent to the feelings of victims;
- **An Illogical Wishful Thinking** about the future, expressed in a belief (despite evidence to the contrary) that they'll never catch me;
- **A Lack of Step-Wise Planning**, so that thieves and murderers often botch even simple crimes. [9]

- **A Selfish, Concrete Ethical Conviction** that it is fine to take or do what is illegal, so long as I don't get caught and punished, so long as there is something in it for me.

One suspects, from this description, that meticulously planned, beautifully executed big-ticket heists are Hollywood fantasies, constructed by grown-up screenwriters who suffer no handicap in fully imagining a goal and working out the steps in an airtight plan. If Samenow is right, moreover, a visit to any cell-block ought to provide variations upon this "criminal mind." Yet what Samenow describes, in essence, is the flawed approach of adolescent immaturity.

The MAMA-p

At Montana Academy we have been developing a measure of maturity, which is needed, because there is no blood level to assay, no cerebral structure (as yet) to scan, and no existing measure (we know about) that gauges maturity in the way we define it. We have been developing a set of standard inferences about a teenager's approach to life—to be drawn by those who know him (or her) well. We began with a parent's assessment of a son or daughter. For if teenagers are themselves oblivious to changes in their approaches to their lives, who better than an intelligent parent to recognize how a young person thinks about the challenges of the adolescent stage of life? The Montana Adolescent Maturity Assessment (the MAMA-p) is a parental assay of a son's or a daughter's level of maturity.

The results that I will describe are preliminary, but unsubtle. Inasmuch as this is an ongoing project, I will simply describe our efforts—so that, preliminary as they are, they can be added to our clinical observations. I will not make too much of these early findings, or make extravagent claims for them. They are what they are.

To start, we constructed a prototype of the MAMA-p by creating, for each element of parents' repetitive description of an immature teenager's approach, a set of descriptive statements about adolescent thinking and behaving. We asked mothers and fathers to rate 58 assertions about their children on a five-point scale:

1 = Never, 2 = Rarely, 3 = Sometimes, 4 = Often, and 5 = Always

Here are a few examples of statements we ask parents to rate:

• Capacity (or incapacity) for *empathy* and consideration:

223

I feel that my child is "too big for his/her britches."

My child needs to be the center of attention.

My child does not understand that sometimes I am tired.

• Capacity (or incapacity) to set goals and make plans:

My child is preoccupied with now, and oblivious to the future.

My child plans ahead.

My child puts off studying until the night before the exam.

• Capacity (or incapacity) for abstract and social ethics:

My child realizes that the rules do apply to him/her.

My child's sense of right and wrong depends on what his/her friends think.

My child understands what "honesty" means.

In this prototype, then, when all responses were aligned so that a "1" reflected the most childish response and a "5" reflected the most mature rating, the lowest (least mature) possible total score was 58 (i.e., 58 questions x 1); and the highest (most mature) total score was 290 (i.e., 58 questions x 5).[10]

At the same time that we asked parents to complete the MAMA-p, we asked them also to assess their daughters and sons on ten dimensions of academic, personal, and interpersonal functioning, as if they were teachers grading a student's performance (A = 5, B = 4, C = 3, D = 2 and F = 1), e.g., on "compliance with rules and schedules," on "academic performance," on "relationships at home," on "relationships with peers," on "relationships with adults outside the family," on "self-esteem, on "vigor in engaging the world," on "ambition and planning for the future," and on an overall rating of a young person's "happiness." At the same time we also asked about the presence of symptoms within seven categories (depressed mood, mood instability, anxiety, substance abuse, and so forth), and about use of prescribed psychotropic medication.

In the past year (at this writing) we have asked parents of new students to rate sons and daughters *prior to enrollment*, i.e., when "things were at their worst." We asked parents of departing students to rate sons and daughters *at graduation*, just as they were preparing to leave the ranch. And we have asked all parents, during parent workshops, to complete a MAMA-p while on campus—so as to rate their sons and daughters, who were at all stages of their treatment at Montana Academy.

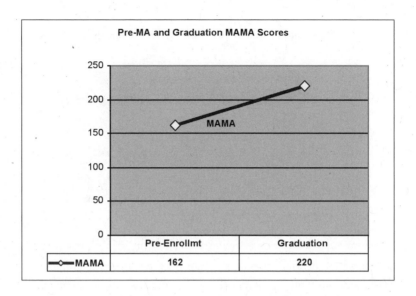

In this year (2005-2006) there were twenty-four new students, who arrived and were rated by their parents, and there were twenty-eight graduates (different students), whose parents completed MAMA-p ratings as their children twenty months later, as they prepared to leave the school. Average MAMA-p scores were 162 (plus or minus 22) prior to enrollment and 220 (plus or minus 17) at graduation—a positive change in the maturity index of +58 points. In other words, on average

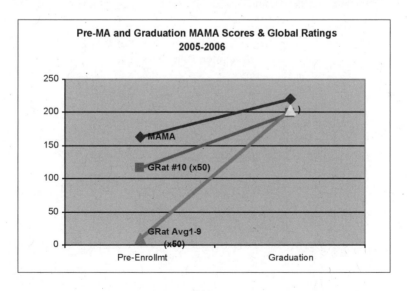

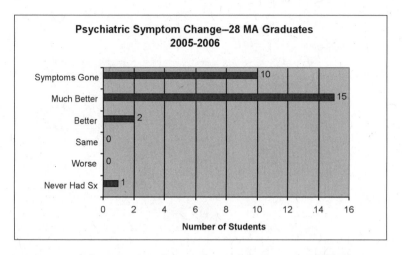

parents rated the maturity of one cohort of their sons and daughters at graduation substantially higher than other parents gauged the maturity of their cohort of students prior to enrollment. That measured difference was very unlikely to have occurred by chance (p < .00000000000002).

With maturity ratings, parental ratings of their sons' and daughters' academic and interpersonal functioning also rose. Both the average sum of the nine specific ratings of academic and interpersonal functioning (dimensions 1-9) and the average rating of "overall happiness" rose dramatically. These shifts in aggregate functional ratings correlated strongly (coefficients were +0.83 and +0.86) with the change in maturity ratings.

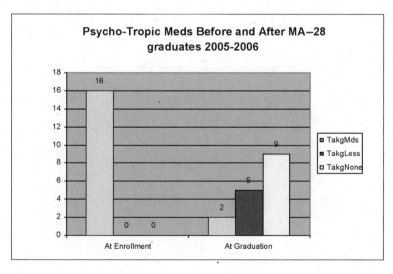

Moreover, as MAMA-p maturity ratings rose and global functioning improved, parents of graduates noted that most psychological symptoms had radically improved or vanished. Parents who had noted multiple symptoms at enrollment in twenty-seven of their children reported at graduation that all symptoms were "gone" in ten students; "much better" in fifteen students; and "better" in two. None reported a son's or daughter's symptoms as "the same" or "worse."

In almost all of the sixteen students (among these twenty-eight students) who had been prescribed psychotropic medications prior to enrollment, as symptoms abated, their need for those medications also diminished or vanished. Among those sixteen graduates, only two (13%) remained on the same doses of psychotropic medications; five (31%) were taking less medication; and nine (56%) had already been taken off all psychotropic medication.

These numbers are small, the instrument (prototype MAMA-p) still blunt, and not too much should be made of these data, except that they are unsubtle and suggestive. The point is that, albeit preliminary, these data support the immaturity hypothesis in a tentative way. They suggest just what the the immaturity hypothesis predicts: that as troubled immature teenagers become psychologically more grown up, they perform better at both academic and interpersonal tasks, their symptoms abate, and (for that reason) those medications that were aimed at relieving those symptoms (e.g., depressed mood, or anxiety, or poor concentration) tend to become less necessary or unnecessary. In this small cohort, this is precisely what happened.

Letters—Karen, Nina, Mona and Phil

In the absence, as yet, of a definitive test of the immaturity hypothesis, there is one other source of relevant observations: the voices of actual parents whose adolescent children have made the transition from much troubled to untroubled, from relatively immature (as I would have it) to mature teenagers. I can make this discussion more real if I publish these parental voices of experience in their own voices, using their own words, to describe their experience—and not rely solely upon composite case reports, as I have done in the cases of Helen and David.

Months ago, to this end—as I wrote the first draft of this book—I corresponded with selected parents of some of the teenagers who had passed through Montana Academy.[11] I explained that in the final pages of this book I hoped to publish their observations. These were anything but a random sample. I asked parents of students that I thought had managed very successfully to grow up. I did not solicit letters from parents of students whom we had failed to help to accomplish this transformation. There are no shortage of such failures, over the years. But in these unhappy cases the later descriptions of continued global failure were not much different from the initial complaints, which I have already described. In choosing sons and daughters who did change, who left the ranch and went on to lives that were much changed from their pre-enrollment trajectories, I was asking parents to describe what it was that they thought had changed during the months those sons and daughters had lived at the ranch, and afterward.

A number of those parents replied, generous with their time and their effort. They wrote to me about their children and about themselves, both with frankness and eloquence. As you will see, some of their children—writing spontaneously, just to keep in touch—also made eloquent contributions. What follows, then, are a few accounts, which I have edited only to prevent identification. If a parent mentioned Cleveland, or a son's name, or a sibling's very specific particulars, I changed all of those details. You can bet that, if in these letters I say that the name of a daughter was "Karen," it was not, in fact, Karen. That said, altered only in these minor ways, what follows are verbatim comments from parents of teenagers who have overcome obstacles to their maturation—and have grown up. With permission, I also have included notes from a couple of these young people, so that you can hear their voices, too. I add introductory or editorial comment, and I have included some disguised but also genuine progress notes, written at the time, sometimes in exasperation, so as to provide you with a telling portraits. Apart from these notes, these are not my clinical accounts. They belong to wonderful, real parents, whose splendid, real sons and daughters lived for a brief time on a remote ranch in northwest Montana.

Karen

Our daughter Karen enrolled at Montana Academy at fifteen. [12] She was essentially a 130-pound, five-foot-tall teenager with raging hormones. She had been diagnosed with bipolar disorder and oppositional defiant disorder and was very heavily medicated. She oscillated between depres-

sion and rage as she tried to cope with a world that expected the maturity of a high-school student while she was in fact still in the stage where "mine" and "no" were her favorite words.

Karen comes from a family where both parents have graduate degrees. Her brother, two years her senior, is very popular and a very good student. Home life was difficult for Karen and, consequently, for us. We basically operated on the "pick your battles" style of parenting. We picked very few battles and generally surrendered. Karen modified our behavior to the point that she ruled, and we lived in fear.

We had sent her brother to boarding school, in part to spare him the turmoil of our home. Karen had always seemed to be quite bright, but was a very poor student, paid little or no attention to her teachers, and had few friends. She did not keep the friends she made, as other kids got very tired of her constant demands to be in control, and each successive group of friends she made were on a lower rung of the scale. We sent her to boarding school, starting in eighth grade, in hopes that smaller class sizes, more attention from teachers, and a new group of friends, who were more academically motivated, would change things.

But Karen continued to do poorly in school, sought out "losers," and was difficult in the dorms. She cut herself on several occasions and entered therapy. Her psychiatrist was treating her for oppositional defiant disorder and bipolar disorder. The private school did not allow her to return after eighth grade. She began her freshman year at the local public high school. Her behavior was so defiant at home that we called the police on several occasions. Twice she moved out to live with friends (whose parents we knew and trusted), but neither family could cope. We arranged for her to live with foster parents in a temporary situation while we looked for alternatives—and found Montana Academy.

There, Karen worked her way through the program slowly, but with consistent progress. Her medications were gradually reduced and discontinued. It was determined that her problems were developmental, not medical. She was treated like a two-year-old (in terms of decision-making, choices, freedom, supervision, and so forth) while being taught how a three-year-old would behave. This process continued until she was acting her age. Her academic work improved dramatically, as did her behavior. Though it was not always easy sailing—and, in fact, our first few visits (to the ranch) were quite painful, and her first visit home so rough

*that she was set back a step in the program—the improvement was little
less than miraculous. She graduated after 20 months.*

*Karen then went to a very fine girls' boarding school, starting as
a sophomore, though by age and years of school she would have been a
junior. She did quite well, and was asked to be a dorm proctor her junior
year. She is consistently on the honor roll in her school, and she is highly
respected by students and faculty. It's a joy to be with her. She is now
starting senior year, looking at some good colleges. She accepts the rules
of her school and behaves beautifully. She is great with us, and considers us among her best friends, as well as parents. This past summer she
and a friend from home made a trip to the ranch to see faculty—and,
in a way, to show them how well she was doing. We are very proud of
our daughter, and shudder to think where she might be now, had she not
spent those months at the ranch.*

Nina

In my impatience with contemporary diagnosis and *DSM-IV*, I did not
mean to imply that mental illness is not a problem for some teenagers.
Surely it can be a serious problem. Mental illness does not reduce
to immaturity, of course, even if immaturity often is mistaken for
mental illness. Like other intrinsic obstacles, mental illnesses can block
development and produce immaturity. Depression, in particular, remains
a common source of adolescent morbidity and mortality.

To illustrate this connection, Nina's father describes a girl struggling
with a very serious depression, which was one pole in a flip-flop course
of (bipolar) mood instability. Nina came to the ranch after a disabling
mood collapse, which had made it impossible for her to go on in her
demanding prep school. Seven years later, well after she left the ranch, her
father answered my e-mail question in this thoughtful way:

*At age fourteen our daughter Nina began to exhibit symptoms that
we tended to hear about secondhand: crying, long periods of silence in
school, confiding to a counselor that she was hearing voices, an interest
in dying. At home, she was very focused on herself, and, as we learned
later, cutting herself. Yet she continued to do well in school, performed at
high levels in her extracurricular activities, and presented to others as a
happy, high-functioning, bright teenager.*

She was evaluated by a psychiatrist, and the diagnosis was that she suffered from a "false self," where she felt one thing (unworthiness) while presenting a happy face, which those around her felt was the real Nina. At this time she started therapy two times per week and taking medications for anxiety, bipolar disorder, and obsessive-compulsive disorder.

By sixteen, however, it was clear that not only was she not better, she was getting worse. We were so concerned about her that her mother began sleeping with her at night. She dropped herself out of high school, unable to function. The school also reported that she appeared to be cutting herself.

After discussions with her therapist, it was agreed that Nina needed more intense treatment, and she was sent to the ranch. She agreed to this, but as soon as she arrived, she immediately rejected Montana Academy and asked to come home. After one month, in a meeting with her psychiatrist and her parents, she was told that her parents had decided this was the best place—and she had to commit.

After that meeting she started to improve, accepting the role of patient, and learning to take ownership of her behavior and illness. After a number of months at MA, she seemed ready to come home to finish high school. After completing her senior year, she went off to a four-year college while attending weekly therapy. As parents, we were both thrilled to see her improvement and very apprehensive about letting her go far away. However, we felt that she had survived in Montana, that in effect we had done what we could for her, and the rest was up to her. We fervently believe that the ranch experience saved Nina's life.

Six years after Montana Academy, Nina graduated from Oberlin, and, to us, has become someone much more comfortable with herself, very good about dealing with emotional issues in non-confrontational ways, able to state what she wants and needs, and in control of her own illness and responsible for its treatment. She is able to face the past with honesty. She needed to be able to acknowledge and confront who she is and to accept responsibility for her actions and emotions. It was at the ranch that this became clear to her, aiding in the transition to becoming a well-functioning adult.

Mona

Some of the most telling accounts of maturation come from teenagers themselves. So often what changes, from their point of view, is the way other people appear. An inner shift changes what is appealing in another person. This shows up in new kinds of relationships, different in character from what went before. The new emotional tone and structure feel auspicious. Mona, at this writing, was a sophomore at one of the Ivy League colleges. She described her collegiate experience this way:

Life is really great. Last year I got straight A's, and I received both dean's list and Excellent Achievement honors. This means I'm eligible for fellowships I am starting to look into. This semester I'm taking linguistics, Italian, ancient government theory (Thucydides, Aristotle, Plato), ballet, and modern dance. It's a load, but I love it all.

I'm not sure if I told you about my boyfriend before. We went to school together in gradeschool. We were not really friends back then, but we sort of always casually got along. We started dating three weeks before I left for college last summer, and decided to try long distance—out on a limb. We made it through the year and have become very serious. He's twenty, and a junior at Amherst. This summer, we went to Mexico and drove cross-country. It's the first healthy relationship I've ever had, which made it really scary, at first—but it's wonderful.

We spent so much time together this summer that both our families now assume whenever one is there that the other one is, too. It's amazing that there's finally a man in my life whom my parents love, too. I know it's sort of cheesy, but my mom and I are still so blown away and appreciative of all this kind of stuff. We joke about it, although we both know how serious and awful it used to be.

Anyway, I'm babbling like a schoolgirl, but that's kind of how I feel. Tell me more about you, and your life.

This remarkable young woman now feels happy "like a schoolgirl," but does not behave or think like one. Her account suggests a disciplined student, a close friend, a romantic partner in a healthy relationship. Without strain she includes her mother in her life whom she once banished. Having escaped from self-absorption she writes now to an aging shrink with a warm consideration—wanting to know about "you, and your life." No longer a patient, she offers the considerate curiosity of a friend.

In response to my e-mail, her mother replied:
During the months after Mona arrived at Montana Academy all

she could think about or talk about was getting out of there. She only wanted to return to the dysfunctional behavior that had motivated us to enroll her. She negotiated hard for immediate release. When we refused, she threatened to release herself on her eighteenth birthday (less than a year away) and then to "divorce" us.

As the months passed, however, Mona gradually became amenable to reason. She came to understand that, if she left the ranch early, she would have to solve the problem of high school graduation some other way. She became interested in the prospect of college, studied for the SAT, and worked on her applications. Two months before her eighteenth birthday, she informed us that she had decided to stay at the ranch for another four months, so that she could graduate from high school and apply to college, which she did.

In addition to her time in Montana, our daughter had been living away from home for most of the preceding year. So it was with great joy and great anxiety that we welcomed her home again. We worried that she was still fragile and unpredictable, and vulnerable to former "friends" who did not have her interests at heart. She recognized our concerns and empathized with us. What an amazing development this was! She acknowledged that she had given us good reason to worry about her and that, although she knew she was different now, we could not know that. Therefore, she voluntarily curtailed her own activities—normal activities for a normal eighteen-year-old—in order to make the transition easier for us.

Our daughter lived at home with us for eight months before going off to college. During that time, Mona did volunteer work in a nursing home and then took a summer job working with kids. She kept her word to live within our comfort zone and never pressured us to give her additional liberties. Nonetheless, we worried about her. She was still troubled emotionally by some of her earlier problems. The important thing was that she was determined now to grow beyond her problems and trusted us to help her do that.

Mona has now completed several years of college. She is an excellent student and a lovely young woman—the wonderful person we always knew she would be. She is still growing and maturing—aren't we all?

Composed in such straightforward English, Mona's mother describes a teenager's rapid maturation: a daughter who becomes amenable to reason, the emergence of a plausible future (college), a new capacity to delay gratification and to carry out a plan (applications, SATs), and a young lady's new and "amazing" capacity to "recognize our concerns and empathize" with adults. Mona now could act on a perception of her own inner experience as separate from the inner experience of her parents, so that, although she knew she was different now (from the way she was in the past), she also recognized that her parents could not be expected to be sure of that yet. Then, with empathy and new consideration, Mona managed without incident to live with her parents over many months. This may not sound like much, but both Mona and her parents were impressed that they could do it.

At the time this letter was written, years later, Mona now takes in stride the academic demands of a first-rate college. She has grown up enough to sustain and enjoy an exciting young-adult relationship. She makes it all sound easy. Teenagers do make it sound easy, once they manage to grow up.

Phil

Some years after his graduation from the ranch, Phil's father wrote a thoughtful reply to my e-mail. To do his transformation full justice, I am going to record my contemporaneous account, in progress notes, of Phil's arrival at Montana Academy and early struggle. I begin with a brief review of Phil's history.

At sixteen, Phil had just been expelled from a boarding school in Seattle. We learned from other clinicians and from his parents that Phil had been sent to the ranch because he would not follow rules, would not (could not?) get to class on time, and would not (could not?) keep his room clean. At his demanding prep school, Phil could not get along with classmates. He was expelled after a nasty altercation.

These, however, were not his first school difficulties. Phil had a history of learning troubles. These seemed related to soft neurological signs, and in second grade he had been diagnosed with ADHD, and prescribed stimulants to help him focus his attention. However, they failed entirely to remedy his impulsiveness and disorganization.

Phil also had sustained a skull fracture in a motor-vehicle accident at ten. He had been riding a four-wheel ATV and rode off the path into a tree. For days he was unconscious, and he was not expected to live. Afterward, noting his god-awful handwriting, left-right confusion, poor concentration, and irascible mood, a neurologist suggested a post-traumatic (post-concussion) syndrome. Moreover, psychiatrists prescribed two antidepressants to help him with deflated mood and impulsiveness. School officials noted Phil was "oppositional," had a "bad temper," and demonstrated "poor social skills." They said Phil was obnoxiously "entitled" and "lacked empathy." Weeks before his expulsion, his grades had gone into free fall.

This was Phil's second expulsion. At his prior school his bomb threat, scrawled in the margin of his algebra homework, seemed unforgivably tactless after the Columbine tragedy. School officials felt that they had no choice but to ask Phil to leave. There was no clear history of drug or alcohol abuse.

Phil arrived at Montana Academy with this *DSM-IV* profile:

I	Conduct Disorder
	Attention Deficit Hyperactive Disorder—
	Combined Type
	Oppositional Defiant Disorder
II	No Diagnosis
III	S/P Head Trauma
	Post-traumatic (neurological) Syndrome

My treatment summaries record a gradually transformed relationship. Phil and I did not start off well. It is uncommon for me to dislike a teenager. I all but always can find something to love, or at least to like. But at first this took some doing. Some of my staff think my progress notes are too frank, but, particularly when it comes to description of the psychology and behavior of teenagers, I have come to value straightforward prose.

At One Month

Just a note to record the continuation of the medications Phil arrived with: Depakote 250 bid; Zoloft 75 mg qAM; Adderall 20 mg qAM, L-Carnitine 500 mg bid; and Tofranil PM 150 mg at dinner. Phil has not done very well. He is convinced he doesn't need to be here. He is rude with staff and fellow students, and he is a bully. He is an angry, hostile boy, who is entitled and seems very spoiled. Review of the record reveals a skull fracture at 10, which might have something to do with his perseveration. He argues about everything and anything!

At Two Months

This sullen, hostile, ungracious young man was on the point of admission to [a locked hospital adolescent unit] because of his insubordination, i.e., his telling staff, "You can't make me do this." I had to make it plain that I cannot have a student on the ranch who won't take basic instructions. I told him that if he persists he will need a locked unit. He is afraid of this, I am glad to say.

Phil finds life at the ranch "not fun" and "just plain BS." He is rude with teachers, rude with his team-leader, rude with his doctor, and rude with his parents—as ugly an arrogant narcissism as we have seen. His insulting behavior with his parents prompted me to urge them to hang up the phone if they heard any more of it. Phil orders them to send this or that from his home, and tells them they are "stupid jerks" if they hesitate. Phil's performance in school has been mediocre for much the same reason. He is unpopular with other students, who don't much like his manners, either. With some vulnerable students, Phil has been cruel, e.g., calling one homesick young man "throw-away boy," saying the boy was "a nobody" because he "doesn't even know who his mother was."

The peculiarity of his clinical picture results not so much from Phil's arrogance, which is not all that unusual, I suppose, but from his tearfulness. The two would not seem to go together. Phil is capable of saying "screw you" to his team-leader while weeping bitter tears. He does the same with his parents. In fact, he does much the same whenever he is told No. He responds in an angry, impulsive, and verbally incontinent way, quick to insult people who do not deserve to be addressed in this fashion, e.g., his therapist or his parents.

Yet he is also tearful. He seems unable to stop crying, and, as best I can tell, the tears are tears of frustration and narcissistic injury. That is, he is actually wounded when told No. He can barely believe his ears. Certainly he feels wounded when criticized. He fights and bites and kicks to avoid the humiliation (to his grand omnipotence, presumably) of someone giving him an order and making it stick. His argumentativeness is epic. He contradicts everything, so if his therapist says, "You did this well," he answers, "No, I didn't." If told he needs to shape up, he argues, "No, I don't." He is an infuriating, obnoxious young man, who provokes anger—and a wish to slap both his ears—in all who spend time with him, particularly if they have any authority.

Thus, the treatment approach is strenuous but simple-minded: to set limits, erect palpable consequences, and mean them. The prescription also includes: empathic recognition, sustained over time. This is the hard part. Of note: I have not yet changed medications, because I have not yet thought of a useful experiment. And I don't want to stress a precarious boy—not yet, anyway.

At Six Months

This week we sent Phil to a wilderness program with the help of his anguished parents, who did what needed to be done, but suffered. Phil left by escort. I awoke him myself at 4 A.M. and took him into the ranch house in the dark for a talk. Wide-eyed, he told me: "I'm scared." I explained that I thought he had made some friends who would miss him; that he had done better in school, which surprised everyone, and earned my respect. But his mean, sadistic teasing, his sneakiness, his concocting some nasty mixture to smoke, all suggested a resistance to rules and a contempt for adults, and a disrespect for other students that was more than I wanted to put up with. He had already had confrontations with me. So I needed to make it plain that I was not kidding—he was to knock it off!

I said he could come back if he wanted to, i.e., if he did well at wilderness, if his attitude suggested he could and would manage here without this kind of contempt for those around him, without his outrageous disrespect for his parents' effort to help him. He took this reasonably well, I thought, and went willingly to the truck with the escort. I hope he will think about what I said.

I have remarked elsewhere that I have come to think that "wilderness" programs can provide the literal and figurative No that very troubled, stuck teenagers often need. Many of the most successful students at Montana Academy have first been to one of those competent programs. It is difficult, I have come to think, even for a concrete and self-preoccupied teenager, to hike around the desert carrying all his belongings on his back, to struggle to start a fire without a match to cook rice and beans (or eat it cold), and not hear the clear parental message: "We are *not* going to go on like this!" As a firmly and vividly set limit, a wilderness trek is an affront to adolescent narcissism. And, oddly enough, most teenagers emerge from the field feeling proud of a demonstrated fortitude, and ready for something a little different.

At Eight Months

Back from wilderness two weeks now, Phil has managed with determination, good humor, and cheerful cooperation to sit in a study carrel during school hours; to work alone on assignments and to submit to questions and discussions with his team-leader. He has stayed constructive in therapy. His team staff complain there is still the "old Phil," so I have had to remonstrate with them that a few weeks in wilderness, while helpful, could not be expected to transform Phil into a saint. I know they are tired—and tired of his abuse. However, I can see he is trying. He can come back at the second level of privileges, having negotiated wilderness and our structured school experience. I have high hopes for him. Certainly his family has stuck it out with him and backed us up, although it made them anxious. I am glad to work with them.

All systems go. We will announce tomorrow that Phil has returned to the community. I have asked staff to make a fuss, to celebrate Phil's success.

Medication Review (eight months)

I see Phil regularly for my stock market experiential. He has been an assiduous student, a courteous young man, a constructive partner (with AS), and has shared his passion. He puts up with looking ignorant relative to AS's expertise. I see no sign of depressed mood, poor self-esteem, inattention, or distracted concentration. Phil has been learning rapidly, sharing his excitement about certain Web sites as wll as his contempt for dubious aspects of American government.

All of this leads me to think a medication-free trial I talked with his parents about is warranted. I have been slow to follow up. He still takes Concerta, Zoloft, and Tofranil, but we agreed to taper and discontinue them. I see no evidence they are needed anymore. I will be particularly ginger about removing Concerta. By the time we stop them all, we will be at the middle of the academic block—a good point to test Phil's attention and concentration. Steady as we go.

At the ranch many of us on staff provide "experiential" courses, which are practical, rather than academic, not usually for school credit, and meant to be fun. These provide a chance for students to pursue for a few months a line of enquiry or an avocation they hope to find engaging.

Moreover, these scheduled encounters permit students to meet in small groups (often three to five students) with a member of the staff they might not otherwise encounter or get to know well. I offered a course in corporate economics and the stock market because this is peculiar psychiatric institution has long been of academic interest to me. Phil, who had become enthralled with Che Guevara, could not resist.

At Nine Months

For my stock-market tutorial, Phil follows the news on sophisticated alternative Web sites. He understands the underside of the Arab-Israeli quagmire, he thinks in interesting ways about Marxism, and he idealizes Che and Ho. He reads books on the Vietnam War and the Cuban Revolution. He thinks about social justice, about anarchy and anarchists, and is interested in government structure. He is beginning to anticipate college—picturing a major in chemistry or government, maybe leaning now toward the latter.

Phil has come to the painful recognition of his father's unhappiness in his career—his sense that his father is skilled but not fulfilled in the business he entered and has done well in. Phil realizes that if his father had it to do over again, he might have gone to medical school.

I am liking Phil very much. He is somewhat standoffish and shy, not convinced that he wants a close relationship with an older bear of an adult like me, but he can't resist having a go, anyway. His relations with his parents have improved. He is off all medications now, and I have yet to see any clinical difference in these first months. This drug-free trial is a success, so far, and Phil seems relieved at this.

Phil shapes up to be a bright, promising, spunky, tough young man, capable of leadership, capable of idiosyncratic independent thinking, and able to ask for a special course from me (the stock-market tutorial) as well as to follow through with reading independently, without my having to chase him around. He is simply interested, engaged, ready to learn. He has become a pleasure to teach.

At Ten Months

Phil is doing well. He has become quite an exemplary student, much to his own surprise—and to the surprise of others. His current grade in U.S. history is 94 percent and he has 89 percent in Spanish. Moreover, he has become a courteous, cheerful student. Who knew?

His social behavior has also improved, although recently Jason re-fused to take him to play soccer in town because he trips and plays in an aggressive, mean-spirited way. On the other hand, he took Jason's criticism with good humor. There were no tantrums, no snit or cussing. One sees Phil walking without his jacket—without the self-conscious worry about his body one used to sense that he felt. Phil is coming along.

Steady as we go.

As Phil's academic horsepower became more obvious and his academic performance earned the admiration of his teachers, Phil became increasingly excited about the prospect of college. His reading became voracious. He worried about the injustices of the world, and he tried to make sense of some of the major ideas, over the past centuries, about how justice could be achieved. You might also guess that, as Phil became less oppositional himself, he would become the more intrigued with those, like Che, who made defiance both glamorous and tragic.

When he graduated and left the ranch, Phil went home to have another go at one of the fine prep schools that previously had expelled him. During that last year of high school there he made a striking academic success. He excelled on the SATs. He wrote witty essays to apply to a number of first-rate colleges and he was offered admission to: Lewis & Clark, Wesleyan, Oberlin, and the University of Texas at Austin, and was wait-listed at Brown.

Here's the father's account, which covers some of the same ground:

I suspect that most parents deliver their child to the ranch with similar feelings of fear, helplessness and desperation. Fay and I would be no exception. Sending Phil off to a wilderness program and then on to Montana Academy were the hardest things we ever had to do. It seemed to us that things with Phil were out of control—we had little influence over him, and he had little control of himself. He had been asked to leave two schools because of impulsive and threatening behavior. At home he was angry, defiant, and verbally abusive. Relationships with both peers and family were deteriorating. Phil was argumentative and dismissive of authority. He had a sense of entitlement and was unable to take responsibility for his actions.

The house was in turmoil as Fay and I tried everything we could think of, resulting of course in undefined boundaries and an inconsistent approach to parenting. Things became more and more dysfunctional, and everybody suffered, including Phil's sister.

As Phil's father describes this broadly based debacle, I probably no longer need to point out that Phil's original difficulties amounted to a global breakdown—as did the difficulties of every one of these former students. Phil struggled with persistent, repetitive failures across the board, which extended to his performance at school, sour relationships with all adults, and social failures with other teenagers. In his enraged, tearful, defiant, arrogant way Phil was profoundly unhappy.

While Phil was at Montana Academy, Fay and I experienced a sense of relief (perhaps in part because we wouldn't have to deal with him daily). For a time we remained fearful that the Montana experience would not be successful and that something terrible and unmanageable could be wrong with Phil—but we became hopeful. We also became determined to trust—and to follow recommendations without deviation.

A pattern arose: just as Phil seemed to be making progress, he would experience a setback. It was an emotional roller coaster for us, as his parents. We would measure a good or bad week by how he communicated during our weekly call. At one point, when things with Phil were not progressing, the ranch therapist proposed that he attend another wilderness program. He was very angry about this, but the experience seemed to be a turning point. When Phil returned to the ranch he became more compliant and respectful. Appointed and elected leadership opportunities lifted his sense of self-worth. We became cautiously optimistic about Phil.

Fay and I also learned from you and others how to set and stick with firm boundaries. Our parenting got more consistent, and, as we worked on our parenting flaws, Phil's "approach" became more reflective and age-appropriate. By the time Phil graduated, Fay and I were less fearful. Some of our concerns were of the more typical variety: How would Phil handle college? But we were also concerned that the good things he had learned might quickly be forgotten.

Now, over two years later, Phil continues to do well. Because he graduated from high school a year early, Phil had the opportunity to study for a year in Rome, and he is now a sophomore at college. He is enjoying himself and making good grades.

Phil is far from perfect, but we see little evidence of entitlement, impulsivity, or threatening behavior. He occasionally loses his temper in a stressful situation, but it is rare. He is open and truthful with us, and he and his sister are close. Certainly family arguments can arise, but issues are resolved with relative calm and respectfulness. Phil's old "flawed approach" is apparently well under control, if not exorcised; issues or problems that arise are typically considered and resolved in a fairly logical fashion, rather than in an age-inappropriate manner. Phil is still shy. This concerns Fay and me. But it seems a relatively minor thing compared to past worries.

In summary, I know there has been a successful shift in maturation, but I find it difficult to express what it looks like. Simply stated, it looks "normal." Except for shyness or social anxiety, Phil handles himself in an age-appropriate manner—in a "normal" and typical way. He no longer needs to be "handled," but is responsible for himself, accountable for his decisions. He can be counted on to reflect before acting and generally to make good decisions—at least as well as any typical nineteen-year-old.

It is a little easier to express how the shift in maturation feels to a parent—at least to this one. It feels absolutely great—the feeling of getting a whole new life and a fresh start. I'm sure you've heard the expression that a parent is only as happy as his or her most unhappy child. Fay and I have high hopes for Phil and for his future happiness—much higher than we did before.

At this writing, more than four years after Phil left the ranch, he is a college senior, and he continues to do well. He has not needed medication since we stopped it all, years ago, and he no longer warrants a psychiatric diagnosis that might imply a need for medication. As his father says, it is not that Phil has become perfect, but he now looks normal.

Actually, he looks better than normal. And I must conclude, after watching this result in other students, again and again, that Phil looks normal because he *is* normal. That is, his maturation, which finally caught up with others his age, simply solved the disabling problems that once alarmed his parents and kept them from sound sleep. He now has turned to the normal tasks of late adolescence: a college education, political passions, friends and girlfriends, and a career.

Phil no longer needs anyone to speak for him, either. Some months ago, Phil sent me a brief e-mail, perhaps on a whim. I was delighted with it. His note says it all:

> *Dear Dr. McKinnon:*
>
> *It's Phil, typing from my father's office. I'm sorry that I haven't been in touch. I wanted to let you know how I'm doing, and to check up on things at MA. This summer I am employed as a file clerk at my dad's office, doing some pretty boring stuff. I took a class in cognitive psychology at UW over the summer, and I found it very interesting. I return to Oberlin for my sophomore year in early September, and I am looking forward to another great year. I am thinking about majoring in history, although I am also finding psychology and philosophy very interesting.*
>
> *College is fun. For the most part I do a good job of balancing work and leisure. I am happy with all the friends I've made—some college buddies are coming to visit next week. It should be a good time. For fun these days I listen to loud, abrasive music and hang out with my wonderful sister. I am a vegan—practicing a cruelty-free lifestyle with minimal environmental impact is something I take very seriously. I also enjoy bugging my parents with lively and hilarious vegan commentary.*
>
> *How are things at the ranch? Drop me a line and let me know what's up. I hope everything is going well for both of you and with the school.*
> *Sincerely,*
> *Phil*

A Normal Prognosis

These young people have grown up. The shift in their way of making sense of the world seems an unsubtle change, hard to miss. It is no longer all about Mona or Rob. Phil is amused by what his parents think and feel, and he has no need to insist that they agree with him. All of them have good friends, and there are few signs of tantrums or mean-spirited retaliation. Karen has plans, goals, and self-discipline. Nina, despite her struggles, takes "responsibility for her own illness." All of these young people can think abstractly, can generalize across contexts—in all the realms of adolescence, starting with the classroom but also including conversations at the dinner table. Phil's wry humor embraces the ironies of his own behavior, and Mona wonders how an aging shrink is getting along.

All of these young people seem now to be launched, heading for college or finishing college, living effectively on their own, employed or taking their studies seriously. They have friends, lovers, important relationships.

Yet they have not put their parents out of jobs, either. Clearly these parents and sons and daughters are very much involved with one another. This is as you might expect, for with troubled teenagers, maturation is a cure, in one way; but in another way, growing up merely returns to parents a normal teenager, soon to be an adult. There continues to be much for parents to do. Neither all the fun nor all the problems are over. As we left him, Phil's college friends were about to arrive at his parents' home.

There will be other arrivals, other big events, other hard decisions, other excitements, other reasons for sadness, other problems to solve. Mona will soon need help with a wedding. Phil is never going to be a bore. Just because they have grown up doesn't mean life will be a snap for any of them, either. This is as it should be.

For the prognosis is no worse, but no better, than for other normal young people. All those whose words I have quoted or whose parents have written eloquently about them—Karen and Mona, Nina and Phil—now have adult lives that lie before them, a brave new world to explore, relationships to forge, lovers to love, educations to complete, careers to pursue. There will be all that to do—no more or less than other promising young people their age who manage to mature and become competent adults. They have the world all before them where to make their way.

Ahead, there will be enthralling intimacies. Surely there will be challenges to their capacities for fidelity, tests of their commitments, marathons of work. They will not escape worry or grief. Most of them, at some point, will suffer the strains of economic exigency. But all of this is normal, expected in our children's lives. I hope they find partners to trust. I hope they manage to create marriages that they will sustain. On that foundation, if they are lucky and feeling strong, may they bring up their own fine children.

Notes

Preface

[1] Erik H. Erikson, "Eight Ages of Man," in *Childhood and Society*, 2nd ed. (New York: W.W. Norton, 1963), 247-274. Erikson published another version of this developmental staging as "The Life Cycle: Epigenesis of Identity," in *Identity, Youth and Crisis* (New York: W.W. Norton & Company, 1968).

1 Point of Departure

[1] No actual person named Pauline was in my mind when I described this fictive composite teenager. In this book, I never deliberately employ the actual name of any person, except my wife, Rosemary, and my partners, John and Carol Santa, and those whose help with this book I have acknowledged. Any reference in any of these clinical descriptions to any student or family at Montana Academy or past patient of mine, in any place or time, can only be coincidence, inasmuch as those descriptions are camouflaged, displaced, and represent a collage—and so rely upon no particular historical event or any person I have ever known.

[2] "Ex" is slang for an amphetamine derivative referred to as "ecstasy"—and so "ex" for short.

[3] Discounted relative to the full retail price an insured person would pay for those services. Medicaid is a governmental monopoly and does not pay the full charges for inpatient or outpatient treatment. Medicaid does not ask a psychiatrist what he will charge but rather announces what he will be paid. The point is that Kenny's estimate of the cost of Pauline's care surely *under*states the retail cost. This low-ball estimate was done in 1996.

[4] This adjustment corrects for Pauline's twelve-week respite from treatment on the streets of Missoula. It does not correct for the discount Medicaid grants to itself at a clinician's expense (see previous note). Medicaid's fee schedule defines what Medicaid will pay for any particular service, whether a provider likes it or not. In those days I would have billed Medicaid $85 for an hour-long session of office psychotherapy, and Medicaid would then send me $28. I had two choices: take it, or leave it. Yet this was not much of a choice, in those days. To leave it meant that I was refusing to help an indigent neighbor's teenager. For years I took it.

However, when we started a private therapeutic school we faced this choice again. This time we decided differently—for two reasons. By this time we had a payroll to meet and could not afford to discount our tuition. And by this time (see chapter 2) we had no intention of letting Medicaid's managed care reviewers bully us about our clinical decisions. I had lost all enthusiasm for accepting paltry pay for doing second-rate clinical work. This time—although Medicaid had paid for Pauline's care more than twice what we proposed to charge at that time for a year's tuition, room, and board at Montana Academy—we left it.

5   Managed care companies contort the English language in some of the ways that made Orwell cringe, so as to frame profitable "determinations" *not* to pay for my care in a diction that suggests they are acting in my patient's best interests, or on the basis of exalted medical best practices. These formulations include "medical necessity," and "least restrictive care," and movement "along the continuum of care." For example, in the act of pushing a girl out of the hospital after she has begun to respond to that level of care, these twisted locutions imply the reviewer fierce protection of a child from being unduly "restricted"—although this protective custody was the whole point. While withholding payment for a girl's care, a reviewer's locution suggests a radical medical economy, or a medical insight unavailable to the benighted doctor, who is actually responsible for the result—to avoid medically "unnecessary" care. And surely to nudge a girl to the next stop along "the continuum of care" sounds better than "giving her the cheaper care" or "throwing her out" of a hospital.

2   Global Disarray

1   Over the years we have been able to accept about one in five unhappy teenagers referred to us. Because of an application process that is strenuous for parents, we try to discourage referrals when we have insufficient space.

In that decade, for various reasons, we admitted only two students from Montana. This was only serendipity, not a reflection of relative economics. We do not enroll local teenagers. We would adopt this policy whether the ranch was in Montana or Massachusetts or Missouri. For local students who are in trouble have local friends, proximate drug connections, innebriated pals bent upon rescue—and so we reduce the risks of a runaway or an unwelcome nocturnal visit. We suggest to local parents that they will do better to take their children to more distant programs—say, in Utah or Texas. I realize this is not the conventional wisdom, and that many ignorant clinicians make a virtue of local treatment. But experience has taught that this seemingly humane idea, which aims to preserve tenuous family ties, simply makes it impossible for students and parents to call time-out from a chaotic debacle.

2   This was not the final irony. There is currently a movement among some outpatient therapists, supported by Congressman Miller from California, whose Committee on Education and Labor recently held deeply biased hearings, to close "those programs" by legislative means. No doubt there are programs that ought close. But the irony is that this expensive level of care, which insurance companies consider too costly, is sought by parents from across the nation who are willing to pay out-of-pocket for the help they think they need. These noisy opponents of residential treatment argue (see above) that this is not the "least restrictive" form of care. However, what troubled teenagers invariably do *not* need is "less restrictive" (less supervised, more lax and permissive) parenting.

3   A generation ago residential or inpatient treatment for troubled teenagers (and for adult psychiatric patients) was much more accessible. The venerable institutions where such treatment took place—the Menninger Foundation (Kansas), Chestnut Lodge and Shepherd Pratt (Maryland), Austin Riggs and McClains (Texas), Timberlawn (Texas), Mt Zion (California) and the Yale Psychiatric Institute (Connecticut)—earned and enjoyed enormous prestige. These hospitals and residential treatment centers were the venerated contexts for intensive, sustained treatment. They were rich clinical contexts for intensively training young clinicians. My older professional friends suspect, not without reason, that Montana Academy is an avatar of the YPI, where I was trained.

4   Perhaps because clients of consultants are well-educated themselves, and our staff are

educated clinicians, consultants referred to us, in our first cohort of students, very intelligent teenagers—whose testing revealed IQ scores that ranged from high-average to extraordinary. As a result, as those students did well, our classrooms became very competitive. And it began to seem a cruelty to put a demoralized, slow student into a highly competitive classroom, crowded with quick, even brilliant, classmates.

5   This is a casual listing that I collected after our first few tens of enrollments. These symptoms and signs and misbehaviors were described in parental applications. The list is not definitive, nor can I add a frequency distribution. But this would, in any event, be a meaningless artifact of our admissions criteria—and would shift as we changed those criteria. On the other hand, this casual list does suggest a striking variety in the surface symptoms that provoke worried parents to seek help.

6   Again this is a casual collection of diagnoses provided (along with parental applications) in psychiatric evaluations, psychological testing reports, and discharge summaries. A typical student's diagnostic profile included more than one *DSM-IV* "disorder."

7   Benedict Carey, "What's Wrong With a Child? Psychiatrists Often Disagree," *New York Times*, November 11, 2006, http://www.nytimes.com/2006/11/11/ health/psychology/11kids.html.

8   Gardiner Harris, "Proof Is Scant on Psychiatric Drug Mix for the Young," *New York Times*, November 23, 2006, http://www.nytimes.com/2006/11/23/ health/23kids.html.

9   Jerome Groopman, "What's Normal?," *The New Yorker*, 9 April 2007, 28-33.

3   A Flawed Approach

1   Robert Kegan *In Over Our Heads: The Mental Demands of Modern Life* (Cambridge, MA: Harvard University Press, 1994) 16-17. Although I have argued that the developmental point of view has gone out of clinical fashion in this era of managed care and the quick fix, it has not vanished entirely from contemporary scholarship. It is no accident that my first footnotes directly concerning the hypothesis of developmental delay is a reference the writings of Robert Kegan, whose two books on this subject have been profoundly influential upon our thinking about adolescent troubles—and in our development of an emotional growth curriculum for our new residential therapeutic school.

His earlier book, *The Evolving Self: Problem and Process in Human Development*, (Cambridge, MA: Harvard University Press, 1982) ought to be mentioned here, at the start, also. I recall that, early in the development of Montana Academy, which I describe briefly in chapter 2, my wife and I left town to visit an old friend in British Columbia. As we packed the car I threw in a paperback I had come across at the Harvard University Press bookshop on Harvard Square. Although I had resolved never again to buy a book with the word "self" in the title, I bought it because of the high praise on its cover from George Vaillant, a psychiatrist I long had admired. So I purchased the book on a whim, but never found time to read it—until this road trip. As we passed through Libby, Montana, heading for the border, I opened *The Evolving Self*, read the first pages in silence—and then re-read them aloud to my wife, Rosemary, and helplessly went on reading to her all the way to Nelson, BC. There I found that I was hoarse, but still I could not stop.

Kegan's brilliant synthesis of past developmental lines proved to be a great help to us and also useful in writing this book. Although these same developmental lines were very much part of my curriculum at Yale, it is impossible to exaggerate my debt to Kegan's scholarship, to his deft synthesis of delayed development.

For this reason I certainly recommend that determined parents attempt this book. But most parents and laymen probably will do better to start with less sophisticated developmental texts. As an introduction to Kegan's formulation of development and its delay, it might be well to start with his second book, *In Over Our Heads*, whose title refers to the predicament of the immature teenager. This, too, is a splendid book, and accessible. I would, with all humility, simply urge parents to read Kegan's *The Evolving Self,* and I would put down my pen, but at Montana Academy our parents confess to me that this expert synthesis is difficult, that it requires a pre-knowledge of many of the referenced texts, that they have trouble getting through it. Therefore, for the sophisticated clinician, who takes care of troubled American adolescents, such as the young people we see at Montana Academy, both of Kegan's books are immediate must-reads. For lay readers and parents coming to the psychology of human development for the first time, I would put *The Evolving Self* further down on my bibliography.

4   Thought and Time

[1] Sigmund Freud, "Introductory Lectures on Psychoanalysis," in vol. 22 of *The Standard Edition of the Complete Psychological Works of Sigmund Freud*, ed. and trans. James Strachey et al. (London: Hogwarth, 1964).

This Psychosexual developmental line, elaborated further by Anna Freud and others, is also classic:

Infant (0-2)	Oral Phase
Toddler (2-4)	Anal Phase
Preschool (4-5)	Oedipal Phase
Schoolboy/Schoolgirl	Latency
Adolescence	Adolescence

[2] Jean Piaget Jean Piaget, *The Origins of Intelligence in Children* (New York: International Universities Press, 1952). See also *The Child's Conception of the World, The Child's Conception of Physical Causality,* and *The Psychology of the Child.*

[3] Margaret S. Mahler, Fred Pine, and Anni Bergman, *The Psychological Birth of the Human Infant* (New York: Basic Books, 1975).

[4] Heinz Kohut, *Analysis of the Self: Systematic Approach to Treatment of Narcissistic Personality Disorders* (New York: International Universities Press, 1971). See also *The Restoration of the Self* (New York: International Universities Press, 1977).

[5] Lawrence Kohlberg, *Collected Papers on Moral Development and Moral Education* (Cambridge, MA: Center for Moral Education, 1973). See also, Robert Kegan's essay, "The Evolution of of Moral Meaning-Making," in *The Evolving Self*, op. cit. (chapter 3, note 1), 46-72.

[6] Erik H. Erikson, *Childhood and Society*, op. cit. (chapter 1, note 1).

[7] Robert Kegan, *op. cit.* (chapter 3, note 1).

[8] Immanuel Kant, *Critique of Pure Reason*, ed. and trans. Paul Guyer and Allen W. Wood (New York: Cambridge University Press, 1999).

[9] Jean Piaget, *o.p cit.*, (note 2).

[10] With all due respect to Piaget, I have simplified his terms. There are probably other reasons why parents have trouble reading Piaget, but one of those reasons is that his diction is difficult. In his original (translated), Piaget refers to these stages: sensorimotor, preoperational, concrete operations, and formal operations (early and late). I have altered this rubric to suit the diction of my own way of explaining these stages. I hope this helps. Purists will prefer to read about this in the original. See note (above) under this chapter for references.

[11] These bracketed terms, matching Piagetian stages, are from Robert Kegan, *The Evolving*

Self, op. cit. (chapter 3, note 1).

[12] Robert Kegan, *The Evolving Self, op. cit.*

[13] These ("accomodation" and "assimilation") are Piaget's terms, for which he provides precise definitions. Those who wish to follow his description of the way a child's experience gets integrated into a child's developing psychology should refer directly to Piaget's accounts of a child's cognitive development, see note 2.

[14] Perhaps children think it is sad, too. This might explain the exhilaration among schoolboys and schoolgirls at Harry Potter's return to this enchanted realm. After all, a two-year-old would feel none of that exhilaration, inasmuch as she would not know the difference—she inhabits that magical world, and no other, every day. For her there can be no revelation, no joke. But ten-year–olds *love* it—and explain the difference on the basis of a "spell" that a two-year-old doesn't need.

[15] See Robert Kegan, "The Unrecognized Genius of Jean Piaget," in *The Evolving Self, op. cit.* (chapter 3, note 1), 38-39.

[16] See Robert Kegan, "The Hidden Curriculum of Youth," in *In Over Our Heads, op. cit.* (chapter 3, note 1), 28-33.

[17] I will omit further discussion of adult cognitive achievements. Although teenagers tend to be skeptical about this, it is something of a relief to know that cognitive and emotional development surpass adolescent ways of making sense of the world. To explore "Fourth Order" or "Systems/Complex" thinking, which Kegan thinks of particular relevance to marriage and parenting, see see "The Mental Demand of Private Life: Parenting and Partnership," which is Part II of his *In Over Our Heads, op. cit.*, 73-136.

[18] Plato, *The Republic*, 1.

[19] Elkhonon Goldberg, *The Executive Brain: The Frontal Lobes and the Civilized Mind* (New York: Oxford University Press, 2001).

[20] To hold two contexts *simultaneously* in mind, so that their relationship can be discerned, is what Robert Kegan calls "cross-contextual" thinking, the radical cognitive achievement of adolescence.

[21] See prior note—this is, again, cross-contextual or cross-categorical thinking.

5 Me, Myself,…and You

[1] I will hyphenate "self-ishness" and "self-ish" to emphasize a normal childhood preoccupation with I, me, and mine—and distinguish this normal self-referential thinking from "selfishness," to which we give a pejorative connotation when we speak of an older child or teenager or adult who persists in this childishness.

[2] Heinz Kohut, who wrote about this partly-separate-but still-connected relationship, calls this a "part-object" relationship. I choose to employ a different term, because in English this talk of "objects" resists common sense. A mother is not an "object" in any familiar sense of either word. A "puppet" relationship, in constrast, is readily understood—both by mothers and by kids. It has the same connotation Kohut intended—a seemingly-separate *other* person who gets treated as an extension of *self*.

[3] This image—of a crawling child or toddler leaving the kitchen, achieving a few feet of separation, literally and figuratively—must stand for a much more complex, much more-protracted process by which toddlers accommodate and assimilate the psychological concept of (partial) distinctness, of (tentative) separation between *self* and *other*—in a psychological differentiation Margaret Mahler described in her classic study *The Psychological Birth of the Human Infant*. In her book and papers she coined elegant terms for the substages of this separation-individuation. All parents should read this

book, but we do not need to rehearse the details of this process, inasmuch as this book is not about infants or toddlers. Yet we need a name for the relationship toddlers achieve with their mothers—in which, to him, she remains an extension of himself, partly separate and partly still attached. I will call this a *puppet relationship.*

4   Puppet relationships are first achieved by toddlers, but, as we demonstrate in chapter 6, they remain ubiquitous at all later stages, too: between friends, between a child and parent, husbands and wives, students and teachers, employers and employees, officers and non-commisioned officers, doctors and patients—everywhere that human beings relate closely to one another.

5   This conception—of differentiation of self from other as a sequence of stages in which the maturing person steps out of a prior self-other fusion, pruning away encumbrances from self and creating (in what has been pushed away) a new kind of *other*—is the essential movement in Kegan's complex, brilliant synthesis, *The Evolving Self.* This is not an easy book. But it is splendid, and it represents a more subtle and precise account of developmental lines that, in this brief chapter, I have only sketched.

6   This chalkboard rehearses a moral developmental line described by Lawrence Kohlberg, *op. cit.* (chapter 4, note 5).

6   Gear Shift & Guitar

1   In framing these composite sketches of the broad stages of development, I have relied upon Erik Erikson and Robert Kegan. Many will find familiar Erikson's eight psychosocial stages of the human life cycle. Albeit less well known, Kegan's summary of stages is wise. In my own summary I use Erikson's developmental crises—*trust, autonomy, initiative, industry, and identity*—and Kegan's constructive-developmental framework to make sense of the evolution of the "self." Kegan's corresponding stages are *incorporative, impulsive, imperial, interpersonal,* and *institutional.*

2   Kegan, *The Evolving Self, op. cit.* (chapter 3, note 1)—emphasis added.

3   Jean Piaget's term for the infant's cognitive mode.

4   *The Evolving Self, op. cit.* (chapter 3, note 1).

5   Again, Erikson's leitmotif from the first crisis—trust vs mistrust.

6   Erikson thought that a child's salutary experience of trust, during her infancy, provided the basis for a later readiness for faith—and considered organized religion to be the institutional support for this universal human experience in adult life. Those who find this idea intriguing may wish to consider James W. Fowler (1981) *Stages of Faith: The Psychology of Human Development and the Quest for Meaning,* HarperSanFrancisco, 1995.

7   Kegan, *The Evolving Self, op. cit.*

8   Selma Fraiberg, *The Magic Years,* Charles Scribner's Sons, New York.

9   Erikson describes the Oedipal dilemma as a tension between a wish to take *initiative* at the risk, in defeated a beloved rival, that a child may become inhibited by *guilt.*

10   When we touch upon limit-setting (chapter 9) and its role in prodding children and teenagers to grow up, I will remind you that after the exile, the Angel Michael guards the gate back to Eden with a flaming sword whose clear meaning is No.

11   Again, this diction—calling attention to a child's emergence from "embeddedness" in the self-object world of the prior developmental stage—is Kegan's way of framing psychological development.

12   Again, Kegan's term, *The Evolving Self, op. cit.* (chapter 3, note 1).

13   Again, for Erikson the adolescent crisis concerns the achievement (or failure to achieve)

a firm sense of *identity*.

[14] Anna Freud, "Adolescence," in vol. 5 of *The Writings of Anna Freud* (New York: International Universities Press, 1958).

[15] Erikson, *op. cit.* (chapter 1, note 1).

[16] Kegan, *op. cit.* (chapter 3, note 1).

[17] Again, Kegan's phrase, *op. cit.*

[18] This parting of ways often is ephemeral. Shortly after marriage many husbands return to fraternal orders, men-only clubs, where wives are not welcome to follow.

[19] Seamus Heaney, *Open Ground: Selected Poems 1966-1996* (Farrar, Straus and Giroux, 1999).

7   Delay

[1] The expected span of time is, of course, a problem, because the normal age for developmental milestones, psychological or physiological, varies a good deal—from milestone to milestone, and from child to child. This variability in the normal course of maturation makes a definition of *immaturity* problematic, too. In practice, parents and clinicians conclude there is a problem when delay becomes a problem, as it does if the delay becomes extreme or, particularly if in modern societies, teenagers have obvious difficulties handling privileges, prerogatives, and responsibilities that, as a function of age and stage, they are given. It is often a disparity between what is socially or personally expected (within a family), on the one hand, and, on the other hand, what a teenager proves capable of delivering that makes relative immaturity a problem that attracts adult concern.

[2] I list these elements separately because parents regularly complain separately about them: self-preoccupation, self-important pushiness, lack of empathy, and lack of any altruistic moral reasoning.

8   Obstacles

[1] Daniel Siegel, *The Developing Mind*, (New York: Guilford Press, 1999), 20.

[2] Ibid, 21.

[3] I call this adult influence "parental," even though I realize that not all parental guidance, not all of the needed apt experience, is provided or managed or choreographed by biological mothers and fathers. In this sense, grandparents, teachers, coaches, therapists and dance instructors provide parenting. And of course adoptive parents are parents. Later in this chapter I will define more precisely what constitutes that needed, apt experience, which "parents," defined in this broader sense, preside over.

[4] Daniel Siegel, *op. cit.* (note 1), 18.

[5] Stanton E. Samenow, *Inside the Criminal Mind* (New York: Times Books, 1984.)

[6] I have described one of these cases in a second book (2008, in press). My lifetime sample of adolescent and adult felons is surely too small to permit generalization across the broad universe of inmates. But a small number of immature inmates may suffice to make the point that it is not inevitable that time will resolve a developmental delay. These convicted men and women, who persist in taking a "flawed approach" to their adult lives, have gone on in a perpetual, no longer amusing, form of childishness.

[7] In the last chapter of *The Evolving Self*, Robert Kegan suggests that the adequacy of a child's or an adult's maturation can be assayed only in the context of the "culture of embeddedness" in which that child or adult must accomplish the tasks of his stage of

life. Here the point is that modern mass society makes relative immaturity more of a problem than it would be, let us say, in a traditional society among the marsh arabs of southern Iraq or in an orthodox Jewish village outside Odessa in the mid-nineteenth-century—in which there are clear, traditional paradigms for solving most of life's social and ethical dilemmas, and where senior members of the community are present and legitimized to answer thorny questions about right and wrong behavior, or to advise about needed skills. This means that the individual need not have achieved the maturity necessary, let's say, to a young mother in an apartment in Cleveland, far from the place of her birth and removed from a supportive culture that provides, in its traditions and prohibitions and values, the already-worked-out answers to human interpersonal and child-rearing questions.

8   Again, I make no claim that the students at Montana Academy are representative of the universe of troubled adolescents. They are highly selected by economics, safety criteria, and parent variables. How far our experience at the ranch can be generalized is, of course, an open question.

9   Oliver Sacks, "Inside the Executive Brain," review of *The Executive Brain: Frontal Lobes and the Civilized Mind, The New York Review of Books*, 26 April 2001, 7-8.

10   This listing (fig. 3c) is neither exhaustive nor definitive. However, it puts in rough perspective the kinds of obstacles to normal maturation that we think we have recognized among our students. This listing could be taken from the table of contents for a psychiatric textbook. That is to say, conventional psychiatry and psychology devote much of their attention to disturbances of brain and mind that, whatever else they do, may obstruct maturation. This is one major reason to consult such experts, i.e., to remove, insofar as possible, any obstacles to a child's developmental progress. This is the potential utility for medications that ameliorate disturbances in mood (depression), attention (ADHD), and anxiety; one reason to achieve sobriety and one's goal for psychotherapy, which ameliorates the disruptive iimpacts of trauma, grief or self-contempt; and why we want special education for children who cannot readily learn in conventional ways. All these interventions may well remove an intrinsic or extrinsic obstacle to maturation. On the other hand, once again, to remove an obstacle may well not be sufficient. For the same intervention that may lessen the impact of an obstacle may not be the same impetus needed to prod development forward again.

11   Non-Verbal Learning Disorder—a neuropsychological eccentricity usually reflected in a particular asymmetry in IQ sub-scores (VIQ – PIQ > 17). Put simply this tilt implies a relative superiority in verbal proficiencies and suggests that a child may be relatively less proficient at visuospatial tasks, including the capacity to make sense of facial expressions and non-verbal social cues. For this reason NVLD is associated with social awkwardness, a tendency to do or say the wrong thing, to misinterpret what others intend or feel. Insofar as this asymmetry is "hardwired," it may constitute a serious (because relatively intractable) obstacle to interpersonal and ethical maturation, which require empathy and a grasp of social nuance.

12   Our clinical experience at Montana Academy tends to emphasize interpersonal and family disruptions, trauama or loss, rather than hardwired "equipment" deficits. But we see enough ADHD and LD and drug abuse to be impressed with their associations with developmental delay.

13   A knock-knock joke turns upon ambiguity—i.e., double-meaning—in a word. It gropes for abstract thinking, but hinges upon a failure to generalize. This humor is logically concrete. It resembles the recognition that two beads are blue—and so belong in the same box. However, to get such a joke or crude pun requires a capacity simultaneously to hear or see two semantically distinct, different words that share a common sound—and so signify two different referents. Thus, the shared word or phrase means two things at

once. This concrete logic is a way station, developmentally, on the way to a recognition that two experiences, or ideas, or historical eras, or people, or relationships, may share the same characteristics—that they are, in this sense, "the same," inasmuch as they demonstrate a common "principle."

I provide this example for those of you who have been hiking solo in Antarctica and so have been spared a ten-year-old's repertoire of knock-knock jokes:

"Knock knock."
"Who's there?"
"Tank."
"Tank who?"
"You're welcome!"

[14] In a casual survey, years ago, we discovered that no student at MA lacked at least one extrinsic or intrinsic obstacle (from these listings), and that, on average, each student could be said to represent at least two of them. However, the particulars of such a frequency distribution are not revealing—except as an gauge of our admissions practices. That is to say, the frequencies have no intrinsic significance, and would change if we altered our admission criteria or experienced some change in our referrals.

[15] Michael Lewis, *Coach: Lessons on the Game of Life* (New York: W.W. Norton & Company, 2005).

[16] For a comprehensive discussion of these two remedial aspects of parenting, see my book (2008) *Why Don't You Grow Up? The Parenting of Teenagers in an Age of Narcissism* (New York: Lantern Books, in press).

[17] "Within" vs "without" is a distinction that is heuristically useful, but not, strictly speaking, valid. As Daniel J. Siegel *op. cit,* (note 1), 19 put it:

> Experience, gene expression, mental activity, behavior, and continued interactions with the environment (experience) are tightly linked in a transactional set of processes. Such is the recursive nature of development and the way in which nature and nurture, genes and experience, are inextricably part of the same process.

[18] This is a large subject. Whole clinical books have been written about trauma's impact upon the subsequent lives of individuals. Literary writers, great and not so great, have devoted epic poems (Homer's Odyssey), memoirs (Siegfried Sassoon's *To My Brother*, or William Manchester's *Goodbye, Darkness*) and full novels (Willian Styron's *Sophie's Choice*, William Kennedy's *Ironweed*, Amy Tan's *The Joy Luck Club*) to the lasting impact of "experiences" that, for their heroes and heroines, turn out to be unforgettable. Presumably because we fear it, we are fascinated by trauma. Newspapers report the "news"—war, famine, epidemic, rape, murder, domestic violence, accidents, natural disasters—of other people's traumas. And, if you had to say metaphorically what lasting legacy trauma leaves, it would be: that a farmer once struck by lightning never leaves the barn, even on a balmy day, without glancing at the sky.

[19] Israeli studies of Holocaust survivors document a persistence of post-traumatic nightmares and intrusive thoughts more than forty years after their emancipation from the death camps. Years ago my colleagues at UCSF and I described a striking delayed post-traumatic reaction in a combat veteran three decades after the end of the war. See Craig Van Dyke, NJ Zilberg, John McKinnon, "Posttraumatic stress disorder: a thirty-year delay in a World War II veteran," *The American Journal of Psychiatry 142* (1985):1070-3.

9   A Two-Step Treatment

[1] There are many other programs—and competent outpatient therapists, inpatient

units—and, of course, there are resilient families, where time-out may be called, a pit-stop effort mobilized, and an effort made to bring the transmission up to date. I mention Montana Academy here only to illustrate the point—that its sustained therapeutic efforts are meant to put the race car back on the road. MA is simply the pit-stop I know very well.

2   For a detailed discussion of this "parental" clinical effort, see *see To Change a Mind: Parenting Teenagers in an Age of Narcissism* (New York: Lantern Books, in press).

3   The specific identifying details are camouflaged, once again, but not the events or the diction, and only enough to protect the privacy of these students and their families.

4   One hurdle in the way of collecting data has been the lack of a validated, reliable measure for "maturity," as we define the term and have conceptualized maturity and immaturity. There are tens of instruments available for one or another useful purpose, but none to measure the adolescent "flawed approach." We, ourselves, have had to develop such an instrument, which is now well into factor analysis and validity testing. We call it the Montana Adolescent Maturation Assessment (MAMA). The parent version has been refined, and a teacher version is in the works.

5   The first reason for this is that there are few data available from comparable programs. As of this writing, however, some fifteen program members of the National Association of Therapeutic Schools and Programs (NATSAP) have created a common database and made available on the internet key outcome measures that all participants may use—and share that pooled, privacy-protected data. This project, which my partner, John Santa, PhD has promoted as president of NATSAP, is in its infancy. But it promises to provide comparative outcome data as well as data that can test various clinical hypotheses.

6   There are now almost 200 therapeutic schools and programs that belong to the National Association of Therapeutic Schools and Programs. To explore this universe, start with the NATSAP website, which you can find at: http://www.natsap.org/.

7   None of our graduates has gone on to MIT, as it happens. But tens have gone on to be accepted and to attend, with many already graduated, first-rate colleges and universities, including, Dartmouth, Brown, University of Chicago, Wesleyan, Smith, Michigan, University of Vermont, University of California (various campuses), University of Oregon, University of Washington, Reed, Lewis & Clark, University of Montana, Willamette, Penn State, University of Massachusetts, Virginia Military Institute, University of Maryland, Beloit, Boston University, Georgetown, Hampshire, Skidmore, Oberlin, Tulane University, Whittier, Ohio Wesleyan—and more. The point is not the prestige of any particular colleges, but rather the implication that so many teenagers who during high school had been failing across the board at all the tasks of adolescence, and invariably at academic tasks, could change their "approach"—in a sufficiently sustained way—so as to go on to gain entrance to and negotiate the rigors of best of the nation's colleges and universities. Not all have managed this, but many have done.

8   I call these formulations tentative because all I have provided the reader are clinical sketches, brief histories of these two teenagers. To confirm these diagnostic impressions certainly required careful interviews, clinical observations (e.g., their relationships with other teenagers and adult staff), and the time to form close relationships, so as to have confidence in what they would confide.

9   Again, for a comprehensive discussion of this prescription, see John McKinnon, *Why Don't You Grow Up? Parenting Teenagers in an Age of Narcissism, op. cit.* (chapter 8, note 16).

10   Ibid.

Helen (B)

11   Here I am not talking about gang crime or brazen sociopathy, but rather the repetitive,

escalating, sneaky misbehavior of a lost teenager, whose parents are not paying (close enough) attention.

David (B)

[12] No doubt wilderness programs need regulatory safeguards and state licensure—as do we, ourselves, and we have lobbied to secure them in Montana. I am not expert about all the alternative adolescent programs in the nation, as an experienced educational consultant must be. I only hear talk about tragic accidents, even deaths, and rumors about shabby or incompetent programs. This is why we sought (and won) accreditation from the Joint Commission on Accreditation of Healthcare Organizations (JCAHO). However, over thirty years of conventional practice, I have learned of suicides inside locked hospital units in conventional hospitals, including university hospitals. I know that treating troubled teenagers is a risky profession. I also know the noisiest, most indignant conventional psychologists know very little about the world of alternative programs. None of them have bothered to visit Montana Academy. We are remote, but not inaccessible. We are visited by parents of 70-100 prospective students every year, and by tens of educational consultants, who tour and sit with our students, and grill us about what we do. And, since we started in 1997, colleagues have always been welcome, and tens of them have come to visit.

10 Outcomes

[1] In *The Logic of Scientific Discovery* (1934) Karl Popper argued that the scientific method was a method for establishing the validity of certain kinds of propositions, namely, those that can be "falsified" empirically. Other kinds of "truth" may command belief, but only propositions that can be put to the test—and which can be framed so as to be proven false—can be proved by empirical science. Here I am making the case that the immaturity hypothesis is a scientific causal theory because it logically implies certain consequences which can be demonstrated to be true—or falsified.

[2] Elkhonon Goldberg, *op. cit.* (chapter 4, note 19). See also Oliver Sacks' review of Goldberg's book, *op. cit.* (chapter 8, note 9).

[3] Elkhonon Goldberg, Ibid.

[4] *Diagnostic and Statistical Manual of Mental Disorders, 4th ed.* (Washington, DC: American Psychiatric Association, 1994).

[5] I say "most" symptoms, but not all. If, let's say, an addiction or a biological mental illness such as schizophrenia were that obstacle that delayed maturation, the consequent immaturity syndrome would not be able to account for *all* of such a teenager's troublesome symptoms and signs. On the other hand, a resumption of developmental momentum after a successful intervention does seem to remedy those signs and symptoms that immaturity itself brings about.

[6] Only preliminary data from trials of the Montana Adolescent Maturity Assessment (MAMA) are available at this writing. But the results are highly suggestive—and not subtle. As parents' ratings of teenaged sons and daughters rise, so do their ratings of their children's academic, familial and interpersonal functioning. As those maturity ratings rise, symptoms also drop away, and much of the previously prescribed medication can be discontinued. These early findings are what the immaturity hypothesis predicts—and precisely what the disorder-to-be-medicated hypothesis does *not* predict. .

[7] Remark attributed to Samuel Clemens, *Readers Digest*, September 1837.

[8] Stanton Samenow, *op. cit.*—note (above) under Chapter 8. Clearly Samenow thought this pathological approach to life derived from genetics—a "bad seed"—or from moral "choices" which, from an early stage of life, *were* choices. Samenow is weary of criminals

making excuses for themselves and adamant that their criminal behavior is their own fault: "Criminals cause crime—not bad neighborhoods, inadequate parents, television, schools, drugs, or unemployment" (6). He came close, nonetheless, to recognizing that this flawed approach may have something to do with a blocked maturation. But instead he ascribes this developmental theory to fooled and foolish parents: "His mother and father... assume that his waywardness is merely a stage of development. This 'stage,' however, never ends" (26).

Despite his missing the point that a stalled development could cause an adult to remain "criminal" in his thinking, Samenow does recognize "patterns" in criminal thinking that constitute a "criminal life style." He is not quick to exculpate parenting (or a lack thereof), as I say; chapter 2 of his book is titled: "Parents Don't Turn Children into Criminals." But he insists (as I would, also) that criminals commit crimes because they end up with "the personality of the criminal." He thinks (as I do) that to make sense of such wretched behavior, "We must understand how criminals think and realize that they have a fundamentally different view of the world from that of people who are basically responsible" (5). I would argue that criminal behavior appears to be the dark consequence of adult immaturity, but Samenow simply blames the criminal, himself, for his "choices."

[9] This is my summary of his description—although Samenow does not put it just this way.

[10] At this writing we have collected 450 parental ratings, which has permitted us to prune the prototype instrument and to notice that the responses tend to cluster around three subscales—narcissism, future-mindedness and ethical primitivism. The data remain preliminary. We need a larger n to validate those subscales, and we are using the Achenbach scales to validate the instrument. But these early data may be worth mentioning, at this writing, because they add an empirical hint in support of an immaturity hypothesis. These early correlations have not been subtle.

[11] I asked parents of a few of our students, who had done very well, to describe this transformation in their own words. I told them I wanted to use some of their own words and their own accounts in place of my own diction—so that readers could hear how parents described success. I did not, I confess, chase after accounts of our failures, although there have been many. When teenagers do badly after leaving the academy, parents try to be polite about their disappointment, but the description is one of persistent childishness—and a regression to that "flawed approach" with which they, and we, had started.

Letters

[12] I had better say this again. I have changed names, designated cities, even the name of a particular college, so as not to give away a family's identity. These are the only alterations, however.